Atomic Assurance

A VOLUME IN THE SERIES

Cornell Studies in Security Affairs

Edited by Robert J. Art, Robert Jervis, and Stephen M. Walt

A list of titles in this series is available at cornellpress.cornell.edu.

Atomic Assurance

*The Alliance Politics
of Nuclear Proliferation*

ALEXANDER LANOSZKA

Cornell University Press

Ithaca and London

First published 2018 by Cornell University Press

Printed in the United States of America

Library of Congress Cataloging-in-Publication Data

Names: Lanoszka, Alexander, author.
Title: Atomic assurance : the alliance politics of nuclear proliferation / Alexander Lanoszka.
Description: Ithaca [New York] : Cornell University Press, 2018. | Series: Cornell studies in security affairs | Includes bibliographical references and index.
Identifiers: LCCN 2018016356 (print) | LCCN 2018017762 (ebook) | ISBN 9781501729195 (pdf) | ISBN 9781501729201 (ret) | ISBN 9781501729188 | ISBN 9781501729188 (cloth ; alk. paper)
Subjects: LCSH: Nuclear nonproliferation—International cooperation. | Nuclear arms control—International cooperation. | Nuclear arms control—Government policy—United States. | Nuclear nonproliferation—Government policy—United States. | United States—Foreign relations—1945–1989—case studies.
Classification: LCC JZ5675 (ebook) | LCC JZ5675 .L36 2018 (print) | DDC 327.1/747—dc23
LC record available at https://lccn.loc.gov/2018016356

To my parents

Contents

Acknowledgments

It took many years for this book to come together. At Princeton University, John Ikenberry was especially helpful and generous; he never let me lose sight of the big picture. Tom Christensen, Keren Yarhi-Milo, and David Carter provided extensive and varied feedback. Aaron Friedberg provided useful commentary and support—through the Bradley Foundation—at a critical juncture when this project was still in its infancy. I also benefited immensely from fellowships at the Security Studies Program and the Dickey Center for International Understanding at the Massachusetts Institute of Technology (MIT) and Dartmouth College, respectively. At MIT, where I was a Stanton Fellow, I am grateful for the mentorship I received from Barry Posen and Frank Gavin. Indeed, Frank has been a wonderful ally over the years. I learned much from Owen Coté, Vipin Narang, and Jim Walsh as well as Henrik Hiim and Julia Macdonald. The Stanton Foundation contributed funding to this project. At Dartmouth, I held a manuscript workshop that saw the participation of Bill Wohlforth, Steve Brooks, Ben Valentino, Jeff Friedman, Brian Greenhill, Joshua Shifrinson, and Katy Powers. Tim Crawford drove up from Boston and took the lead at that workshop, providing me with a new vision for the manuscript.

I have many other friends and colleagues to thank, whether for the support they provided or for the feedback they gave when I was working on this book. They include Alexander Alden, Dan Altman, Danny Bessner, Matthew Fuhrmann, Kiichi Fujiwara, Kate Gheoghegan, Mauro Gilli, Andrea Gilli, Tsuyoshi Goroku, Brendan Green, Kristen Harkness, Matthew Kroenig, Raymond Kuo, Akira Kurosaki, Christine Leah, Andreas Lutsch, Rupal Mehta, Rohan Mukherjee, Leah Sarson, Jonas Schneider, Luis Simón, Henry Sokolski, Jeffrey Taliaferro, Nobuhiko Tamaki, and Simon Toner. Michael

Hunzeker, in particular, read numerous drafts over the years. I could not have asked for a better friend. Sandy Hager, Leonie Fleischmann, Iosif Kovras, Ronen Palan, Inderjeet Parmar, and Madura Rasaratnam are among the many scholars and friends who have made City, University of London a wonderful place to work. I apologize to those whom I forgot to mention. I also thank Roger Haydon, for his superb assistance, and the staff at Cornell University Press. They are all consummate professionals—it was a pleasure to have the opportunity to work with them. Robert Art and the reviewers gave terrific feedback that helped me to clarify and to improve key parts of the book.

Emmanuelle Richez entered my life when this book was already under review. She has been a tremendous source of love and comfort, motivating me always to see the bright side of things and to power through the work that needed to be done when this project was in its final stages. I am very grateful to have her support.

Finally, I want to thank my family. I have treasured their emotional support and encouragement. Some of the issues raised by this book acquired a personal significance for my relatives and me, as we have become alarmed by the geopolitical developments in Poland's region that began in 2014. I especially thank Danusia, Kasia, Rafał, and my grandparents Marianna and Tadeusz. Most of all, I thank my parents, Anna and Marek, to whom I dedicate this book. Their love and unconditional support were never in doubt.

Atomic Assurance

Introduction

The Alliance Politics of Nuclear Proliferation

Tensions were high on the Korean Peninsula. Fears of nuclear proliferation were rife, and a newly elected American president had gone on record saying unflattering things about the South Korean government. Such was the context in mid-1977 when the American ambassador in Seoul met with various government officials and scientists, in part to discuss what could be done to prevent South Korea from undertaking nuclear weapons activities. During that meeting, a nuclear scientist proposed that one solution would involve the United States extending the same "nuclear umbrella policy" to South Korea as that given already to Japan. This proposal struck the ambassador as nonsensical. After all, South Korea benefited from a nuclear umbrella thanks to its treaty alliance with the United States and the tactical nuclear weapons that American forces had stationed on its territory. The only change to the alliance was the full withdrawal of American ground forces from South Korea—a policy for which President Jimmy Carter had advocated during his presidential campaign. And so the ambassador wrote back to the State Department in Washington, decrying "the evidence of ignorance at very senior government levels of either costs or risks [*sic*] involved in the weapons development program over and above seriously adverse impact on US relationship [*sic*]."[1]

Carter ultimately decided against his planned troop withdrawal, and South Korea did not acquire a nuclear weapons capability, but the episode raises important questions that continue to resonate into the twenty-first century. Why did the alliance break down so as to create proliferation risks? And to what extent was the alliance responsible for restraining South Korea's nuclear ambitions? These questions in turn speak to a much larger concern: what is the relationship between alliances and nuclear proliferation?

Ever since the United States forged its alliances with partners around the world at the beginning of the Cold War, many experts agree that alliances have yielded important strategic benefits. Alliances enable the United States

1

to manage local conflicts, to prevent arms races, and to reassure partners that the United States will defend them in a military crisis that involves a shared adversary. The result is that recipients of these security guarantees feel less need to acquire their own nuclear weapons. Even when allies have pursued nuclear weapons development, the United States would coerce them into halting their ambitions. Such is the emerging narrative of the American experience of the nuclear era: that alliances are effective nonproliferation tools and that the Cold War is largely a story of American nonproliferation success. This nonproliferation mission could become more challenging to undertake if predictions of American decline are true and allies are growing in power relative to the United States.

This book challenges this emerging narrative by making two related claims. The first claim is that military alliances are important tools for thwarting nuclear proliferation, but they are more susceptible to breakdown and credibility concerns than some accounts in the international relations literature presume. Indeed, why alliances should ever be a viable solution for nuclear proliferation is puzzling, since international agreements ought to be fundamentally unbelievable in the absence of a world government that can enforce them. Even if we accept that strong commitments are possible, those very commitments risk emboldening those allies to undertake aggressive foreign policies that are contrary to the interests of the United States.

The second claim is that although the United States has played a key role in enforcing the nuclear nonproliferation regime, we should be careful not to attribute too much success to the United States. It encountered severe difficulties in curbing suspect nuclear behaviors of key allies like West Germany and Japan, to say nothing of Great Britain and France—allies that feared American abandonment yet succeeded in acquiring nuclear weapons. South Korea often serves as an example of the effectiveness of American coercion, but the state of its nuclear program made South Korea an easy target at a time when the United States wanted to demonstrate its commitment to nuclear nonproliferation. Moreover, the proliferation scare that took place during Jimmy Carter's presidency happened after the United States had seemingly shut down South Korea's nuclear weapons program and strong-armed Seoul into ratifying the Nuclear Non-Proliferation Treaty (NPT). That nonproliferation campaign took place between 1974 and 1976. Safeguard violations persisted into the early 1980s. Put together, from the perspective of Washington, deterring nuclear weapons interest is easier than eliminating it once it has become activated. This is the main message of this book.

This book expands on these arguments by investigating the link between alliances and nuclear proliferation using a series of case studies drawn from the Cold War. I consider two main questions. The first question is, how do alliances prevent nuclear proliferation? To answer it, I examine why some states that received security guarantees have tried to acquire nuclear weapons and why many of them ultimately renounced such efforts by making nonproliferation commitments. Both France and Great Britain successfully acquired nuclear weapons, but only France does not need technological support from the United States to maintain them. Japan and West Germany do not have nuclear weapons but have enrichment and reprocessing capabilities. South Korea has agreements with the United States that forbid it from having reprocessing capabilities to this day. We thus arrive at the second question: what was the role of the United States in its allies' decisions to renounce nuclear weapons? To consider these questions even further, it is worth clarifying the puzzle of nuclear proliferation from an alliance perspective.

The Puzzle of Alliances and Nuclear Proliferation

The standard view among international security experts is that guarantors like the United States face a conundrum when designing alliances. The so-called alliance dilemma is as follows. By offering a strong commitment, the guarantor demonstrates that it will back its ally in the event of a militarized crisis that involves a shared adversary. However, the ally might exploit this favorable situation by pressing its claims against the adversary harder than it otherwise would, thereby raising the likelihood of starting a war that the guarantor does not want. Because the guarantor wishes to protect its reputation for upholding its commitments, it might find itself intervening in this war to support its ally. All things equal, the risk of entrapment—that is, of being dragged into an undesirable war—increases with the strength of the alliance commitment.[2] Yet weakening the alliance commitment to lessen entrapment risks introduces new problems. The ally might fear abandonment when it starts to doubt the credibility of the guarantor and its security pledges. A weakened commitment might tempt the adversary to attack the ally, which may thus feel compelled to launch destabilizing preemptive measures.[3]

As a tool for preventing nuclear proliferation, the alliance commitment must be strong enough for the ally to view it as a credible deterrent against the adversary. Otherwise, doubts about the guarantor's stated pledges would lead the ally to discount the military value of the alliance and to reconsider its own armament choices. For the guarantor, the policy challenge becomes acute: how does one craft a security commitment that at once resolves the alliance dilemma and discourages nuclear proliferation–related behavior?

The difficulty of this policy challenge has led scholars to adopt conflicting positions regarding the relationship between alliances and nuclear proliferation. Some scholars downplay the alliance dilemma and emphasize the stabilizing impact alliances have for international politics. These scholars see formal defense alliances as credible and thus the most desirable security institutions states can have. Because formal alliance treaties are public and thus known to all other states, guarantors incur high reputation costs for violating them.[4] These alliances are the best for deterring adversaries and reassuring allies. Democratic states like the United States are especially good allies: the transparency of their institutions makes them more predictable, and the difficulties of shepherding alliance treaties through domestic ratification processes make their commitment choices stronger and more selective.[5] Entrapment concerns are overstated, since guarantors can attach conditions and specify the terms in which the alliance would be activated.[6] Accordingly, written and public security guarantees (particularly those issued by democratic countries) are credible, allay abandonment fears, and reduce incentives for nuclear proliferation. Yet other scholars see abandonment concerns as a pervasive feature of alliance politics, no matter the political system of the state that dominates the alliance. These scholars argue that such concerns encourage states to seek nuclear weapons in order to deter adversaries on their own.[7]

The problem with many existing alliance-based arguments is that they expect either too little or too much nuclear proliferation. Scholars who see democratically led alliances as relatively free of pathologies have trouble explaining the proliferation record of American alliances. Of the thirty or so states that at least considered getting nuclear weapons at one point since 1945, over half of them were aligned with the United States.[8] In contrast, only three nuclear proliferators had defensive alliances with the Soviet Union: China, North Korea, and Romania. Five of fourteen NATO allies at least considered getting nuclear weapons by the 1970s, but only one out of seven Warsaw Pact members committed the same offense. Scholars who see alliances as inherently problematic face a different challenge. If abandonment concerns are so acute, then why do allies only seldom move to acquire nuclear weapons? Unfortunately, we are yet to have an account that specifies the precise conditions under which states *sufficiently* fear abandonment so that they begin desiring nuclear weapons.

Many allies ultimately renounced their efforts to acquire nuclear weapons, but to what extent were such reversals the result of alliance politics? The academic literature is also divided on this question. Some scholars dismiss security explanations of nuclear proliferation altogether, emphasizing instead such variables as leaders' beliefs or economic growth strategies.[9] However, a school of thought has recently emerged—one that stresses the restraining role of American alliances with respect to nuclear proliferation. Nicholas Miller claims that the threat of American sanctions has deterred nuclear proliferation, especially after the United States demonstrated its commitment to nonproliferation by suppressing South Korean and Taiwanese nuclear activities in the 1970s.[10] Gene Gerzhoy similarly maintains that threats of alliance abandonment—meted out by the United States—have curbed proliferation risks, whereas Francis J. Gavin concludes that nonproliferation has been as much a pillar of American grand strategy as containment (in the Cold War) and openness (since 1945).[11] Yet close scrutiny reveals important shortcomings in these claims. American nonproliferation efforts against South Korea and Taiwan were done quietly so as not to alarm China and Japan, making it debatable as to whether those efforts signaled American nonproliferation interests widely and clearly. Those states have also relapsed into nuclear proliferation–related behavior after having been sanctioned. Moreover, if abandonment fears provoke nuclear interest, then how can credible threats to abandon an alliance altogether reverse that interest? Finally, nuclear nonproliferation may have been a by-product of American foreign policy, rather than a core aim of it. Ridding South Korea of nuclear weapons helped ensure stability on the Korean Peninsula when the United States pursued rapprochement with China. For diplomatic and possibly economic reasons, the Ford administration did not push Japan as hard as it could have for Japan to make clear nonproliferation pledges. Whether nuclear reversals resulted from alliance politics remains an open empirical question.

THE ARGUMENT

How do guarantors like the United States design commitments that at once mitigate the alliance dilemma and reduce nuclear proliferation risks? To what extent are alliances responsible for curbing the efforts of those states interested in acquiring nuclear weapons? I advance a new theoretical framework in chapter 1 that begins with the observation that nuclear security guarantees contain much ambiguity despite involving existential stakes. The recipients of these guarantees have good reason to worry about abandonment: no world government exists to ensure that their received commitments would be honored, and the written commitments that they receive are often vague. Consequently, as much as allies pay attention to the foreign policy doctrines of their guarantors, they desire more than simple pledges of support.

Allies thus tend to believe that in-theater conventional military deployments are necessary for bolstering commitments to extend deterrence. These deployments are not just "trip wires" that help deter an adversary by threatening the involvement of the guarantor should its ally be attacked. They have war-fighting capabilities and are tangible representations of the nuclear security guarantees that these states receive.[12] States see the credibility of their security guarantees tied to such deployments as troops more so than even tactical nuclear deployments, despite how the latter matter for extended nuclear deterrence. As long as these commitments appear stable, abandonment fears will not intensify, and the temptation to develop nuclear weapons will be limited. Moreover, these troops have the additional benefit of helping to restrain the ally's foreign and defense policies. For example, those troops' participation in joint military planning with the ally's own armed forces reduces entrapment risks. And so alliances are useful for deterring nuclear proliferation. However, if allies anticipate or suddenly experience unfavorable conventional redeployments (i.e., large, unilateral troop withdrawals), then their abandonment concerns rise to a level much higher than normal. They begin to doubt their security guarantees enough to embark on a set of behaviors related to nuclear proliferation, which range from hedging strategies to the active pursuit of a nuclear weapons capability.

Unfortunately, the guarantor will experience severe challenges in its efforts to reverse the nuclear proliferation–related behavior of its ally. To begin with, the guarantor needs to repair the security guarantee that the ally now perceives as sufficiently broken to warrant nuclear weapons pursuit. To reassert its security guarantees and to soothe intensified abandonment fears, new agreements that credibly restore or preserve troop levels are necessary. Yet these agreements are difficult to forge if the underlying circumstances that broke the security guarantee in the first place still exist. Other diplomatic levers have limited efficacy and could be counterproductive: threatening the withdrawal of more troops or the termination of the alliance altogether so as to isolate the ally will only exacerbate abandonment concerns. I thus argue that the best possible recourse available to the guarantor is its economic and technological power over the ally. If the ally depends on those nonmilitary goods from the guarantor, then the ally might have to reconsider its nuclear activities in the interest of its own welfare. Absent such leverage, the guarantor will have trouble getting the ally to renounce nuclear weapons credibly. In the event that the ally decides to reverse its nuclear behavior, it may do so for reasons that have little to do with the coercion—threatened or applied—by its guarantor.

In going about these nonproliferation efforts, the guarantor must have a clear and strong interest in preventing nuclear proliferation and perhaps even in preserving its security guarantees. At first glance, an eagerness to limit the spread of nuclear weapons seems to dominate American foreign policy. The United States withheld major atomic secrets from its biggest coalition partner in World War II and the Manhattan Project, Great Britain. In 1946, Congress passed the Atomic Energy Act so as to restrict other countries' access to nuclear information possessed by the United States. A later amendment to this act still reiterated its nonproliferation principles, thus becoming a source of frustration to some presidents who contemplated nuclear-sharing arrangements with other countries. Indeed, Congress has passed laws like the Nuclear Non-Proliferation Act of 1978 and the Pressler Amendment to advance nonproliferation objectives. Nevertheless, I contend that American interest in nonproliferation is variable. Although American decision makers may agree in principle that nuclear proliferation is highly objectionable, the desire to satisfy other foreign policy interests could have the potential to undercut nonproliferation efforts. As the American campaign against Taiwan's nuclear weapons program indicates, sometimes narrow foreign policy interests—in this case, improving relations with China to exploit the Sino-Soviet split—can strengthen nonproliferation efforts.

To evaluate my argument, I use a qualitative research design that I elaborate toward the end of chapter 1. The empirical bulk comprises three intensive case studies on West Germany, Japan, and South Korea. These three American allies also represent most-likely cases for when an alliance with the United States inhibited nuclear interest. For each of these cases, I rely on deep archival research. The primary documents I collected and discovered serve as process-tracing evidence. They allow me to test the causal mechanism and the implications of my theory against several leading alternative arguments that prioritize adversarial threats, domestic politics, and the prestige that states might see in nuclear weapons. Because I am skeptical of how alliances can halt nuclear weapons activities definitively, I allow for the possibility that these other causal processes can affect a state's decision to cease its proliferation-related behavior.

Chapter 2 sets up the main case studies of this book by reviewing the history of American security guarantees during much of the Cold War. I show how and why American presidents from Harry Truman to Jimmy Carter designed their alliance commitments and implemented their strategic doctrinal visions. Of interest in this chapter is President Dwight Eisenhower's adoption of the New Look, the stated emphasis of "flexible response" in the Kennedy and Johnson administrations, and President Richard Nixon's articulation of the Nixon Doctrine. American presidents consistently preferred a military strategy whereby the United States provides the "nuclear sword" and allies supply the "conventional shield." Nevertheless, the implementation of this strategy varied over time and in intensity between Western Europe and East Asia. We thus have variation in how allies might assess the security guarantees they receive.

Chapters 3 and 4 together form a controlled case comparison of West Germany and Japan. Both countries are similar along several key dimensions: their roles in World War II, liberal democratic political regimes, spectacular economic reconstruction and growth in the postwar period, and hosting of a large-scale American military presence. Despite these similarities, West Germany began considering nuclear weapons development in the mid-1950s. Thereafter it had an ambiguous stance with respect to nuclear nonproliferation.[13] Japan started its nuclear hedging behavior about a decade later. Differences in their strategic situations led those two allies to vary in how they perceived changes in their security guarantee and in their subsequent behaviors.

Chapter 3 shows that, as a mostly landlocked country, West Germany was affected by Eisenhower's stated objectives of relying more on nuclear weapons at the expense of such conventional military deployments as ground power. Its abandonment fears intensified when news reports appeared in the United States that suggested large-scale troop withdrawals from West Germany and Europe were being planned. Shortly afterward West Germany entered a short-lived trilateral initiative with France and Italy to develop nuclear weapons. Because the policies of the Kennedy and Johnson administrations exhibited important continuities from those of the Eisenhower administration, West Germany had little motivation to renounce nuclear weapons fully. I show that the United States attempted various alliance solutions to little avail and had difficulty leveraging its economic power to secure various agreements from West Germany during the 1960s. I provide evidence that alliance coercion might not have been so decisive in curbing West German behavior as now presumed. Explanations that emphasize domestic politics better account for West German decisions regarding the NPT.

Chapter 4 demonstrates that Japan was attuned to Eisenhower's New Look because of its geography. Indeed, Japan remained quiescent until China's first nuclear detonation in 1964—an event that shook the Japanese leadership and forced it to attend more carefully to American security guarantees. As the American military involvement in Vietnam slowly unraveled, Japanese leaders became apprehensive of American alliance support and began to ratchet up their nuclear activities, giving national priority to a centrifuge program. Though Japan relied on the United States for the development of its civilian nuclear program, such dependency was not enough to eliminate American unease regarding its nuclear policy. Like West Germany, Japan ratified the NPT because of domestic politics and an international safeguards agreement that it was able to secure.

Chapter 5 addresses South Korea, a *critical* case for my theory because the American government initiated plans for major troop withdrawals from the peninsula on several separate occasions. In fact, the United States barely consulted with South Korea when it openly sought troop withdrawals in 1970 and 1977. Moreover, the first of these troop withdrawals reflected the Nixon Doctrine—an important shift in American defense policy. The magnitude of these unwanted redeployments should have provoked a response from South Korea. Therefore, my theoretical framework must have empirical validity in this case. I demonstrate that South Korea's nuclear efforts are comprehensible only from the perspective of its alliance with the United States. That is, South Korea first explored and later began a nuclear weapons program in reaction to Nixon's troop withdrawals from its territory. South Korea tried to operate this program secretly. Yet once Washington discovered it, it pressured Seoul to cancel the primitive nuclear weapons program. South Korea's nonmilitary dependence on the United States contributed to this result. Underscoring the difficulties of mounting a nonproliferation campaign, the story does not end there. Carter sought to withdraw all American forces from South Korea—a move that some observers speculate incited further efforts by South Korea to develop nuclear weapons secretly. Safeguard violations persisted into the early 1980s.

Chapter 6 reviews a set of smaller case studies to expand the variation of my study. These cases are Great Britain, France, Norway, Australia, and

Taiwan. I argue that my theory can illuminate why both Great Britain and France sought nuclear weapons and why only France succeeded in acquiring an *independent* nuclear deterrent capability. I show that Norway largely abstained from nuclear proliferation–related behavior for domestic political reasons. For its part, Australia was alarmed that its received security commitments were not backed by military power. It subsequently tried to acquire nuclear weapons, only to cancel the project when the Labor Party came to power. Taiwan feared abandonment due to the prospect of Sino-American rapprochement and the waning of its received military commitment from the United States. I highlight how Taiwan evaded many coercive efforts by the United States to shut down its nuclear weapons program.

Chapter 7 summarizes the main argument and discusses the broader implications of this study for both international theory and policy. The core message of this book is that alliances are more effective in deterring *potential* nuclear proliferation than in curbing *actual* cases of nuclear proliferation. This book thus has implications for how we think about such topics in international relations theory as credibility, coercion, American primacy, and the great power management of weaker states, more generally. For policy makers and practitioners, the findings demonstrate that the retraction of such military assets as troops can provoke intense abandonment fears even if the nuclear basis of extended deterrence remains unchanged. Upholding alliance commitments is insufficient: such pledges need to be coupled with credible military support. Though no one seriously argues that nuclear nonproliferation is easy, the record of alliances is much more mixed than commonly presumed with respect to being tools for curbing actual nuclear activities. A lot depends on the economic and technological leverage that the United States might have over the proliferating ally. If its relative global position continues to erode, Washington will experience greater difficulties in reversing the nuclear undertakings of its allies. As such, it will need to be even more forward-looking and careful in adjusting its alliance commitments.

How Alliances (Mis)Manage Nuclear Proliferation

When we think of nuclear proliferation, the countries American leaders have recently seen as adversaries often come to mind: Iraq, Iran, and North Korea. And yet when we take a historical perspective, we see that many American friends and allies have at least considered acquiring nuclear weapons. France and Great Britain even succeeded in developing their own nuclear arsenals. Contemporary efforts made by the United States to reassure South Korea and Japan often serve to stifle their potential appetite for nuclear weapons, since they both face the dual threat of a rising China and a nuclear-armed North Korea. These observations suggest that the connection between alliances and nonproliferation is not straightforward. How can alliances best reduce nuclear proliferation risks? And how have these security institutions curbed the efforts of those allies that have pursued nuclear weapons, if at all?

This chapter develops a theoretical framework of how alliances are useful for preventing nuclear proliferation–related behaviors among their members but less useful for stopping a program once it has started. Five propositions flow from my account. First, military alliances might not keep allies from acquiring nuclear weapons as much as the conventional wisdom suggests. Second, in-theater conventional forces are crucial for making American extended nuclear guarantees credible. Third, the American coercion of allies who started, or were tempted to start, a nuclear weapons program has played less of a role in forestalling nuclear proliferation than assumed. Fourth, the economic or technological reliance of a security-dependent ally on the United States, if utilized, works better to reverse or to halt any ally's nuclear bid than anything else. Put together, these claims suggest one more proposition: that is, deterring an ally from initiating a nuclear program is easier than compelling an ally to terminate a program. In making these claims, I do not offer a unified account that illuminates both the start and stop of an ally's nuclear interest. Indeed, my argument allows for the possibility that nonsecurity motivations could explain why such interest ends.

My framework also allows for greater variability in states' abandonment fears than do existing accounts.

This chapter proceeds by describing first what my book seeks to explain: the nuclear proliferation–related behavior of a treaty ally. I then review current understandings of alliances and nuclear proliferation before developing my own theoretical framework. Last, I discuss my research design as well as several alternative explanations.

Key Definitions

I strive to explain the nuclear proliferation–related behavior of treaty allies. By "treaty allies," I mean those states that receive a formal security guarantee via a formal alliance treaty. This type of treaty formalizes a "relationship of security cooperation between two or more states and involving mutual expectations of some degree of policy coordination on security issues under certain conditions in the future."[1] By "nuclear proliferation–related behavior," I refer to those nuclear activities undertaken by an ally that deliberately serve to develop an indigenous capacity for producing explosives that use fissionable materials. Sometimes an ally might indeed have an explicit and dedicated nuclear weapons program. Alternatively, an ally might be trying to acquire enrichment or reprocessing capabilities in the absence of proper safeguards or international agreements so that it could one day activate a nuclear weapons program when necessary—that is, the ally is seeking a latent nuclear capability. Table 1 lists all the nonsuperpowers—along with their geopolitical alignments and Nuclear Non-Proliferation Treaty (NPT) status—known to have nuclear weapons programs or enrichment and reprocessing capabilities.

My dependent variable differs from standard measures used in statistical studies of nuclear proliferation. Drawing on a commonly used dataset, many researchers code nuclear proliferation in terms of whether states do nothing, explore the nuclear weapons option, pursue a nuclear weapons program, or acquire nuclear weapons.[2] Yet this approach has problems. To begin with, scholars disagree over how to measure nuclear proliferation effort, since distinguishing empirically those states that have "explored" from those that have "pursued" is difficult.[3] Rather than using systematic measurement criteria to code states' nuclear activities, datasets often rely on ex post facto statements and secondary sources. The result is that they can include Indonesia on the basis of its leaders' statements but miss such cases as Japan, Italy, and West Germany despite their efforts to acquire reprocessing and enrichment capabilities while deflecting international scrutiny.[4] Moreover, the states that have acquired the capacity to enrich uranium, to reprocess plutonium, or to do both overlap with the states coded as nuclear proliferators (see table 1). Sometimes states have no intention to acquire nuclear

11

Table 1 Nonsuperpower nuclear proliferation, 1945–2012

Country	Alignment[a]	NW Years[b]	ENR Years[c]	NPT[d]
Algeria	Soviet	1983–2012	1992–2012	D: 1995
Argentina	US	1968–90	1968–73; 1983–89; 1993–94	D: 1995
Australia	US	1956–73	1972–83; 1992–2007	S: 1970; D: 1973
Belgium	US	—	1966–74	S: 1968; D: 1975
Brazil	US*	1953–90	1979–2012	D: 1998
Canada	US	—	1944–76; 1990–93	S: 1968; D: 1969
China	Soviet	1955–2012	1960–2012	D: 1992
Czechia	Soviet/US*	—	1977–98	S: 1968; D: 1969
Egypt	Soviet/US*	1960–74	1982–2012	S: 1968; D: 1981
France	US	1946–2012	1949–2012	D: 1992
(West) Germany	US	—	1964–2012	S: 1969; D: 1975
India	None	1954–2012	1964–73; 1977–2012	Never signed
Indonesia	None/US*	1965–67	—	S: 1970; D: 1979
Iran	US*; None	1976–2012	1974–79; 1985–2012	S: 1968; D: 1970
Iraq	Soviet*	1976–95	1983–91	S: 1968; D: 1969
Israel	US*	1949–2012	1963–2012	Never signed
Italy	US	—	1966–90	S: 1969: D: 1975
Japan	US	—	1968–2012	S: 1970; D: 1976
Korea, North	Soviet/China	1965–2012	1975–93; 2003–12	S: 1968; O: 2003
Korea, South	US	1959–78	1979–82; 1997–2012	S: 1968; D: 1975
Libya	Soviet*	1970–2003	1982–2003	S: 1968; D: 1975
The Netherlands	US	—	1973–2012	S: 1968; D: 1975
Norway	US	—	1961–68	S: 1968; D: 1969
Pakistan	US*	1972–2012	1973–2012	Never signed
Romania	Soviet	1985–90	1985–89	S: 1968; D: 1970
South Africa	US*	1969–1991	1967–2012	D: 1991
Sweden	None	1946–69	1954–72	S: 1968; D: 1970
Switzerland	None	1946–70	—	S: 1969; D: 1977
Syria	Russia	2000–12	—	S: 1968; D: 1969
Taiwan	US; US*	1967–77; 1987–88	1976–78	S: 1968; D: 1970
United Kingdom	US	1945–2012	1952–2012	S: 1968; R: 1968
Yugoslavia	None	1954–65; 1974–88	1954–78	S: 1968; D: 1970

[a] * indicates non–treaty alignment. See Herbert K. Tilemma, "Cold War Alliance and Overt Military Intervention, 1945–1991," *International Interactions* 20, no. 3 (1994): 270–277.

[b] Years of nuclear weapons (NW) activities from revised 2012 list of nuclear proliferators for Sonali Singh and Christopher R. Way, "The Correlates of Nuclear Proliferation: A Quantitative Test," *Journal of Conflict Resolution* 48, no. 6 (2004): 866–867, http://falcon.arts.cornell.edu/crw12/documents/Nuclear%20Proliferation%20Dates.pdf. Some of these dates are debatable.

[c] Enrichment and reprocessing (ENR) plant operation years from Matthew Fuhrmann and Benjamin Tkach, "Almost Nuclear: Introducing the Nuclear Latency Dataset," *Conflict Management and Peace Science* 32, no. 4 (2015): 443–461.

[d] S: signature; D: deposit; O: withdrawal. Data from United Nations Office for Disarmament Affairs, *Treaty on the Non-Proliferation of Nuclear Weapons*, http://disarmament.un.org/treaties/t/npt.

weapons, but they may be pursuing hedging strategies that leave policy options open in the event that their security environment deteriorates further.[5] Accordingly, because I specify that any effort to acquire enrichment and reprocessing capabilities without proper safeguards or international agreements constitutes nuclear proliferation–related behavior, my definition helpfully excludes benign cases like the Netherlands and Belgium. Of course, being party to the NPT does not always imply peaceful nuclear intentions, but that is for case study research to sort out.

Prevailing Understandings of Alliances and Nuclear Proliferation–Related Behavior

Treaty alliances involve written-down, and often public, pledges to aid an ally following an attack by a third-party aggressor. Accordingly, rational choice perspectives take such alliances to be credible institutions. For one, reneging on written pledges that are publicly visible damages a state's reputation. By breaking a promise to support an ally, the unfaithful state will find it harder to form new alliances or craft new agreements.[6] Adversaries could become bolder and challenge the other alliance commitments of the guarantor. For another, violating an alliance treaty can incur domestic costs. Alliance treaties must be shepherded through domestic legislative bodies—a process that usually requires building coalitions and burning political capital. Governments should endure the pain of this process only if they believe in the importance of the alliance for national security reasons. Democracies should thus be the most reliable security partners that states can have. Their leaders are more constrained by their formal agreements to follow through on their promises, whereas autocratic leaders might approach their commitments more cavalierly.[7] When promises of military support are verbal or tacit, as in the case of informal alliances, the guarantor can disclaim responsibility for the ally without risking domestic backlash or reduced international standing.[8]

Still, alliances should be neither too credible nor too incredible due to what Glenn Snyder calls the alliance dilemma.[9] Making too strong a security guarantee shields the costs of aggressive behavior for that receiving ally. A moral hazard problem thus arises. From the perspective of the guarantor, it fears entrapment—the risk that it would be dragged into a conflict against its wishes. However, if the guarantor makes too weak a guarantee to an ally, then it could leave the security concerns of its ally unaddressed. From the perspective of the ally, the unreliability of its guarantor makes it fear abandonment when confronted with a threatening adversary. Several solutions for managing this dilemma are available to the guarantor, such as specifying conditions and using precise language in the alliance treaty.[10]

One benefit of resolving abandonment fears is a reduced risk of nuclear proliferation. In arguing that states might seek nuclear weapons for reasons of security, domestic politics, and prestige, Scott Sagan conjectures that a powerful security motive for nuclear interest is the worry that a major power guarantor will not fulfill its commitments.[11] Avery Goldstein elaborates on this argument, contending that middle powers like France and Great Britain under bipolarity and anarchy have a strong strategic rationale to discount the protection offered to them by a superpower and to acquire their own nuclear arsenals.[12] Dan Reiter finds that troop deployments can bolster alliance commitments and curb nuclear proliferation.[13] Similarly, Philipp Bleek and Eric Lorber highlight the importance of security guarantees in limiting the spread of nuclear weapons.[14] Nuno Monteiro and Alexandre Debs claim that strong allies would act on abandonment fears and acquire nuclear weapons.[15] These accounts are unclear as to how strong commitments can prevent proliferation and entrapment risks simultaneously.

This research has generated important insights, but several key issues remain. Formal alliances backed by democratic guarantors like the United States are allegedly very credible, yet many countries aligned with the United States have tried to acquire nuclear weapons (see table 1). As for Goldstein's study, not all middle powers under bipolarity or anarchy succeeded in acquiring nuclear weapons, if they had tried to do so at all. Statistical research has also yielded mixed findings on alliances. One analysis finds that having an alliance with a major dampens the likelihood that a state will acquire (or even consider) nuclear weapons, whereas another notes that "nuclear defenders do discourage a deepening of nuclear proliferation among protégés, but there is not much difference between states possessing or lacking nuclear defenders in terms of the likelihood of having a nuclear weapons program."[16] Nevertheless, a stress test has found that alliances are weakly correlated with different measures of proliferation.[17] We thus need a rigorous and predictive theory that takes a more sophisticated view of how abandonment fears wax and wane. In many accounts abandonment fears are constant, resulting either from the institutional design of the alliance or from idiosyncratic circumstances. Consequently, arguments about abandonment fears causing nuclear proliferation are difficult to falsify. The challenge then involves identifying the conditions under which abandonment fears reach a certain threshold whereby states become especially likely to seek their own nuclear weapons.

How Alliances Affect Nuclear Weapons Interest

In this section, I address the foregoing analytical issues. I first discuss how alliances best reduce the likelihood of states from wanting nuclear weapons. I then describe how guarantors can adjust their alliances in a way that creates proliferation risks. Thereupon I illuminate the challenges that guarantors face in suppressing nuclear interest.[18]

HOW ALLIANCES BEST PREVENT NUCLEAR PROLIFERATION

Because no central government in the international system exists, states have to optimize between arming (internal balancing) and forming alliances (external balancing) to obtain security.[19] Following World War II, when the United States and the Soviet Union were striving to acquire and improve their nuclear capabilities, weaker states came to depend more on alliances for their security. They thus received nuclear security guarantees—a form of extended deterrence whereby the guarantor dissuades an adversary from attacking its ally by threatening unacceptable costs.[20] Yet those weaker states could not take their received nuclear security guarantees for granted. Unlike in previous historical periods, alliances in the nuclear age often feature vague commitments regarding collective defense despite the existential stakes involved,[21] and so states continuously evaluate whether and how their guarantors would aid them in a possible militarized crisis that involves a nuclear-armed adversary. I argue that states determine the credibility of their nuclear security guarantees with reference to their guarantor's strategic posture. Two factors are critical: foreign policy doctrine and conventional military deployments. Of these two factors, conventional military deployments are more important.

Foreign policy doctrine helps allies to understand the security orientation and interests of their guarantor. It allows them to evaluate the extent to which their interests converge with those of the guarantor. If interests converge, insofar as the survival and security of the ally are deemed vital to those of the guarantor, then the guarantee will seem believable.[22] However, states do not wish to rely on rhetoric alone: interests can change and even diverge with circumstances. States want to determine whether the guarantor is bearing costs to support the alliance—is the guarantor putting its money where its mouth is?

Hence the importance accorded by the ally to the in-theater conventional military deployments of the guarantor, particularly those on the ally's territory. Such forward basing reflects the degree to which the guarantor is sinking costs into the ally's security. Troops are also hostages that convey commitment—they bind the guarantor in future decision-making so that the guarantor follows through on its promises.[23] These deployments can include ground troops and non-nuclear-armed (perhaps dual-capable) aerial and naval forces. Conventional military deployments matter because they constitute a credible commitment device on the part of the guarantor to respond militarily on its ally's behalf. Any act of aggression against the ally implicates the involvement of the guarantor's armed forces stationed on that ally's territory. The guarantor has "skin in the game" such that it would face pressure to respond if its forward-deployed forces are threatened. This logic existed even before nuclear weapons. Prior to World War I, when asked how many British troops were necessary for augmenting France's security, French general Ferdinand Foch quipped that "one single private soldier" was sufficient and that "we would take good care that he was killed."[24]

Yet a major reason why forward conventional military deployments matter is that they bolster what security experts call *deterrence-by-denial:* they directly raise the cost of war to the adversary. If the guarantor's conventional forces have the ability to hold off an attack just long enough for reinforcements to arrive, the adversary faces a lower likelihood of winning on the battlefield without using nuclear weapons. Those forward deployments might even defeat the invading force. In contrast, in the absence of such forces, a nuclear security guarantee hinges on *deterrence-by-punishment—* that is, the promise that the guarantor would impose unacceptable costs on an aggressive adversary by way of a devastating nuclear riposte. International relations scholars generally agree that deterrence-by-denial is more effective than deterrence-by-punishment. Robert Pape argues that successful coercion depends on disrupting the target militarily rather than hurting its population, whereas John Mearsheimer contends that failures in conventional deterrence are likely when the adversary believes a blitzkrieg—or lightning attack—is easy.[25] Paul K. Huth offers statistical evidence that denying an adversary the ability to win on the battlefield quickly and decisively enhances deterrence.[26]

Making deterrence-by-punishment strategies believable is difficult precisely because nuclear weapons are involved. Consider how the nuclear balance can shape perceptions regarding the credibility of a security guarantee when we consider only nuclear weapons. If the adversary has nuclear supremacy, whether in terms of more or better nuclear weapons, then it could blackmail the guarantor at the ally's expense. If the guarantor and the nuclear-armed adversary each possess a survivable second-strike capability, then the guarantor might be tempted to surrender the ally under nuclear parity in order to avoid nuclear devastation. In other words, the security interests of the guarantor and those of its ally become decoupled. Indeed, many American allies engaged in nuclear proliferation–related behavior when Washington was losing or had lost nuclear supremacy over Moscow. In contrast, deterrence-by-punishment may be more credible when the guarantor has nuclear supremacy such that it can launch a disarming first strike against the adversary. Under these circumstances, the adversary might not risk armed conflict, even with the guarantor's ally.[27] However, the benefits of nuclear supremacy should not be overstated if both sides incur unacceptable damage in a nuclear war.[28] In one analysis, Matthew Fuhrmann and Todd Sechser find that stationing nuclear weapons on an ally's territory does not bolster deterrence effects, because those nuclear weapons represent sunk costs rather than provide constraints on future decision-making.[29] Accordingly, an unfavorable nuclear balance matters to the degree that it would make allies even more attentive to the doctrinal and conventional military foundations of their received security guarantees.[30] Unless the adversary can certainly disarm the guarantor with a bolt-from-the-blue strike without incurring unacceptable harm—an extremely difficult task—the conventional military protection that the guarantor offers its ally remains valuable.

Conventional military deployments also benefit the guarantor because they attenuate the entrapment risks normally associated with strong alliance commitments.[31] To bolster deterrence of a shared adversary, forward-deployed forces should coordinate their operational planning and engage in joint military exercises with the host government's military. That way they can fight together as an effective, integrated force on the battlefield. Some alliances exhibit tight coordination: the American-led Combined Forces Command retains wartime operational control of the South Korean military, having relinquished peacetime operational control in 1994.[32] All things being equal, the greater the depth of planning coordination and integration, the better the guarantor can detect and restrain unwanted behavior by the ally. Moreover, conventional military deployments mitigate some of the weaknesses associated with measures that experts have identified as helpful for reducing entrapment risks. Consider, for example, the use of greater treaty precision and conditions to specify narrowly the circumstances under which an alliance commitment becomes active. Though these tools are helpful by themselves, the guarantor may have difficulty assigning culpability when an unwanted dispute begins. Conventional military deployments can complement these measures, because they monitor certain aspects of the ally's own defense planning as well as its command and control structures. Military attachés could assist intelligence efforts in processing local armed forces' messages and providing human intelligence.[33] During the Cold War, military intelligence units accompanied American and British forward-deployed forces in frontline states like West Germany. Some overseas military installations even served as intelligence bases.[34]

To be sure, the extent to which conventional military deployments reduce entrapment risks must not be exaggerated. Although "U.S. basing agreements do, of course, limit aspects of a host country's sovereignty," Alexander Cooley and Daniel Nexon argue that "beyond occasional provisions for joint consultations over security arrangements, [basing agreements] do not generally govern other host-country institutions."[35] Indeed, host governments often regain sovereignty rights over time by renegotiating their basing agreements with Washington.[36] Furthermore, embassies offer a better resource for intelligence gathering. According to Michael Herman, "Cold War espionage was closely linked with the position of intelligence officers as agent-runners and recruiters, operating from embassies under diplomatic cover."[37] At the American embassy in Seoul, for example, foreign service officers and intelligence analysts collaborated in evaluating South Korean proliferation risks. Conventional military deployments have the capacity for reducing entrapment through joint planning and intelligence, but these deployments do not eliminate its possibility.

HOW ALLIANCE ADJUSTMENTS CAN PROVOKE
NUCLEAR PROLIFERATION

Despite their benefits, forward deployments can be materially and financially costly for the guarantor. They can strain defense budgets and take money out of the domestic economy. To be willing and able to shoulder these costs signifies commitment.[38] They are thus sensitive to changes in its strategic posture, whereby the guarantor changes its foreign policy objectives to diverge from those of the ally. Nixon's attempt at rapprochement with China and its effects on Taiwan is one such instance. Alternatively, domestic economic concerns might induce the guarantor to exploit the relatively inexpensive substitution effects of nuclear weapons to replace manpower unilaterally. The Eisenhower administration partly implemented the New Look for this reason.[39]

Whatever their cause, these changes can adversely affect the security of the ally and stoke abandonment fears, especially if they are major, unforeseen, or unilateral from the ally's perspective. I hypothesize that such changes make recipients of nuclear security guarantees more likely to seek their own nuclear weapon arsenals.[40] Proliferation seems to be a drastic response, yet it has a strategic logic. When an ally confronts a nuclear-armed adversary, nuclear weapons provide the ally with a deterrent capability so that one day it can resist the coercion of that adversary.[41] In other words, the ally engages in "true self-help" behavior in balancing against the adversary.[42] Even if the ally decides to pursue a hedging strategy instead by actively developing latent nuclear capabilities, the ally could still position itself in such a way as to gain certain coercive benefits.[43]

My argument assumes that in engaging in nuclear proliferation–related behavior, the ally has a bona fide interest in obtaining technologies related to the development of nuclear weapons. That is, it is not using the threat of nuclear proliferation as a bargaining chip for extracting new security assurances from the guarantor without any intention to acquire nuclear weapons. Admittedly, states have incentives to represent their resolve and capabilities to get better agreements with friends and enemies in the absence of a world government. Since guarantors like the United States appear to have a strong interest in nuclear nonproliferation, the ally might believe that it could bluff and exploit that interest in order to draw additional assurances.[44] However, I believe that my assumption is tenable. As one of Aesop's fables warns us, crying wolf is dangerous when no wolves are around. The ally would have to send a nuclear signal loud enough for the guarantor to receive and interpret in the intended manner before responding favorably. Yet nuclear feints are difficult and even dangerous to do effectively: if the signal is too loud, the ally could catch the unwanted attention of an adversary and cause an incident; if too quiet, the signal could have no effect whatsoever.[45] Finally, the argument that the ally is exploiting the guarantor's interests in nonproliferation is paradoxical. How can uncertainty over the guarantor's future behavior provoke the use of a strategy—nuclear bluffing, in this case—that relies on the ability to predict the behavioral responses of the guarantor?

HOW ALLIANCES MIGHT REVERSE NUCLEAR PROLIFERATION

The guarantor could lose a lot from the spread of nuclear weapons, even among its allies. Nuclear weapons undercut the ability of the superpower guarantor to project its power and influence as well as to control escalatory dynamics.[46] Accordingly, when it learns or suspects that its ally might be seeking an independent nuclear deterrent, the guarantor has incentives to thwart such ambitions as quickly and as comprehensively as possible. To begin with, diplomatic relations with affected allies and adversaries are at stake, especially if the guarantor is seen as not doing enough to restrain the proliferating ally. It could even be seen as culpable if its (perceived) inaction benefits the proliferator at the expense of others. Local security dilemmas could subsequently intensify.[47] Although the ally seeks nuclear weapons to satisfy its defense needs, others could see its behavior as sufficiently threatening that they acquire their own new weapons. As such, the guarantor prefers its ally to dismantle its nonpeaceful nuclear program. It might perhaps wish to monitor all nuclear activities, denying its ally enrichment and reprocessing capabilities as well. Such a comprehensive nonproliferation campaign would address any international doubts about the ally's willingness and ability to restart its nuclear weapons program. How can the guarantor get the nuclear genie back into the alliance bottle?

I argue that pursuing this task is extremely challenging for the guarantor. States that have decided to undertake a nuclear weapons program typically do so recognizing and accepting the risks and costs involved. And so the guarantor is no longer deterring its ally from seeking nuclear weapons. The guarantor is instead trying to compel that very ally to stop its proliferation-related behavior—a harder undertaking, since scholars agree that deterrence is easier than compellence.[48] Moreover, the alliance bottle is broken and must be fixed first, requiring the guarantor to undo the harm inflicted on the security guarantee that prompted the ally to desire nuclear weapons in the first place. Reasserting security guarantees is challenging when the affected ally has had its faith in its received commitments badly shaken at a time when it faces a hostile threat environment. The guarantor might have to make credible commitments to restore troop levels or to retain existing troop levels. Yet making such commitments believable is difficult when the guarantor has already revealed an interest in limiting them. Alternatively, the factors that led to the unfavorable alliance adjustments in the first place could still exist. The guarantor might have enduring economic problems or irrevocably different foreign policy interests.

Certain proposed alliance solutions are also counterproductive. Military action is one option, but using military force against an ally would lack credibility and make the guarantor look unhinged to its other security partners.[49] Gene Gerzhoy identifies another option. He claims that threats to abrogate the alliance altogether could compel a proliferating state to renounce having an independent nuclear arsenal.[50] Yet such threats risk deepening abandonment fears even if they are conditional on the disavowal of nuclear weapons. A paradox also arises: how can abandonment fears trigger nuclear weapons interest but abandonment threats end it? Moreover, terminating an alliance is difficult. Besides, public alliance treaties cannot be removed on a whim: in the case of the United States, a major procedural process that involves Congress and multiple government outfits is necessary for dismantling them. The decade spanning Nixon's overtures to China and the termination of the American alliance with Taiwan is instructive. Finally, if carried out, ending an alliance could have undesirable diplomatic repercussions among other allies. They might begin to fear abandonment themselves, whereas the adversary could perceive a "window of opportunity" to attack.[51]

Disruptive, nonmilitary policy instruments hold slightly more promise. One potential avenue available to the guarantor is the extent to which the ally depends on the guarantor for economic growth—that is, how exposed is the ally's economy to the coercion of the guarantor. The higher the ratio of trade with the guarantor to gross domestic product is one metric for evaluating this level of vulnerability. Alternatively, the guarantor might cut off or promise forms of aid that the ally believes is necessary for the ally's goals, be it the maintenance of domestic rule or the viability of its economic programs. The ally could also be susceptible to the manipulation of financial flows that it receives from the guarantor. Monetary sanctions are another tool. By attacking the value and stability of the ally's currency, the guarantor could create inflation, increase debt burdens, and disrupt local economic planning. Alternatively, the guarantor could seize highly valued assets belonging to the ally.[52] All things being equal, the ally wishes to avoid these types of economic sanctions because it does not wish to experience economic difficulties that weaken its hold on power at home and empower potential opposition groups. It might desire avoiding such hardship if it already faces a hostile threat environment.[53] Because it derives more from the relationship than does the guarantor, the dependent ally should be more willing to concede when coerced strongly.[54] Absent such leverage, the nonproliferation challenge for the guarantor will be severe.

Economic sanctions still have limited efficacy in absolute terms even if they are relatively more effective tools. Robert Pape argues that economic sanctions are ineffective because "pervasive nationalism often makes states and societies willing to endure considerable punishment rather than abandon what are seen as the interests of the nation." Furthermore, states are institutionally adept at working around the sanctions that could be leveled against them.[55] Indeed, the ally should anticipate the sanctioning effort of its guarantor, thus factoring this expected cost into its decision to seek nuclear weapons. Nevertheless, complete skepticism over sanctions would be unwarranted. After all, the empirical record of sanctions is highly biased because they are implemented in the hardest cases. Just as it is easier to deter than to compel, the best sanction is one that does not have to be used.[56] Nevertheless, as Daniel Drezner shows, states might infrequently use sanctions against their allies, but when they do, they are more likely to extract concessions from them than from adversaries.[57] Moreover, the ally might underestimate the likelihood or costs of a sanctioning effort when it decides to embark on a nuclear weapons program. The benefits of such a program could outweigh those potential costs amid a hostile security environment. Finally, and most importantly, sanctions can be especially effective if they directly target the nuclear activities of the proliferator. Sometimes allies also desire nuclear energy in order to sustain economic growth. Rather than threaten to harm the economic interests of the ally directly, the guarantor could block access to the credit, technologies, and resources necessary for developing nuclear power whether for military or for civilian purposes.[58]

So far this discussion presumes that the guarantor has an overriding interest to halt an ally's nuclear interest. Despite the strategic incentives involved for valuing nonproliferation and despite how some scholars postulate that nuclear nonproliferation has been a key pillar of American grand strategy for much of the Cold War and after, I believe that such an assumption is unwarranted.[59] I argue that interest in the nonproliferation mission depends on whether key decision makers are pursuing foreign policy goals that are complementary or inimical. Sometimes foreign policy goals are complementary with nonproliferation. Consider, for example, a situation in which the guarantor wishes to improve relations with an adversary, either for their own sake or to balance against another adversary.[60] In so doing, the guarantor might wish to restrain the nuclear ambitions of an ally because the guarantor wants to assure the adversary of its bona fide intentions to cooperate or to prevent that ally from sabotaging the rapprochement effort. However, foreign policy goals can work at cross-purposes with nonproliferation: the guarantor may wish to retrench and thus retract certain military and political commitments. Although the guarantor would prefer not to see nuclear weapons spread for strategic reasons, it might have difficulty striking a balance between reassurance and geopolitical divestment. The ally will recognize that the guarantor is pursuing conflicting foreign policy goals, thereby complicating any nonproliferation effort.

To the extent that an ally does end up renouncing nuclear weapons, my argument is open to the possibility that it does so for multiple, even non-alliance, reasons. To be sure, I do not argue that alliance considerations are unimportant in an ally's decision to reverse its nuclear proliferation–related behavior. Nevertheless, alliance coercion could be one factor among many—it may not even be decisive for the final outcome. If the ally has adopted a hedging strategy, then it might stop its nuclear activities once it assesses the security environment to be such that nuclear weapons have become undesirable. Alternatively, the ally might find that rejecting international demands for inspections or antinuclear treaty commitments are no longer useful, either because their complaints regarding a nonproliferation agreement have been addressed or because their foreign policy orientation has changed. Finally, the ally might have succeeded in acquiring certain technologies—such as the ability to enrich uranium or to reprocess plutonium—it had always wanted while stopping short of building nuclear weapons. The ally might have simply wished to be in a better position so as to acquire those weapons in the future if international circumstances might necessitate them.

FIVE PROPOSITIONS

Five propositions flow from this discussion. First, alliances are less useful than often presumed with respect to the prevention of nuclear proliferation among their members. Second, in-theater conventional military forces are key for boosting American extended nuclear guarantees. Third, alliance coercion—though it may still be important—has played less of a role in nuclear nonproliferation than some accounts suggest. Fourth, the best tool available to the United States, if it decides to use this tool, is leveraging the economic or technological dependence the security-dependent ally has on it. These propositions ultimately suggest a fifth proposition: deterring a nuclear weapons program is easier than compelling the reversal of one.

Alternative Arguments

Aside from pushing back against the view that American nonproliferation efforts were decisive, I evaluate my argument against several alternative explanations for nuclear proliferation: the adversary thesis, the domestic politics thesis, and the prestige thesis. With respect to why states might renounce nuclear weapons, these arguments do not necessarily rival my own. My skepticism over how alliance coercion can definitively stop actual nuclear programs allows other factors to be influential.

THE ADVERSARY THESIS

The adversary thesis posits that threat emanating from the adversary is alone sufficient to explain nuclear proliferation. To clarify, my theory assumes that an adversarial threat exists, since abandonment fears would have no salience in its absence. Hence the United States could withdraw large numbers of forces from Western Europe in the 1990s without much risk of nuclear proliferation. Yet some might argue that adversarial threat—irrespective of the guarantor's own actions—drives nuclear proliferation. When the adversary poses a threat, the ally ratchets up its nuclear weapons activities. When the adversary poses less of a threat, the ally reduces those activities. This alternative argument narrowly reflects Stephen Walt's assertion that states respond to threats rather than capabilities in making alignment decisions.[61]

Both my theory and this counterargument are "realist": they each see states engaging in nuclear proliferation–related behavior as a response to external stimuli. They also assume conflictual preferences and unitary statehood.[62] However, my theory is distinct in assuming that states would prefer to depend on their alliances and that adversarial threat is at most a necessary but not a sufficient factor for their nuclear interest. In contrast, the adversary thesis assumes that states believe that their alliances are always unreliable and only serve as a temporary expedient in a self-help world. States react more to the conduct of their adversary than to that of their guarantors.

Of course, a state might view an adversarial threat as more severe when facing possible abandonment by a major power. Conversely, the ally might be more dismissive of the threat if it is adequately assured of its received security guarantees. To disentangle these overlapping variables, I examine how leaders construe their threat environments before substantive changes in security commitments occur. For my theory to be empirically valid, leaders should see the severity of the adversarial threat as a function of the reliability of the alliance support they receive. Alternatively, their evaluations of the adversarial threat should remain unchanged when the guarantor unfavorably adjusts its security commitment made to the ally. If perceptions of the adversarial threat drive nuclear proliferation–related behavior before any such changes, then my argument would be invalid.

THE DOMESTIC POLITICS THESIS

The domestic politics thesis offers a more contrasting perspective on nuclear proliferation. By asserting that international state behavior results largely from internal stimuli, the domestic politics thesis emphasizes regime survival rather than state security. Specifically, as Etel Solingen argues, decisions to acquire nuclear weapons after the NPT entered into force reflect governing leaders' preferences over their state's role in the global economy. Outward-looking regimes favor greater integration with the global economy in order to increase their domestic legitimacy through economic growth. They eschew nuclear weapons development because it could reduce their country to pariah status and cause trade-destroying security dilemmas. Inward-looking regimes legitimate themselves through nationalism and thus favor economic self-sufficiency. These regimes are more likely to develop nuclear weapons, since they serve not to deter attack but to rally their populations, to stir nationalist rhetoric, and to divert attention away from domestic problems.[63] The domestic politics thesis thus postulates that nuclear interest is insensitive to changes in the external threat environment. A nuclear weapons program could cease with the emergence of an outward-looking regime. To be sure, Solingen restricts her analysis to the NPT period, but the motivation for doing so is unclear given the perceived fragility of the nonproliferation regime during the 1970s. Governments wishing to engage with the international community might have been disinclined to acquire nuclear weapons even before the NPT was signed in 1968.

THE PRESTIGE THESIS

The final alternative argument is the prestige thesis, whereby leaders do not implement rational and materialist cost-benefit calculations in their nuclear decision-making. Leaders instead might perceive nuclear weapons as being intrinsically valuable, because those weapons confer prestigious status on the states that possess them.[64] In Jacques Hymans's schema, leaders who are oppositional nationalists are prone to nuclear weapons interest, because they have heightened threat perceptions and exhibit excessive confidence in their country's ability to face adversaries. For this rare type of leader, "the decision to acquire nuclear weapons is not only a means to the end of getting; it is also an end in itself."[65] Other leaders might hold contrary views—namely, that nuclear weapons are so fundamentally distasteful and immoral that no conceivable strategic situation could merit having them. Such leaders might believe that these weapons could even undermine national prestige. Leaders drawn from societies steeped in antimilitarist norms are more likely to hold such views. These antimilitarist norms could be politically manifest in social movements, large-scale protests, public opinion polls, and even independent media coverage on issues relating to nuclear policy, alliance politics, and the defense industry.[66] The prestige thesis overlaps with the domestic politics thesis, not least because antimilitarist norms are likely to be salient in democracies, which in turn are likely to be outward-looking.[67] Nevertheless, the prestige thesis allows leaders of inward-looking regimes to vary in their beliefs about the value of nuclear weapons.

THE NONEXCLUSIVITY OF ALTERNATIVE ARGUMENTS

These alternative arguments do not necessarily rival my own framework. I argue that alliances might not be the effective instruments for thwarting actual cases of nuclear proliferation, as they are sometimes heralded for doing. Accordingly, decisions to cease proliferation-related behavior can have different or complex causes.[68] For example, the ally might desire nuclear weapons following a perceived breakdown in its alliance but then renounce those desires to mollify its adversary. Alternatively, alliance adjustments might spark nuclear interest, but a change in regime type or leadership could lead to a cessation of proliferation-related behavior. In such instances, alliance coercion might have been not a primary factor in the nonproliferation outcome but at best a secondary factor, especially if the guarantor experiences significant difficulties in obtaining the ally's compliance. Indeed, I generally share Scott Sagan's observation of "nuclear weapons proliferation and restraint have occurred in the past for more than one reason: different historical cases are best explained by different causal models."[69]

Empirical Strategy

The following chapters evaluate how alliances can inhibit nuclear proliferation by investigating the five propositions outlined earlier. Three intensive cases on West Germany, Japan, and South Korea are the empirical core of this book (chapters 3, 4, and 5, respectively). Complementing these cases is a set of smaller cases contained in chapter 6. This chapter expands the variation of my study by considering whether and how alliance politics can explain the French and British cases of proliferation success as well as the varying levels of nuclear interest exhibited by Australia, Norway, and Taiwan. Because this complementary chapter strives to determine the external validity of my framework, it does not draw on the same level of theory-testing and deep archival work as the three intensive cases do. Why, then, did I choose the cases of West Germany, Japan, and South Korea for intensive analysis?

These three cases are all most-likely cases for alliance ties to matter for curbing nuclear proliferation risks. Some scholars have called West Germany and Japan "effectively semi-sovereign states," meaning that they have had little foreign policy autonomy in the Cold War so as to render them susceptible to American pressure.[70] With respect to West Germany and South Korea especially, scholars have even argued that these allies were coerced into renouncing any nuclear interests that they might have had. If alliances are imperfect instruments for managing nuclear proliferation risks in these most-likely cases, then one wonders about states that are less dependent on their relationships with the United States.

Other methodological reasons lead me to prioritize these three cases. The cases of West Germany and Japan together form a *controlled comparative case study* research design. They exhibit important similarities on several key dimensions that plausibly affect their foreign and defense policies. They were both defeated aggressors in World War II and subsequently hosted a large American military presence that was originally an occupying force but evolved to become "trip wires" against communist aggression. They are also postwar success stories: they became wealthy liberal democracies that provide extensive social benefits to their citizens, who in turn have cultivated strong antimilitarist norms. But despite these similarities, their geographical differences made them diverge in their susceptibility to changes in American grand strategy and force posture. These changes had varying implications for how both states should perceive their received nuclear security guarantees.

Though South Korea owes its existence to a Cold War partition similar to the one that created West Germany, I analyze South Korea for different reasons. For one, South Korea is a *critical* case for my theory because the United States initiated plans for several major troop withdrawals without much, if any, consultations with the South Korean government. Both of these plans for troop withdrawals reflected important changes in American grand strategy and so should provoke the nuclear response that my theory expects. For another, the South Korean case exhibits high values on those independent variables that reflect the alternative explanations. South Korea faced a hostile international environment during the 1960s and the 1970s due to the double threat posed by Maoist China and North Korea. At this time, the nationalist Park Chung-hee led an authoritarian regime in South Korea. Finally, South Korea was a security-dependent ally that also needed economic and technological support from the United States, thus making it highly vulnerable to alliance coercion.

For all three intensive case studies, I rely on extensive archival evidence that I gathered from multiple archives, the *Foreign Relations of the United States* documentary record, and the secondary historical literature. Unfortunately, direct "smoking gun" evidence is often difficult to obtain when researching such sensitive issues of national security as nuclear weapons policy. This problem is especially acute for countries like Japan and South Korea, where ongoing security concerns have made those governments unwilling to be fully transparent on how they dealt with these issues in the past. Although the evidence is sometimes circumstantial, these documents still provide insights into the decision-making process of American leaders and their interlocutions with their allied counterparts.

I structure my analyses in the following manner. I first review the strategic and domestic contexts of each country. I then describe the nuclear proliferation–related behavior that they undertook. Thereupon I examine evidence that alliance adjustments prompted those allies to engage in such activities before considering the alternative arguments. Specifically, I investigate whether abandonment fears animated decisions to ratchet up nuclear proliferation–related behavior so as to determine the validity of the first and second propositions of my argument. The deck is admittedly stacked in favor of the first proposition by examining cases of supposed alliance breakdown. Yet I still assess the alliance explanation against the alternatives to make sure that the connection is not spurious. After I summarize the findings regarding why allies initiated such actions, my focus turns to why they stopped so as to address the validity of the third and fourth propositions of my argument. I look at how the United States might have used various alliance-related nonproliferation tools—reassurance, nuclear sharing arrangements, abandonment threats, and nonmilitary tools—to compel states into renouncing their nuclear interests. To determine whether allies ended their nuclear interest due to American-led coercion, the evidence must do more than to show that security assurances and economic ties framed the nonproliferation effort. For example, the actions and rhetoric of the ally's leadership should reveal a sensitivity to actual or threatened applications of nonmilitary sanctions, bowing to such pressure by canceling suspicious nuclear programs or adopting stronger international safeguards. Conversely, the guarantor should be hamstrung in its efforts to coerce a much more economically resilient ally. Once I assemble the evidence, I summarize the main findings and consider again the alternative arguments. By checking whether the four propositions all have empirical validity, support is built for the broader argument that deterring proliferation-related behavior is easier than compelling a reversal of it.

This chapter explains how alliances are more effective in deterring potential nuclear proliferation than in compelling nuclear reversals. For the first part of my argument, I emphasize the doctrinal and military infrastructure that supports the security guarantees that allies receive. The original treaty underwriting the partnership does not fully determine the scope of subsequent entrapment and abandonment concerns—indeed, abandonment fears constantly exist. What varies is their intensity. And so guarantors invest in their alliances with varying levels of conventional military commitments and rhetorical pledges. In-theater conventional military commitments also have the benefit of addressing entrapment risks. Nor do democratic guarantors have a unique advantage in credibly extending nuclear deterrence. After all, the stakes are existential: recipients of treaty commitments are looking for more than pieces of paper when they evaluate whether their guarantor would support them in a militarized conflict with a nuclear-armed adversary. They want to see that their guarantor has "skin in the game" and can provide deterrence-by-denial. They are thus acutely sensitive to major and unfavorable conventional military redeployments that the guarantor might make for economic or geopolitical reasons. When such events occur, their abandonment concerns intensify so as to stimulate nuclear proliferation-related behavior. Unfortunately, the guarantor will have difficulty in trying to end such behavior, if it is so inclined to stop it. Of course, no one argues that it is easy, but some scholars do assign special powers to military alliances in curtailing proliferation efforts. In the event that the ally does renounce nuclear weapons, it could do so for reasons unrelated to alliance coercion. Finally, this chapter describes the alternative arguments and outlines my empirical strategy. Before I turn to the cases, however, a historical overview of American security guarantees between 1945 and 1980 is necessary.

American Security Guarantees during the Cold War, 1949–1980

Because chapters 3 through 6 address the nuclear proliferation–related behaviors of major American allies, I should chronicle the evolution of American Cold War strategy. I show how American decision makers constructed and adjusted their security commitments overseas between 1945 and 1980. As such, this chapter has two purposes: first, to introduce important concepts, historical events, and topics that will be frequently mentioned throughout the empirical chapters; and second, to outline variation in how decision makers implemented changes in American strategic posture and, by extension, the security guarantees provided to American allies. Of course, several basic continuities characterized American strategy during the Cold War. Aside from broad agreement on the need to contain the Soviet Union, American decision makers believed that nuclear superiority over the Soviet Union was necessary for securing American strategic interests. Nevertheless, the nuclear balance evinced important changes throughout the Cold War: the United States lost nuclear superiority by the time Lyndon Johnson had left the presidency. The United States began designing and developing weapons systems in the 1970s so as to try regaining nuclear supremacy by the late 1980s. Some presidents like Dwight Eisenhower and Richard Nixon wanted to rely more than others on the nuclear deterrent while its allies bear more of the conventional defense burden. All presidents wanted to reduce the American troop presence abroad—either in Europe or in East Asia—at some point when they were in office.

Still, the extent to which American decision makers successfully adjusted their alliance commitments varied. This variation matters for the empirical chapters, since I will use it to explain why and when key allies began to distrust American security commitments sufficiently to desire nuclear weapons. To organize the following discussion, I divide the historical period under review into four distinct phases: 1949–1952, 1953–1960, 1961–1968, and 1969–1980. For each of these periods, I consider several issues that bear on the individual case studies, including American military planning for nuclear and conventional wars, force posture changes, threat perceptions, and the economic factors that constrained American Cold War strategy.

1949–1952: The Beginning of Commitment

Geopolitical circumstances compelled Washington to provide regional security outside the Western hemisphere after World War II. Whereas the United States had retreated to its own neighborhood when World War I ended, the expansionist threat posed by the Soviet Union now raised the perceived costs associated with isolationism.[1] The devastation wrought in Europe and advances in weapons technology combined to negate the sense of insularity that the United States had long enjoyed. With industrial centers vulnerable to conquest by the Soviet Union, the United States could no longer afford to be disinterested in the security of others lest transnational communism expand its global reach. In early 1949, the United States signed the North Atlantic Treaty with Canada and ten Western European countries to form the North Atlantic Treaty Organization (NATO). A few months later, the Soviet Union detonated a nuclear device for the first time, much earlier than expected.[2]

Washington would have had the upper hand over Moscow in a nuclear war at this early stage of the Cold War. Strategic Air Command had over 120 nuclear-capable aircraft, and the size of the stockpile was projected to grow to four hundred bombs by 1951.[3] Yet this edge was tenuous. A 1949 report commissioned by the Joint Chiefs of Staff found that an atomic air offensive would not "per se, bring about capitulation, destroy the roots of Communism, or critically weaken the power of Soviet leadership to dominate the people." To the contrary, such an attack would be counterproductive, because "for the majority of the Soviet people, atomic bombing would validate Soviet propaganda against foreign powers, stimulate resentment against the United States, unify the people, and increase their will to fight." This report estimated that an aerial campaign would "only" reduce Soviet industrial capacity by 30 to 40 percent. As a result, the Soviet Union could still exploit its conventional military advantage by conquering areas of Western Europe and elsewhere, though it would face massive logistical challenges amid likely fuel shortages. And so the United States would have experienced difficulties defeating the Soviet Union with nuclear weapons alone thanks to Soviet conventional military power.[4] That Moscow came into possession of nuclear weapons sooner than expected in 1949 meant that it could become bolder in taking the initiative and intimidating Western Europe.[5]

Countering the growing Soviet threat required the United States to mobilize extensive resources in order to strengthen its allies, to establish both a conventional and a nuclear deterrent, and to prepare its population for possible war. However, American decision makers realized that any successful policy of containment would be expensive to maintain and would require extensive state intervention in the American economy. The political willingness for undertaking these actions was absent. Congress passed two tax cuts in the late 1940s, even overriding a presidential veto in 1948, and denied Truman's request for tax increases to finance military expenditures.[6] Attempts by the executive branch to legislate universal military training failed.[7] Indeed, early American Cold War foreign policy was subject to intense partisan debate over the extent to which the United States should provide military and financial assistance to Western Europe.[8] Even American defense planners and strategists were unsure of what parts of the world necessitated American protection. George Kennan famously distinguished between the advanced military-industrial core and the periphery so as to argue for the vital importance of the former. Yet other writings of his seem to reveal his support for curbing communist expansion anywhere it happened.[9] When decision makers did converge on the desirability for an aggressive military policy of containment, as articulated in a major policy paper called National Security Council Report 68 (NSC-68), they were hamstrung by concerns over costs and practicality given the lack of domestic support for such an expansive strategy.[10]

North Korea's invasion of South Korea in June 1950 removed these constraints by clarifying for many the seriousness of the Soviet threat. It gave the Truman administration ample justification to increase defense expenditures dramatically and the political capital to strengthen its alliance commitments.[11] Until 1950, the institutional form of NATO was weak, consisting largely of written pledges of members to come to an ally's aid in the event of an attack per article 5 of the alliance's founding document, the Washington Treaty. Formal policy coordination bodies were largely absent, and the alliance had neither a central headquarters nor a secretariat to manage its operations.[12] The Korean War provided new impetus for the expansion of alliance commitments in Western Europe. The United States deployed greater numbers of troops in Western Europe and pushed for improved policy coordination in NATO. Alongside these changes were institutional upgrades to the alliance such as a centralized administrative body located in Paris. The Korean War also dispelled doubts about the desirability of defending East Asian countries against communist aggression.

The incipient nature of pre-1950 American security guarantees partly reflected uncertainty over how to deal with the now-vanquished aggressors of World War II. The defeat of Nazi Germany in May 1945 and Imperial Japan in August 1945 marked the beginning of occupation in both countries. In Germany, the allied coalition had agreed at the Yalta Conference to divide the conquered territory into American, British, French, and Soviet zones of occupation. By contrast, the United States exercised exclusive administrative control over Japan. These allied zones of occupation could not last forever; despite their role in World War II, these occupied societies had to reacquire some form of political sovereignty eventually. Nevertheless, because tensions mounted between Washington and Moscow, geopolitical realities circum-scribed the extent to which these defeated states were able to determine their domestic and foreign policies. In 1949, the Western powers consolidated the non-Soviet Zones into West Germany. The Soviet Union established a communist satellite state that would become East Germany. Japan regained independence in 1952.

American (and other Western) decision makers soon faced an urgent di-lemma when reconstituting the political sovereignty of these defeated socie-ties. West Germany could not remain weak vis-à-vis a strong and persistent Soviet threat. Yet it was unclear how a strong and independent West Ger-many could be liberal democratic, amenable to American geopolitical in-terests, or, most optimistically, both. To resolve this dilemma, American de-cision makers adopted several measures. First, the Western powers would maintain an extensive troop presence in West Germany, thereby limiting the West German government's foreign policy options while posing a (limited) conventional deterrent to the Soviet Union. Second, West Germany would become a member of NATO and rearm under its auspices. In the famous words of Lord Ismay, these alliance commitments served to "keep the Sovi-ets out, the Americans in, and the Germans down." Third, the United States ultimately obliged the new West German government to make formal com-mitments not to acquire certain weapons in exchange for the restoration of its politically sovereign rights. The Final Act of the London Conference pro-vides that West Germany was "not to manufacture in its territory any atomic weapons, chemical weapons, or biological weapons."[13] The agreement also noted how NATO would closely monitor West Germany's armament activi-ties. West Germany was independent but restrained. Marc Trachtenberg best describes the situation facing West Germany: "Germany was to be tied to the West, and in important ways was made part of the West, but her free-dom of action was to be curtailed, and she was not to have the same sover-eign rights as the other western powers."[14]

A similar fear regarding Japan confronted American decision makers. They did not want to see Japan reemerge as an aggressive military power. Nevertheless, Japan could not remain completely defenseless, especially after communist forces took political control of the Chinese mainland in 1949. American and Japanese decision makers found a useful compro-mise. Tokyo adopted a constitution that renounced war and the acquisition of military forces, but it also entered into a bilateral security agreement with Washington when the Security Treaty Between the United States and Japan came into force in 1952. Similar to West Germany's participation in NATO, this treaty with Japan advanced American interests because it would perform the dual task of maintaining a bulwark against communist aggression while inhibiting Japanese militarism.[15] Moreover, it contained several provisions that delineated American basing rights on Japanese ter-ritory. For example, article 1 of the Security Treaty stipulated that Tokyo would grant Washington the "right" to "dispose United States land, air and sea forces in and about Japan" in order to satisfy their mutual security needs.[16]

The Korean War thus prompted the expansion of American security commitments around the globe. Aside from NATO and the Security Treaty with Japan, the United States contributed to the formation of the Australian, New Zealand, United States Security Treaty (ANZUS) in 1951. It went on to sign bilateral alliance treaties with South Korea (1953) and Taiwan (1955) in addition to the Southeast Asia Treaty Organization (SEATO; 1954). This last alliance entailed American security commitments to the Philippines, Thailand, and Pakistan.

Contemporaneous with these new alliances was a significant expansion of the American military. Between June 1950 and December 1952, all the services saw their forces increase. The number of Army divisions doubled from ten to twenty, the Navy saw an 80 percent increase in its ships, the Marine Corps added a third division, and the US Air Force more than doubled the number of wings. Total manpower increased from 1.45 million to 3.5 million.[17] With this military buildup, American troop deployments overseas grew considerably. In 1950 over 120,000 American military personnel were stationed in Western Europe. This number rose to almost 400,000 by 1954. Unsurprisingly, the Korean War also precipitated major increases in troop numbers in East Asia, from 147,000 in 1950 to over half a million in 1953.[18] Because of their numerical inferiority to Soviet forces, the enlarged American forces stationed in Europe likely would not have prevailed in a war. As such, nuclear weapons appreciated in their deterrent value as they become more sophisticated, more powerful, and more plentiful toward the end of the Truman administration.[19] According to war plans from this period, the Air Force would deliver nuclear weapons not only against industrial centers but also against a growing list of targets that included nuclear facilities, airfields, and even "Soviet ground and tactical air forces."[20]

Threat perceptions made the military buildup palatable, if not desirable, but it still represented a radical and expensive departure in American foreign and defense policy. The Truman administration earmarked $13 billion for defense spending in 1950, yet estimations of the defense budget would increase the number several-fold over the next few years. The Truman administration surmised that the "total annual bill for national security programs would stand at around $60 billion" by about 1955.[21] When the fiscally conservative Eisenhower and the Republican Party won the presidency in 1952, how such high levels of defense spending could last became uncertain.

1952–1960: Commitment and Nuclear Superiority

Ideas and beliefs over political economy influenced Eisenhower's foreign policy. Eisenhower wished to maintain balanced budgets, to control inflation, and to avoid deficits.[22] Even with respect to national defense, his strong personal opposition to "statism" made Eisenhower want to control government spending.[23] Because of the drastic uptick in military expenditures during the Truman administration, Eisenhower confronted a stark choice upon becoming president. One option involved repudiating his beliefs and raising taxes to maintain his country's military posture. The other option involved spending cuts that could endanger American national security. To overcome this conundrum, Eisenhower advanced a new approach to American foreign policy: the New Look.

Outlined in a policy document dated October 30, 1953, the New Look contained at least two key features. First, though maintaining that the Soviet Union represented a significant threat to American national security interests, the New Look shifted emphasis away from conventional military forces. Instead, the United States would rely on "the capability of inflicting massive retaliatory damage by offensive striking power." Accordingly, Washington would respond to Soviet aggression with the overwhelming use of its atomic capability—a strategy called "massive retaliation." Second, the United States would assist its allies in becoming more capable of their own defense. Despite calling for reductions in American military assistance to Western European countries, the New Look contended that "it is essential that the Western European states, including West Germany, build and maintain maximum feasible defensive strength."[24] The New Look was to provide an adequate deterrent to the Soviet Union without jeopardizing the American economy.

Relying on nuclear weapons also served a strategic rationale, since Western decision makers recognized that they would not be able to match Soviet conventional forces in Europe. British defense planners observed later in the 1960s that "any attempt by NATO to base its strategy for the defense by conventional means is impossible, unless the Western nations drastically lower their living standards."[25] In deterring Soviet attack with the threat of using nuclear weapons at an uncertain threshold, the United States was also reassuring its Western European allies—especially West Germany—that it had their security in mind. Moreover, matching Soviet conventional military power on the continent required military expenditures that the United States would not and could not pay. NSC-162/2, the principal document that describes the New Look, emphasizes this point in outlining the basic problems confronting American national security. Its opening section notes the need "to meet the Soviet threat to US security" without "seriously weakening the US economy or undermining our fundamental values and institutions."[26] The document later stresses the health of the American economy as the sine qua non of allied perseverance over the Soviet Union.[27] With the New Look, Eisenhower hoped to reduce spending from $43 billion to about $33 billion.[28] Cutting the size of the armed forces was necessary for fulfilling this objective.[29]

The New Look depended on Washington maintaining nuclear superiority over Moscow. Nuclear superiority compensated for Soviet conventional military superiority on the continent. If the Soviet Union could threaten a devastating nuclear strike on the American homeland, then Massive Retaliation would lose credibility. Nuclear war would have to involve the United States trading one of its own cities for Paris or Berlin—something that European statesmen would have trouble believing. For this reason the so-called missile gap that emerged in the late 1950s between the two superpowers unnerved American allies. Vulnerability to a Soviet nuclear strike might induce the United States to strike some bargain at their expense. To allay such worries, the United States invested extensively in its stockpile and delivery capabilities. Thus, from 1949 to 1960, the American nuclear arsenal grew from 250 primitive atomic weapons to eighteen thousand atomic and thermonuclear weapons. Even as late as 1962, the Soviet Union possessed "only" several hundred nuclear warheads as well as a limited delivery capability served by bombers and rocket-fueled missiles.[30] Pavel Podvig reports that the Soviet Union in 1962 "had about 100 Tu-95 and 60 3M bombers, which could deliver about 270 nuclear weapons to U.S. territory." Ballistic missile development continued apace, but the deployment and readiness of Soviet intercontinental ballistic missiles (ICBMs) still remained very limited despite the "missile gap" controversy.[31]

The result was that at this time a nuclear war would have been especially unbearable for the Soviet Union. Consistent with the New Look, any conventional aggression made by the Red Army would elicit a response that combined strategic and nuclear forces. MC-48—NATO's strategic planning document that was approved in 1954—envisaged the "early use of nuclear weapons to stop a Soviet invasion" while NATO forces were positioned on a forward defense line at the Weser, Fulda, and Lech Rivers. These conventional forces were not expected to repel the Soviet invasion. Rather, their placement would "force the Soviets to concentrate their forces to break through and thus provide lucrative targets for NATO nuclear weapons."[32] NATO revised these plans with MC-70 in 1958, but it still called for the early use of nuclear weapons against a large-scale invasion force.[33]

The force requirements for the United States to defend East Asia from communist aggression were smaller. The Soviet military presence in this region was far more limited than in Europe. Communist China posed a threat with its massive army, but its military was qualitatively weak such that it had trouble projecting military power over the Taiwan Straits, to say nothing of the South China and East China Seas.[34] Still, in the mid-1950s, the United States did use the threat of nuclear force to defend the Kinmen and Matsu island groups in the Taiwan Straits.[35] Indeed, the United States stationed nuclear-capable Matador missiles in Taiwan in addition to a troop garrison.[36] The same was true in South Korea, where in 1958 the United States placed

280-mm nuclear cannons and Honest John nuclear-tipped missiles. A year later the US Air Force deployed a squadron of nuclear-tipped Matador cruise missiles capable of hitting targets in China and the Soviet Union.[37] These forces strengthened deterrence. After all, the attritional nature of the Korean War revealed the inability of the United States to prevail against Chinese forces in a purely conventional war.

Reliance on nuclear weapons did not just result from Eisenhower's fiscal conservatism and geopolitics. The economic problems facing Eisenhower were structural: changes in the global economy were making the status quo regarding overseas American deployments difficult to uphold. Specifically, the United States was beginning to incur a balance-of-payments deficit that threatened to complicate its ability to pay for its military expenditures abroad.[38] Balance-of-payments refers to the net payments made for a state's imports and exports of goods, services, and financial capital. A balance-of-payments deficit means that the current account is negative, reflecting how the state is a net debtor in the global economy. Though market mechanisms should automatically correct any imbalances, one tool that a government can use to address a balance-of-payments deficit is to depreciate its national currency. By lowering the value of the national currency, the country's exports should increase as its imports decline. This option was not available to American decision makers during the 1950s. At the time, governments fixed their exchange rates in keeping with the Bretton Woods system—an international economic regime that emerged after World War II. Under a fixed exchange rate system, states can make changes within their domestic economies in order to rebalance payments, thereby satisfying their obligations to exchange their currencies at fixed rates. For deficit countries, the required adjustments have to exert a deflationary effect on internal prices so as to increase exports. For many Western governments during the 1950s and 1960s, such adjustments were politically unattractive because they meant compromising on social spending and high standards of living.

Compounding this situation was how the global economy relied on a two-tiered system in which states could use the American dollar (and the British pound sterling) in lieu of gold in international transactions. The reason for this system was straightforward. Global economic growth requires the expansion of international liquidity, but relying on gold exclusively, as is the case under a gold standard, is problematic due to the limited supplies of this valuable metal. Though a two-tiered system was an appropriate solution to this problem, it had an important weakness. If the country whose currency can be used in lieu of gold runs extensive balance-of-power deficits, then it risks stoking such inflation that other states would switch to gold. A consequence of the attendant lack of liquidity is downward pressure on the world economy.[39]

Starting in 1950, the United States ran a large balance-of-payments deficit as its financial capital outflows exceeded its inflows. Paying for its global presence contributed greatly to this deficit. By spending money on its military bases abroad, for example, the United States was increasing other countries' supplies of foreign exchange and accumulating greater debt. Though the United States was favorably predisposed to supplying international liquidity, the balance-of-payments deficit began to exert deflationary pressure on the American economy in the mid-1950s.[40] Furthermore, American allies were using their expanding foreign exchange reserves to purchase gold. These gold purchases narrowed the supply of international liquidity, increased the vulnerability of the greenback, and, by extension, enhanced the political power of surplus countries.[41]

1961–1968: Losing Nuclear Superiority

During his successful bid for the American presidency, John F. Kennedy campaigned on boosting economic growth and strengthening defense. Eisenhower, he charged, focused too much on controlling the budget. An important consequence of this inappropriately stringent fiscal policy was a neglect of military power. Eisenhower had allowed the alleged "missile gap" to grow unfavorably between the United States and the Soviet Union.[42] The Republican president had also neglected conventional forces. Kennedy declared that his presidency would rectify these mistakes. "Arbitrary budget ceilings" will now no longer compromise American national security.[43] A new doctrine—flexible response—would now replace the New Look, allowing for a greater range of military options when confronting Soviet aggression.

The extent to which the Kennedy administration would be able to meet the practical demands of flexible response was unclear. The policy was too expensive to implement. To be sure, spending on conventional weapons did increase during the Kennedy years. National defense outlays rose from $48 million in 1958 and $54 million in 1964. During those years, NATO's conventional forces improved relative to Warsaw Pact forces. Thanks to improved weaponry and the West German buildup, NATO could even plausibly defend against a Soviet invasion.[44] With some small tweaks to NATO forces, American military defense planners even believed that a robust conventional defense against Soviet belligerence was possible and that an immediate recourse to nuclear weapons was unnecessary.[45] But despite his earlier criticisms of Eisenhower's austere fiscal policy, Kennedy soon found himself facing both old and new financial constraints. He initially felt pressure to balance the annual budget by controlling spending and later stimulating aggregate demand with tax cuts. Expanding social programs were also costly.[46] Thus, before his assassination, Kennedy was in fact calling for fewer defense outlays. The Johnson administration heeded his worries. By 1965, the increase in outlays to support flexible response had all but disappeared—with defense spending falling to $50.6 million only to rise again to support the military effort in Vietnam ($81.9 million in 1968).[47]

Flexible response was also premised on unrealistic assumptions. Providing adequate civilian protection against nuclear attack was prohibitively costly and probably infeasible. Within two years the administration had to scuttle ambitious plans for an extensive network of underground shelters.[48] Indeed, administration officials became convinced that managing nuclear escalation was impossible. Francis Gavin offers evidence that Secretary of Defense Robert McNamara and other decision makers no longer believed that escalation control was possible by targeting only the military assets of the Soviet Union. This nuclear doctrine ended up being only a fiction that the administration maintained to ease tensions within the Western alliance.[49] As such, American defense planners still envisioned a devastating nuclear war that would begin with the United States targeting Soviet launch silos, airfields, and other military bases with nuclear weapons in addition to urban industrial areas.[50] Even Kennedy believed that American conventional forces in Europe were useful only for ensuring the free status of West Berlin. Once the Berlin crisis was resolved, he thought, no further need for them existed because any war with the Soviet Union would entail nuclear weapons use.[51]

The other constraint binding the Kennedy administration was the deepening balance-of-payments crisis. Early in his presidency, Kennedy established a committee tasked with devising a policy to manage the problem. The resulting policy comprised three measures. First, the United States asked that those states that acquired surplus dollars as a consequence of American military spending abroad would desist from buying American gold. Instead, these states would use their surplus dollars to acquire new military equipment, thereby offsetting—as it were—both American financial costs and their contributions to the deficit. Second, Washington would explore various initiatives aimed at reforming the global monetary system. Third, it sought tariff reductions from Western European allies.[52]

This policy did not represent the full extent to which the United States would address the deficit. The Treasury Department also dedicated itself to an additional measure: under the direction of Secretary Douglas Dillon, it examined which government outlays overseas could be cut. Specifically, Dillon advocated cuts to military expenses overseas. McNamara agreed, even pledging to cut these costs by a third.[53] Although these reductions would improve balance-of-payments savings, they contradicted flexible response's supposed emphasis on conventional military power. Had Washington been seriously committed to this strategic doctrine, it would have at least maintained the six divisions stationed in Western Europe without any suggestion of their redeployment. Instead, debates ensued within the American government over the appropriate number of American troops in Western Europe and whether any changes would have to be made.[54] Decision makers even explicitly linked balance-of-payments considerations with the

American conventional military presence when they met their West European counterparts.[55]

The Kennedy administration still paid lip service to flexible response. One reason for maintaining this fiction was to ease intra-alliance tensions in Western Europe, especially those centered on the "German question"—that is, how to empower West Germany without threatening its neighbors. If American decision makers openly acknowledged the problems associated with implementing flexible response, then the credibility of the American security guarantees would be severely compromised, and allies like West Germany would want their own nuclear weapons. American decision makers thus understood that a connection existed between nuclear strategy and the risk of nuclear proliferation by allies. Indeed, had Washington been more honest and declared that its conventional military presence was unnecessary for deterring Soviet aggression, the thinking went, then Western European allies would decide against both improving their own conventional forces and relying on American security guarantees.[56]

The rhetoric of flexible response was also useful in East Asia. The dual threat posed by a nuclear-armed Soviet Union and a non-nuclear-armed China implied that escalation could be rapid. The nuclear threshold was presumably even lower in an armed confrontation that would involve only China. Accordingly, McNamara believed that the local strategic environment presented another opportunity to cut defense expenditures.[57] Yet the concept of massive retaliation was unsavory in East Asia. Many critics were pointing out (misleadingly) that the United States used nuclear weapons on Asians rather than on Europeans in 1945.[58] Moreover, the growing antinuclear and antimilitarist movement in Japan would have complicated efforts by the United States to legitimate its use of bases if extended deterrence remained exclusively nuclear. Flexible response was thus more palatable to East Asian allies.

The one area in which the Kennedy administration's policy was consistent with flexible response was in seeking centralized decision-making over tactical nuclear arrangements. Centralized decision-making was necessary for ensuring that armed escalation would proceed appropriately in response to Soviet levels of aggression rather than ratchet up inadvertently. Nevertheless, the desire for centralization in this domain also conformed to the general American desire to monopolize western nuclear decision-making authority and intolerance for other countries' nuclear weapons programs.[59] Illustrative of this view is the "no-cities" speech given at the University of Michigan: McNamara charged that "limited nuclear capabilities, operating independently, are dangerous, expensive, prone to obsolescence, and lacking in credibility as a deterrent."[60]

Seeking control over nuclear-sharing arrangements was manifest in one key policy: the Multilateral Force (MLF). The MLF was a formal nuclear-sharing arrangement that the Eisenhower administration had put forward in December 1960. Such arrangements appealed to members of the American government because it addressed growing concerns that Western European governments had an unfairly minimal role in nuclear decision-making in NATO. Prompting these concerns was the emergence of medium-range ballistic missiles (MRBMs). In order not to risk diffusing these weapon systems, American decision makers were resistant to basing MRBMs in Europe despite calls from the Supreme Allied Commander Europe. To preserve deterrence while permitting some form of European participation, the MLF represented a favorable solution. Of course, the United States had already begun to implement informal nuclear-sharing arrangements in Western Europe in the form of the "dual-key system." Under this system, the United States managed nuclear warheads, whereas European allies had control over the missiles on which they would be mounted. In the event that both states agreed to launch a nuclear weapon, Washington would turn control of the warhead over to its ally. Nevertheless, this arrangement was becoming technologically outdated. The nuclear weapons used in the dual-key system were tactical and thus unable to meet the threat posed by the expanding Soviet arsenal of MRBMs.[61]

Another perceived benefit of the MLF is that it would enhance American credibility by institutionalizing further the American military presence in Western Europe. It would also leverage and sustain the superiority of the American nuclear arsenal. After all, an emerging preoccupation of American decision makers at this time was the development, actual and potential, of national nuclear forces in Western Europe. Such programs would undermine alliance cohesion.[62] As an exemplary nuclear-sharing arrangement, the MLF would comprise a multinational fleet of ships and submarines manned by NATO crews and armed with multiple nuclear-armed ballistic missiles. Participating countries would jointly own the fleet and give their unanimous consent before firing any missile.

Notwithstanding its origins in the Eisenhower administration, the Kennedy and the Johnson administrations took up the MLF as a major component of their defense policy in Western Europe. Kennedy highlighted the importance of seaborne nuclear forces in a speech delivered before the Canadian Parliament in Ottawa on May 17, 1961.[63] Yet the United States began a major effort to rally NATO members into supporting this initiative in 1963 following the resolution of the Berlin crisis and a nuclear weapons system agreement with Great Britain.[64] The same motivations underpinned the Kennedy administration's interest in seeing the MLF succeed despite the delay: permitting a robust European nuclear role in NATO, averting European nuclear proliferation, and addressing fears of discrimination among allies like West Germany.[65] Resolving the nuclear status of West Germany was critical. Kennedy informed Macmillan that "if [the MLF] fails, the Germans are bound to move in much more dangerous directions. In the long run even toward some partly clandestine arrangement with the French, or if this should not work, toward an independent nuclear effort in Germany—not now but in time."[66] Despite Kennedy's stated fears over the effects of the MLF's failure, the State Department most vigorously promoted the initiative to Western European allies during the Johnson administration.

The Johnson administration faced many of the same challenges and adopted similar policies as its predecessor. Shortly after becoming president, Lyndon B. Johnson met with West German chancellor Ludwig Erhard in Texas to discuss military offset arrangements and balance-of-payments problems. An internal document that provided Johnson with talking points for this meeting captures the continuity nicely: "The US faces heavy pressure to reduce the overseas cost of its armed forces (e.g., Eisenhower proposal of drop-back to 1 division in Germany), and full offset is an absolute necessity if 6 division force is to be kept intact in Germany."[67] In another memorandum prepared ahead of Erhard's visit, Dillon asserted that "our own balance-of-payments weakness is the most serious present threat to the maintenance of our military and political leadership in the free world."[68] Such themes—balance-of-payments problems and the difficulty of maintaining existing military commitments—dominated Johnson's foreign policy toward Western Europe.

Though the Soviet Union and the United States were nearing nuclear parity by this point, the Johnson administration abided by its predecessor's strategic and doctrinal thinking regarding nuclear weapons.[69] After all, many of Kennedy's leading decision makers like McNamara, Rusk, and Dillon retained their cabinet posts under Johnson. Thanks to this bureaucratic continuity, foreign policy officials still adhered to the rhetoric of flexible response. Within the Defense Department, McNamara still sought to streamline the American military and threaten reductions in American commitments in Western Europe. The State Department remained wedded to the MLF as the future basis on which an American-led European deterrent force would be organized. Finally, by participating in negotiations for a nuclear nonproliferation treaty, the administration shared Kennedy's goal of preventing further nuclear proliferation.

Johnson's interest in advancing global nuclear nonproliferation objectives was more intense than Kennedy's, however. China was one reason why this nonproliferation effort intensified. To be sure, Chinese efforts at acquiring nuclear weapons dated back to Eisenhower's presidency, but by the 1960s many states had become apprehensive of Beijing's nuclear ambitions. The Soviet Union quickly withdrew its support for the program before attempting to thwart it.[70] American decision makers themselves feared that nuclear weapons would not only embolden an already aggressive and revisionist China but also trigger wider nuclear proliferation, particularly among American allies. At one point, the Kennedy administration even explored whether to use military force to disrupt China's nuclear program. The Johnson administration revisited this option after China first detonated a nuclear device in October 1964.[71]

Also distinguishing Johnson from Kennedy was the war in Vietnam. Aside from containing communism in Southeast Asia, Vietnam mattered to Johnson partly because of alliance politics. Defending Vietnam was critical for demonstrating American resolve in supporting weaker allies against foreign depredations, especially in areas that were not vital to American security. Fredrik Logevall argues that credibility concerns—personal and domestic in addition to national—influenced Johnson's decision-making.[72] Indeed, the belief that commitments were interdependent was in vogue among policy experts at this time.[73] Accordingly, in the months after China's nuclear detonation, the Johnson administration began seriously contemplating whether to Americanize the war. Retreating from Vietnam during this time might have, for example, hinted to China—and other aspiring nuclear proliferators—that de-escalation or withdrawal was a consequence of its newfound nuclear capability. Thus, in July 1965, Johnson chose to escalate the American military presence in the Vietnam War. The number of American military advisers and soldiers grew from sixteen thousand in 1963 to over half a million in early 1968. National defense outlays expanded dramatically. The United States was spending about $82 billion on defense by 1968, an increase of about 50 percent from 1965.[74] Military attention shifted away from Western Europe and turned toward Southeast Asia.

Within several years, it became evident that uncertain American victory in the Vietnam War would be prohibitively costly in both blood and treasure. Domestic opposition to the war intensified, particularly among young adults who feared that they would be selected in the national draft and shipped overseas. Protests rocked university campuses and cities across the United States. After an antiwar candidate finished seven points behind him in the New Hampshire Democratic primary, Johnson declared his decision not to seek reelection. In the same speech, made on March 31, 1968, he announced that he would unilaterally suspend aerial bombings over North Vietnam so as to pursue peace talks. In the presidential election that year, both Democratic candidate Hubert Humphrey and Republican candidate Nixon pledged to end the Vietnam War. But how would the United States withdraw from Southeast Asia without signaling a full retreat from its global commitments?

1969–1980: Nuclear Parity and the Consequences of the Vietnam War

By the time Johnson left office, the United States and the Soviet Union were at nuclear parity. Because both superpowers had a survivable second-strike capability, nuclear war would be suicide for both sides under mutually assured destruction (MAD). Worsening this situation further for the United States was that even a European conventional war had become more difficult. The fighting power of the US Army was depleted in Vietnam. The domestic public opinion was turning against an activist American foreign policy.

The Vietnam War thus preoccupied Nixon's presidency. That conflict was the center around which all other issues revolved, including relations with the Soviet Union and China. Because tensions between Washington and Moscow had eased over the course of the 1960s through détente, Nixon concentrated on developing a political solution to Vietnam. His signature foreign policy achievement—rapprochement with China—also had Vietnam in mind.

Positive diplomatic relations with *both* communist powers would take time to develop, and so more immediate and direct solutions in the Vietnam War were necessary. After all, when Nixon became president, the military situation facing the United States appeared futile. The attritional warfare produced high casualties for both sides of the conflict. Partly because the military relied on conscription to support the campaign, members of the American public became increasingly critical of their country's involvement in the war. Taking advantage of these sentiments, Nixon pledged to end the Vietnam War. This promise became a signature aspect of his successful presidential election campaign in 1968. Nevertheless, the war could not end at any cost. Nixon believed that American withdrawal from Vietnam could be achieved only if a workable arrangement would guarantee South Vietnam's security.[75] Amid faltering negotiations with North Vietnam and domestic demands for pulling out of Vietnam, Nixon initiated a strategy of phased troop withdrawals and greater reliance on Vietnamese troops.[76]

This policy, known as either "Vietnamization" or the Nixon Doctrine, was the cornerstone of a general theme of Nixon's first term of office. In a speech delivered at Guam on July 25, 1969, Nixon announced that although the United States would maintain its treaty commitments and continue to provide nuclear umbrellas, it would ask its allies to contribute more to satisfy their own security needs.[77] On November 3 that year, he clarified that "we shall furnish military and economic assistance when requested in accordance with our treaty commitments. But we shall look to the nation directly threatened to assume the primary responsibility of providing the manpower for its defense."[78] Transferring military responsibilities to South Vietnamese forces was one aspect of this policy, but the Nixon administration also sought to implement similar changes in East Asia. Indeed, the Nixon Doctrine articulated explicitly the principle that allies must bear more of the conventional defense burden while the United States would rely more on its nuclear deterrent.

As if détente and the Nixon Doctrine did not signify the retraction of American alliance commitments enough, strains on the American economy intensified. Spending on the Vietnam War and the Great Society—Johnson's program to eliminate poverty and racial injustice—drove up inflation. Domestic unemployment was increasing. The Bretton Woods system teetered as gold outflows from the American economy persisted. It finally collapsed in August 1971 when Nixon signed an executive order that unilaterally made the dollar no longer directly convertible to gold outside of the open market. Indeed, the negative balance-of-payments crisis and growing public debt had finally overwhelmed the American ability to manage the international monetary regime. The most significant consequence of the "Nixon Shock"— as Nixon's decision came to be called—was that many fixed currencies became free-floating in world markets, thereby eliminating a key pillar of the Bretton Woods system and rendering obsolete (at the time) the International Monetary Fund. For many observers, the United States seemed no longer able to manage the global economy. That Nixon issued his executive order without consulting either his own government officials or allied decision makers also signified that American leaders had no qualms with upending international arrangements for their own benefit.[79]

This display of executive power notwithstanding, Congress was asserting its power over foreign policy. Most famously, it passed the War Powers Act in 1973, whereby the White House could not commit to an armed conflict without the consent of Congress.[80] From an alliance perspective, a more relevant piece of legislation was the failed Mansfield Amendment. Introduced by Democratic senator Mike Mansfield in 1971, this amendment called for the number of American troops in Europe to be halved. Although the Senate defeated this motion 61–36 within months of its appearance, the amendment fueled concerns that the United States was declining and contemplating a global retreat.[81]

Amid these dismal developments, the United States was embracing nuclear arms control. Under Nixon's leadership, the United States negotiated the Strategic Arms Limitation Treaty (SALT) I, the Anti-Ballistic Missile Treaty, and the Biological Weapons Convention. His successors Gerald Ford and Jimmy Carter negotiated SALT II and canceled the neutron bomb, respectively. Because the rival superpowers were at roughly nuclear parity, fears of accidental nuclear war and relaxed tensions seem to have driven the pursuit of arms control. Yet the documentary record reveals that Nixon was dismissive of these treaties. He admitted, "I don't give a damn about [SALT]; I just couldn't care less about it." Nixon construed the Biological Weapons Convention as "the silly biological warfare thing, which doesn't mean anything."[82] Indeed, Nixon began his presidency by stirring public debate on the development of a ballistic missile defense system intended to neutralize the Soviet SS-9, a liquid-fueled ICBM capable of carrying multiple warheads.[83] He privately lamented nuclear parity with the Soviet Union, because he thought that nuclear weapons would not only deter but also compel adversaries. Moreover, he and Kissinger believed nuclear superiority was what made American security guarantees believable. For Nixon, the "nuclear umbrella in NATO was a load of crap," whereas Kissinger observed how "Europeans don't realize American nuclear umbrella depended on first strike."[84]

Unfortunately for Nixon, breaking out of MAD was not a viable proposition due to the associated costs and technical barriers. When Nixon became president, multiple independently targetable reentry vehicle (MIRV) technology was available. This technology was attractive because it allowed a ballistic missile to carry a payload containing several warheads, each of which could be aimed at an individual target.[85] Yet the Soviets also had MIRV capability, and the nuclear stalemate meant that a general nuclear war would have been suicide for all involved. Nevertheless, the Nixon administration tried to develop limited nuclear options. The result of these efforts was the so-called Schlesinger Doctrine, leaked to the press in 1974. This nuclear strike policy consisted of using a set of limited strikes against Soviet military targets so as *not* to foreclose a diplomatic solution. Whether American decision makers believed in the practicality of these ideas remains unclear.[86]

With time, the United States could increase the deployability of its nuclear arsenal, reduce Soviet retaliatory capabilities, and escape MAD. MIRV technology thus gave the United States a possible first-strike advantage, but it was only by the late 1970s that the nuclear balance began tipping in favor of the United States. Despite initial congressional concerns about the vulnerability of the system, President Jimmy Carter reinstated a major land-based MIRV missile called the Missile-eXperimental (MX) in 1979. His investment in counterforce was especially surprising given Carter's stated opposition to nuclear weapons on the election campaign and the first half of his presidency. After some controversy that saw the MX program canceled in the early 1980s only to be later reintroduced as the Peacekeeper, counterforce capabilities saw major upgrades under the Reagan administration. This administration also sought to dampen MAD with a ballistic missile defense project popularly known as Star Wars.

Why the United States would invest heavily in expensive counterforce capabilities is a puzzle for another book. One possibility is that American leaders believed that counterforce gave them political leverage over the Soviet Union. That is, nuclear superiority would inspire confidence among American allies that the United States possessed a powerful deterrent.[87] Certainly, Nixon felt this way. Giving credence to this claim is the controversy that arose among European allies over Soviet intermediate range ballistic missiles (IRBMs) in the late 1970s. Their deployment suggested to some Western European leaders that their countries became vulnerable to the military buildup in the Warsaw Pact, since SALT I and SALT II circumscribed American nuclear capabilities. Because the Soviet Union could hold the United States hostage with ICBMs, the United States could become less willing to defend Europe in the event of a localized nuclear attack. Security interests between both sides of the Atlantic became decoupled, in other words. The Carter administration and NATO resolved this controversy by implementing the "dual-track" decision, whereby the United States introduced more IRBMs in Europe but would promise (threaten) to withdraw (increase) them should negotiations for banning these weapons entirely succeed (fail).[88]

The dual-track decision concluded a decade in which American power was in general crisis. Military defeat in Vietnam fostered doubts in the ability of the United States to win wars. The collapse of the Bretton Woods system and two oil shocks made global markets volatile. The United States also loosened its alliance commitments first by withdrawing troops from East Asia, then by allowing the dissolution of SEATO and terminating the alliance with Taiwan, and finally by advocating human rights at the behest of authoritarian allies like South Korea. The domestic political situation in the United States also appeared dismal. Nixon's presidency ended ignominiously after the Watergate scandal. Carter seemed to offer a decisive break from the policies of Nixon and his successor Gerald Ford. However, economic malaise and the Carter administration's mishandling of the Iran hostage crisis limited Carter to a single-term presidency.

The American experience in the first three decades of the Cold War follows an arc. At the beginning, the United States expanded its alliance commitments around the world. NATO preceded the Korean War, but it became more institutionalized and saw massive military investments after that conflict. Elsewhere the United States established several bilateral and multilateral alliances, backing them with major troop deployments, a large and growing nuclear arsenal, and vague threats against the conventionally superior Soviet Union.[89] Over time, however, these commitments came under duress. The balance-of-payments crisis made large overseas deployments and defense outlays untenable unless allies would spend their American dollars so as to offset the costs. American participation in the Vietnam War initially served to convey American resolve, but it seemed to engender American decline instead. By the late 1970s, the United States was undoing some of the alliance commitments it had made after the Korean War.

This trajectory notwithstanding, two desires were common among American decision makers during this part of the Cold War. One was to depend more on the nuclear deterrent of the United States than on conventional military deployments to thwart communist aggression. This preference was most pronounced during the Eisenhower and Nixon years, but Kennedy and Johnson at times indicated their frustration with maintaining troops in Europe. The other related to nuclear superiority. Eisenhower's strategy required a favorable nuclear balance. By the late 1960s, the nuclear balance entered a phase of rough parity—something that Nixon resented because he felt that it deprived him of leverage.

Chapters 3, 4, and 5 show how the nuclear interest of allies depended on whether and how the United States was able to retract its conventional military commitments in light of the nuclear balance. As such, this chapter has several implications for what we can expect from the following three cases of West Germany, Japan, and South Korea. One is that credibility problems will become more salient in Europe much sooner than in East

Asia. For one, deterrence was easier in the latter region owing to geography and the threat environment. For another, economic constraints had greater ramifications for American ground power—a form of military power that West Germany valued as a deterrent force more than Japan, at least. Another implication is that credibility concerns will be persistent in Europe despite declared changes in American foreign policy doctrine and military strategy. American reassurances to allies should have had limited effectiveness in addressing their abandonment concerns, thereby hampering efforts to curb their nuclear interest.

West Germany, 1954–1970

A major American ally on the front lines, West Germany was the focal point of major power tensions during the first half of the Cold War. It benefited from extensive military commitments from the United States, ranging from NATO membership to large numbers of American nuclear weapons and foreign troops stationed on its own territory to deter Soviet aggression. Indeed, given the large-scale military presence that the United States has maintained in Germany to this day, some international relations scholars assert that this country has had limited foreign policy autonomy, especially during the Cold War.[1] According to such assessments, alliance coercion should have been most effective in curbing any West German nuclear proliferation–related behavior.

Yet the record suggests a different story. West Germany joined a trilateral partnership with France and Italy in 1956 so as to develop a European nuclear weapons arsenal. Prompting this action was the anticipated withdrawal of American troops from West Germany and the rest of Europe. Despite problems with its credibility, the New Look did not alarm decision makers in the West German capital of Bonn enough to make them to desire nuclear weapons. Rather, what intensified abandonment fears among West German leaders were (unsubstantiated) newspaper reports of imminent cuts to the American military and its manpower. The New Look mattered insofar as nuclear vulnerability made West Germany sensitive to any indication that the United States would loosen its "trip wire" and weaken local deterrence-by-denial. Although France unilaterally decided to terminate this trilateral initiative, West Germany still avoided making clear commitments renouncing nuclear weapons until signing the nonproliferation treaty in 1969 and ratifying it in 1975. By this time, West Germany had extracted treaty concessions from the Soviet Union and the United States while acquiring reprocessing and enrichment capabilities. Contrary to some American accounts of this nonproliferation episode, West Germany did not actually intend to acquire nuclear weapons, but it caused sufficient doubt—intentionally or not—about its motives among Soviet and American decision makers.

The propositions drawn from my framework apply in this case. First, the alliance with the United States was less useful for curbing West German nuclear ambitions than was commonly presumed. Second, in-theater conventional forces mattered for bolstering American extended nuclear guarantees to West Germany. Third, American coercion of West Germany was important, but it played a much less direct role than assumed. And fourth, economics provided the United States some leverage over a defeated West Germany that was still recovering from World War II, but American decision makers had difficulty applying such pressure effectively to obtain offsets, to say nothing of nonproliferation commitments. Other factors—especially domestic politics—drove West Germany's final choices. That is not to say that the alliance had no effect whatsoever: without NATO at all, West Germany's security environment would have been dramatically worse such that it might actually have had a full-fledged nuclear weapons program. Nevertheless, the alliance did break down and provided American decision makers with few effective means for extracting nonproliferation commitments.

Before examining the case, I outline West Germany's strategic and domestic political environment. The analysis proceeds in two parts. The first investigates West Germany's decision to embark on nuclear proliferation–related behavior in the mid-1950s. The second examines why West Germany ultimately made nonproliferation commitments in the late 1960s. Each part assesses the validity of alternative arguments.

The Strategic Context

West Germany emerged as the product of allied decisions taken between 1946 and 1949 to amalgamate the British, French, and American zones of occupation. It was largely land locked, with its eastern borders abutting two communist states (East Germany and Czechoslovakia) and, after 1955, neutral Austria. Its position in Central Europe thus exposed it to the Soviet Union. Despite lacking a significant air and naval capability during the 1950s, the Soviet Union was a land power that concentrated much of its armed forces in Central and Eastern Europe. These conventional forces outmatched those aggregated by NATO. Although it first detonated a nuclear device in 1949, the Soviet Union did not develop an ICBM capability until the late 1950s. West Germany on its own faced a severely unfavorable conventional balance of power with the Soviet Union that an allied military presence could significantly (but not fully) redress.

Implemented by the Eisenhower administration, the New Look was important for West Germany, since it emphasized substituting nuclear weapons for conventional military power. This substitution was a mixed blessing. Nuclear weapons compensated for the conventional superiority of the Soviet bloc because they were the deterrent that the United States could best provide. Still, as Soviet nuclear capabilities improved toward the end of the 1950s, West Germany risked being the battleground on which the major powers could wage nuclear war if deterrence failed. Notwithstanding these existential stakes, West Germany had little to no input in NATO or American nuclear decision-making. As long as the United States retained a troop presence on West German soil, West German leaders could be assured that the United States very likely would be involved in any localized aggression in Central Europe.

My theory understands the Soviet threat as a necessary condition for West German nuclear proliferation–related behavior. Whether rooted in real or anticipated changes in American force posture, abandonment fears should be the key driver of any movement toward nuclear weapons. In contrast, the adversary thesis stresses the Soviet threat, irrespective of American actions, as the principal influence on West Germany's nuclear interest.

The Domestic Context

The domestic politics thesis sees outward-looking regimes as favorable to nonproliferation norms and agreements and inward-looking regimes as inclined to embark on nuclear proliferation–related behavior. Of course, only one regime—the Bundesrepublik—ruled West Germany, yet what were the preferences of the major distinct political groups in West German politics? Thomas Berger describes three: the Atlanticists, the West Europeanists (sometimes called the Gaullists), and the Central Europeanists. The Atlanticists were ambivalent about the formation and rearmament of the Bundeswehr (the West German armed forces), backed the United States, and doubted the early prospects of German reunification. They valued NATO over other European collective security arrangements, seeing the alliance as the best provider of deterrence despite endorsing European integration. The West Europeanists, too, supported an alliance with the West and rearmament, but they doubted that the United States would fulfill its commitments. They believed that European collective security arrangements would better serve West German strategic interests over the long term. Radicals even preferred the European Defense Community (EDC) and the Western European Union to NATO.[2] Finally, the Central Europeanists disliked the United States, rejected nuclear deterrence altogether, embraced geopolitical neutralization, espoused socialist principles, and opposed European integration.[3] Simply put, the Atlanticists and West Europeanists were outward looking, whereas the Central Europeanists were inward-looking even if they were not nationalists.

Applying these three categories to ascribe prestrategic preferences to individual leaders and their parties is challenging. The political parties themselves straddled major political cleavages. Consider the main political parties in West German politics during the 1950s and 1960s. The Christian Democratic Union (CDU), steeped in socially conservative values informed by interconfessionalism, contained both Atlanticist and West Europeanist factions. Coalition governments present another complication. The CDU often partnered with its Bavarian counterpart, the Christian Socialist Union (CSU). This party espoused values similar to those of the CDU but was more nationalist and socially conservative. Though this ideological overlap made these parties coalition partners, their main political leaders—Konrad Adenauer (CDU) and Franz Josef Strauss (CSU)—still disagreed over West German foreign policy. Moreover, geopolitical developments could empower certain ideas while discrediting others. The CDU and CSU were dominant in West Germany partly because the Cold War made socialism politically undesirable both at home and with anticommunist allies. Accordingly, after suffering successive electoral defeats, the Social Democratic Party (SDP) adopted in 1959 the Godesberg Program, renouncing Marxism so as to broaden its appeal among members of the middle and professional classes. It even embraced a pro-Western policy supportive of the United States.[4] Party identification notwithstanding, however, individuals are purposive. Though influenced by the discursive practices in which they are embedded, leaders may still adjust and manipulate ideas to suit their agenda, sometimes even moving between political categories. Konrad Adenauer was one such leader. Berger regards him and Strauss as being both West Europeanists, but Adenauer was the more Atlanticist of the two.[5] Strauss should make West Germany more likely to engage in proliferation-related behavior when he has a greater share of decision-making authority vis-à-vis Atlanticist chancellors like Adenauer and his successor Ludwig Erhard.

The prestige thesis emphasizes the degree to which leaders believe that nuclear weapons have intrinsic value. In a society where antimilitarist norms were only beginning to take root in the 1950s, this thesis may not seem applicable to West Germany.[6] Nevertheless, West German leaders might have seen nuclear weapons as status markers within NATO in light of the capabilities possessed by the United States, Great Britain, and France. Normative inhibitions on nuclear weapons could have intensified as antimilitarist norms grew more pervasive in West German society toward the late 1960s. The prestige thesis would thus look to normative considerations as drivers of West German nuclear weapons interest.

Nuclear Proliferation–Related Behavior: The F-I-G Initiative Followed by Hedging

The West German government, in exchange for political sovereignty, renounced domestic nuclear weapons production at the Paris and London Conferences in 1954. Still, West Germany partnered with Italy and France in

1956 to develop a nuclear weapons arsenal. By the time this trilateral initiative came into being, Chancellor Adenauer was already countenancing some form of a nuclear program during the second half of 1956. He sought to pass legislation in the Bundestag—the West German federal parliament—to remove domestic legal strictures against having a nuclear weapons program. In October 1956, Adenauer promoted his minister of atomic affairs, Franz Josef Strauss, to become the minister of defense, indicating his personal understanding regarding the connection between nuclear policy and defense.

West Germany was not entirely discreet in its conduct. At a February 1957 press conference, Adenauer referred "to the possibility of organizing a Franco-German co-production of nuclear weapons on French territory."[7] By December 1957 West Germany quietly began its collaborative project with France and Italy, called the F-I-G (French-Italian-German) initiative.[8] Although American decision makers knew that these three governments were engaged in some joint initiative, they were uncertain of the extent to which it involved nuclear weapons. And yet even with this secrecy, the three governments did not intend their project to work at cross-purposes with NATO.[9] For Adenauer, the protection that Washington could offer remained desirable despite its flaws. And so shortly after this project started, Adenauer made private and coded requests to the United States for "the most modern and effective weapons" while denying to the Soviets any interest in such weapons.[10] In January 1958 Adenauer successfully oversaw legislation pass in the Bundestag to permit the acquisition of delivery vehicles, which members of the opposition suspected was a reflection of a desire to seek nuclear weapons.

Bonn's pursuit of the bomb was brief. Upon returning to power, French president Charles de Gaulle unilaterally terminated the F-I-G initiative in June 1958.[11] West Germany did not reattempt a nuclear weapons program after de Gaulle's abrupt cancellation of the trilateral initiative. Indeed, de Gaulle's actions imposed a new constraint on any new nuclear weapons project that West Germany could pursue. Another initiative with its European neighbors was unlikely, whereas a unilateral West German program risked international detection and censure. Notwithstanding this constraint, West Germany hedged diplomatically so as to improve its status within the burgeoning nuclear order, even if it did not intend on acquiring its own nuclear weapons.[12] For one, it criticized and resisted early international drafts of a treaty banning the spread of nuclear weapons. Some West German politicians even understood a nonproliferation treaty as being designed *against* them. For another, Bonn strongly backed the nuclear-sharing arrangements that Washington was considering in the early 1960s. One reason why American leaders contemplated such concepts as MLF as long as they did was their concern for how West Germany would behave in the absence of these initiatives. West German leaders sometimes exploited these fears that their successors might want nuclear weapons.[13] Often forgotten, however, is that

West Germany still proceeded to acquire nuclear technologies amid these diplomatic efforts. George Quester estimated in 1970 that within several years West Germany "will have enough installed nuclear electrical power facilities to produce plutonium for 200 atomic bombs a year."[14]

Contemporary international observers and decision makers themselves were uncertain of West Germany's nuclear intentions. Take, for example, a correspondence between Kennedy and British prime minister Harold Macmillan. Kennedy wrote Macmillan that "the Chancellor made very clear his conviction that German unilateral ownership or control over nuclear weapons is undesirable, and [Minister of Defense Franz Josef] Strauss expressed the same view; they agreed that their needs could be met within a multilateral framework."[15] The basis of these impressions was a conversation that Kennedy had just the previous day with Adenauer. During this meeting Kennedy asked the chancellor directly whether he would continue to abide by the terms of the 1954 renunciation of the experimentation of nuclear, biological, and chemical weapons. Adenauer reaffirmed these commitments but added that the obligation had legal validity as long as "circumstances remain unchanged."[16] According to Adenauer, former secretary of state Dulles himself endorsed this application of the legal principle of rebus sic stantibus (things thus standing).

And so despite the confidence he conveyed to Macmillan, Kennedy was privately unsure. In a 1964 interview, Kennedy adviser Charles E. Bohlen recalled: "I think that [Kennedy] had a certain reservation as to the German future and the danger of German militarism. I think he was very conscious of the possibility that given a few turns or twists of events, you could be headed back into another situation where Germany could again become a menace."[17] These fears encouraged various probes into West German nuclear interest. One American government study explored the meaning of Adenauer's statement to Kennedy and its significance for West German policy. This 1962 report failed to confirm whether Dulles had enunciated the principle of rebus sic stantibus and noted that its status in international law was dubious.[18] While this report was being drafted during the summer of 1962, American government officials investigated whether Paris and Bonn were cooperating in nuclear weapons development. A December 1961 telegram had already cautioned that "if continued integration of scientific and technical resources of France and Germany goes on at its present rate, and the economic cooperation of both countries continues in EEC [the European Economic Community], surely US must realize it is very likely that France will provide technical nuclear information to Germans."[19] With British collaboration, however, the State Department found "no concrete evidence now exists confirming any such cooperation." Nevertheless, the American ambassador in Bonn observed that the British found it "prudent to assume that, even in absence of direct collaboration in weapons field, probability is great that French and German scientists do in fact cooperate at theoretical level on matters of nuclear physicals which cld [*sic*] be related to nuclear weapons technology."[20] Investigations into possible Franco-German nuclear cooperation continued until at least December 1962.[21]

Other statements by American government officials highlight a shared sense of unease over West Germany's nuclear policy. A telegram from the American embassy in Bonn for Secretary of State Dean Rusk captures the prevailing attitude at the time: "At present there does not exist deliberate intention in [West] Germany to embark on nuclear weapons program, either alone or with French, but caution requires us assume [*sic*] that latent intention exists that any responsible German leader must keep possibility in back of mind as possible answer to future contingencies for which no concrete anticipation now required."[22] One such contingency was the successful acquisition of a nuclear arsenal by the French government. In a memorandum to Kennedy, Rusk explained that the United States opposed French nuclear efforts because of the risk it created for West German nuclear proliferation.[23] Furthermore, Washington understood the domestic influences on West Germany's foreign policy. State Department officials in May 1961 commented that "we can best settle the German issue in Adenauer's, not Strauss', time" since Strauss was thirty-nine years younger than Adenauer.[24] A State Department study group warned that a future West German government might have to demonstrate to its electorate that it faces no international discrimination in nuclear policy.[25]

Fears of a nuclear West Germany persisted into the Johnson administration and became salient after October 1964 when China detonated its first nuclear weapon. Indeed, two months later Johnson indicated to British prime minister Harold Wilson that failure to resolve West Germany's status would have significant implications for continental security, warning that "if we cannot solve this problem . . . there was [*sic*] some 17-year-old right now in Germany who would be a 20-year-old little Hitler in another three years."[26] Others in his administration were less dramatic but still apprehensive. A 1966 State Department report listed West Germany as a possible proliferator. Though this report argued that West Germany had little reason to proliferate thanks to domestic politics and existing collective security arrangements, ensuring that Bonn would credibly commit to nuclear nonproliferation was a major preoccupation of the Johnson administration.[27]

West Germany's nuclear ambiguity also made the Soviet bloc nervous, especially East Germany and Poland. In 1957, the Polish foreign minister Adam Rapacki proposed a nuclear weapons–free zone in Central Europe that would comprise Poland, Czechoslovakia, and the two Germanies.[28] During early negotiations for a nuclear nonproliferation treaty, some Warsaw Pact leaders expressed concerns regarding the apparent Soviet inclination to accommodate NATO nuclear-sharing arrangements.[29] Consequently, Moscow adopted a tougher stance by advocating for an agreement that would explicitly forbid the possession or transfer of nuclear weapons to Bonn.[30]

To be sure, West Germany did acquire key nuclear technologies during this time. By 1976, West Germany was operating seven nuclear power reactors, with twelve more under construction and another eight ordered.[31] It even possessed reprocessing and enrichment capabilities, having also made investments in gas centrifuge technology. As such, West Germany was able to sell sensitive nuclear technology to Brazil in the mid-1970s, much to the dismay of the United States.[32] West Germany's nuclear hedging amounted to more than just deflecting calls to sign international agreements. It also encompassed the development of a robust nuclear industry.

Explaining West Germany's Behavior: Initiation and Persistence

By signing onto the Trilateral Initiative in 1956 with France and Italy, West Germany did not violate the letter of the London and Paris Conferences. After all, the Final Act of London only prohibited West Germany from building nuclear weapons on its own territory. Still, although this program lasted briefly, Bonn's stance toward nuclear weapons became internationally suspect. Only in 1969 did West Germany publicly renounce nuclear weapons by signing onto the NPT. Before analyzing this decision, I address why West German began, and continued, to engage in nuclear proliferation–related behavior. In this section, I demonstrate how the West German case indicates the limits to the ability of alliances to restrain nuclear interest on the part of its members as well as the importance of in-theater conventional deployments for the credibility of extended nuclear guarantees. Since the military infrastructure buttressing alliance commitments should affect West Germany's nuclear weapons interest, I first discuss the New Look before addressing flexible response.

THE NEW LOOK AND THE AMERICAN SECURITY
GUARANTEE TO WEST GERMANY

With its emphasis on Massive Retaliation, the New Look concerned West German decision makers. Yet this apprehension pulled in opposite directions. On the one hand, the retaliatory threat of overwhelming nuclear weapons use lacked believability. Uncertainty abounded over what forms of communist aggression—if any—would incite a dramatic nuclear response from the United States. West German leaders were not unique in expressing unease over this doctrine; American strategic thinkers had their own reservations.[33] Eisenhower himself admitted that "in the defense of the United States itself we will certainly use nuclear weapons, but to use them in other situations will prove very difficult."[34] On the other hand, concern existed over whether the United States would pursue a reckless foreign policy at the expense of Western European security. Accordingly, West German anxiety was unique insofar as its leaders felt that in the event of Soviet aggression West Germany would be the site of either foreign occupation or nuclear devastation. Nor did they want the West German military to provide merely "foot soldiers marching in the middle of (tactical) nuclear units."[35] These anxieties were justified. A 1955 NATO military exercise, code-named Carte Blanche, simulated a nuclear conflict over NATO territory that resulted in over five million West German casualties. The publication of these results sparked popular furor over NATO nuclear strategy in West Germany.[36]

The New Look served to deter the Soviet Union, but it reinforced the impression that the allies were becoming unwilling or unable to maintain troop deployments in West Germany. In the mid-1950s, American decision makers saw high defense expenditures and balance-of-payments issues as increasingly problematic. British decision makers were already struggling with fulfilling military commitments in West Germany while crafting monetary policy. Great Britain's high debt, incurred during World War II and the subsequent recovery, made the sterling—the second reserve currency of the Bretton Woods system—susceptible to crises of confidence, devaluations, and exchange rushes. Though Great Britain agreed to maintain four divisions and the Second Tactical Air Force in the West European Union Treaty of 1954, it began demanding the next year that West Germany cover seventy million pounds in troops' foreign exchange costs.[37] Bonn resisted such demands, arguing that they reinforced West Germany's "second-class status" within the alliance. Furthermore, British troop redeployments would have weakened Western European defense, perhaps even precipitating an American withdrawal. Both nuclear-armed allies, after all, were exploring how to substitute relatively cheap nuclear weapons for expensive conventional military assets in Europe.[38]

Mindful of these issues, American decision makers did not naively believe that Bonn would unquestioningly embrace the New Look. They recognized that West German—and other European—leaders might see the strategy as a symbol of declining commitment. In a 1953 National Security Council (NSC) meeting, Eisenhower noted: "The presence of our troops there is the greatest single morale factor in Europe. You cannot therefore make a radical change so quickly. Besides, the physical cost of bringing back these troops will be so high as to effect very little savings in the course of next year, even if considerable numbers were to be redeployed."[39] He had also noted in a separate memorandum that "while it is true that the semi-permanent presence of United States Forces (of any kind) in foreign lands is an irritant, any withdrawal that seemed to imply a change in basic intent would cause real turmoil abroad."[40] An "educational campaign" and a "new general program for European defense" were necessary before such withdrawals could occur. In the meantime, Dulles averred, "no impression should be allowed to get about that we may be thinking of pulling troops out of Europe."[41] Nevertheless, Eisenhower personally recorded Dulles's view that the United

States should avoid "ground deployments in Asia" and that the United States "should begin to withdraw ground troops from Korea." Air and naval power were sufficient to deter future communist aggression. Eisenhower agreed in principle that "some reduction in conventional forces" was justifiable thanks to nuclear weapons.[42]

The rhetoric of the New Look seemed to suggest American withdrawal, but Washington refrained from taking active steps to make the proposed change in American force posture reality. Absent such concrete measures, Adenauer may have felt that he lacked sufficient cause to fear abandonment truly. However, when news reports appeared during the summer of 1956 that Washington planned to downsize the military, the New Look seemed finally to be coming into fruition. The Eisenhower administration found itself having to dispel a rumor put forward by an unsubstantiated *New York Times* report on July 13, 1956 that the chairman of the Joint Chiefs of Staff sought to reduce the size of the US Army by a third. The so-called Radford Plan sufficiently disturbed Adenauer that he responded by launching a "major diplomatic effort" to curb these reductions.[43] West German diplomats wanted reassurances from their American counterparts over the status of American troop deployments in West Germany, since the news reports constituted the "greatest concern to the German Government."[44] Adenauer personally wrote to Dulles, warning that "Europe including Germany is losing confidence in the reliability of the United States," since such plans as the Radford Plan "are regarded as clear proof of the fact that the United States does not feel strong enough to keep at least on a par with the Soviet Union."[45] As Hubert Zimmermann writes, "for [Adenauer] these troops were the fundamental symbol of the American commitment to Europe."[46]

To be sure, the Eisenhower administration recognized that the geopolitical situation was too dangerous to permit large-scale troop reductions. Just weeks before the Hungarian Revolution broke out in October 1956, Eisenhower asserted that "he felt very definitely that we cannot take divisions out of Europe at this time. The effect on Adenauer would be unacceptably damaging. He could not agree with a Defense position contemplating such reductions."[47] American diplomats reported the widespread unease regarding the international threat environment at a NATO conference held in December 1956.[48] With its handling of the Hungarian Revolution, the Soviet Union demonstrated its willingness to use force to suppress liberalizing movements within the Soviet bloc. Cold War tensions soon intensified. In November 1958, Soviet premier Nikita Khrushchev issued an ultimatum to the West, decreeing that Berlin should be a free, demilitarized city from which all non-Soviet forces had six months to evacuate. Indeed, during this phase of the Cold War, Khrushchev often used inflammatory rhetoric to emphasize the Soviet Union's military and political advantages over NATO.[49] Circumstances forestalled any major troop redeployment. Thus, Eisenhower stated that "nothing could be more fatal than to withdraw our troops from Europe or to say we are about to withdraw them" despite how "it was high time that the population of Europe did its part with respect to ground forces."[50]

Adenauer's alarm over the New Look and the Radford Plan gives context to his decisions, first, to promote his minister of atomic affairs to be the minister of defense and, second, to enter a tripartite initiative with France and Italy to research and develop nuclear weapons.[51] That abandonment fears were manifest in West German decision makers' repeated requests for assurances demonstrates that Adenauer became increasingly worried by Washington's policies and how they related to the safeguarding of West German interests.[52] Concerns over American commitments persisted throughout the remainder of Eisenhower's presidency.

FLEXIBLE RESPONSE AND THE AMERICAN SECURITY GUARANTEE TO WEST GERMANY

Talk of flexible response by the Kennedy administration did not allay West German worries. As defense minister, Strauss found flexible response objectionable for several reasons. First, flexible response risked emboldening the Soviet Union into taking limited conventional actions against West Germany. Because the Berlin crisis was still unfolding in 1961, West German leaders felt that enhancing the alliance's conventional capabilities risked signaling that the United States was not willing to engage in a nuclear confrontation with the Soviet Union.[53] Second, Strauss opposed flexible response because it contradicted his goal to arm the Bundeswehr with dual capable weapons— that is, platforms that can execute both conventional and nuclear missions.[54] Third, recognizing that not every communist aggression should provoke a nuclear response, Strauss nevertheless felt that the notion of a firebreak—a neat division between conventional hostilities and nuclear war—was inapplicable to the Central Front, the main area of the Soviet threat in Central Europe.[55] A war would not stay conventional for long before tactical nuclear weapons would be needed to frustrate Soviet offensive operations.

This last point reflected a fundamental disagreement between American and West German decision makers about how a war with the Soviet Union would be fought and the circumstances under which NATO would use nuclear weapons. Consider this extract from a West German Ministry of Defense memorandum drafted in September 1966: "Deterrence must on the one hand be comprehensive, on the other hand differentiated, in order to be credible and effective in peace, [in] times of tension and even after the outbreak of hostilities. Presupposition: modern armed, conventional and nuclear forces. The strategic means is thus the credible deterrence of escalation by the defender. The question of risk plays a decisive role. The real purpose of deterrence is therefore, to create uncertainty [in the mind of] the adversary. Fear of escalation and political concerns (e.g., mutual interests with the USSR) appear to create on the part of the USA a hesitating and uncommitted attitude."[56] For West German observers, war-fighting in Central Europe *had* to involve nuclear weapons. Yet flexible response implied that American defense planners now accepted that the Soviet Union could use its conventional superiority against West German interests without eliciting a nuclear response under certain circumstances.

To be sure, the West German position had its weaknesses, not least because its leaders knew that nuclear conflict would have terrible consequences for West German society. An irony exists here. On the one hand, the New Look reflected a willingness to turn Europe into a nuclear wasteland should war occur. Caught in the crossfire, West German decision makers valued American conventional military deployments on the continent for their trip-wire effect, reacting negatively to signs that those forces would be withdrawn. On the other hand, flexible response might have lowered the likelihood of Europe becoming a nuclear wasteland, but it undercut the credibility of American nuclear security guarantees. This observation raises an important question: if the New Look undermined conventional deterrence and flexible response undermined nuclear deterrence, then were West German leaders irredeemably doubtful of American assurances? How could the United States signal credible commitment if seemingly opposite strategies provoked similar abandonment fears?

The answer is that American *behavior* undercut the believability of flexible response. For one, some West German decision makers were unimpressed with the American handling of the Berlin crisis in 1961. West Berlin mayor Willy Brandt was incensed at the delays characterizing the American military response to the Soviet blockade. When American military patrols arrived in Berlin twenty-four hours after the Soviets began erecting the Berlin Wall, he exclaimed: "Those shitheads are at least finally sending some patrols to the sector borders so that the Berliners won't think they are totally alone."[57] Indeed, Brandt's indignation points to the perception that the United States seemed unable to assure even with conventional forces, let alone nuclear forces. For another, despite increases in American conventional forces in Western Europe during the Berlin crisis, American decision makers by 1962 reverted back to the notion that allies should bear the conventional defense burden within NATO. Flexible response was largely a rhetorical ploy to elicit higher alliance defense spending while leaving basic war plans unchanged. Later in 1965, McNamara admitted to the West German defense minister that "there exists no rational plan for the use of nuclear weapons located in Europe."[58] Hence the fear of allies like West Germany regarding an unfavorable military division in which the United States would be responsible for the management and deployment of nuclear weapons (i.e., the sword), whereas the Europeans would supply conventional military power (i.e., the shield). If conventional forces were so important for deterrence, the thinking went, then why was Washington emphasizing nuclear weapons instead?[59] This division became more intolerable as Moscow was developing capabilities that could threaten North America and thus make Washington unwilling to use its nuclear sword lest it suffer nuclear strikes as well. The United States did not help to allay abandonment fears when it staged a major airlift exercise intending to demonstrate its ability to dispatch an armored division to Europe quickly.[60]

West German leaders had yet another reason to fear the military division of labor that Washington was apparently trying to establish. If the British and the French were to retain their nuclear capabilities, and continental European allies were to provide the conventional military defense, then West Germany would occupy a subordinate status within the alliance. The Kennedy administration anticipated this concern. During internal deliberations over Adenauer's allusion to rebus sic stantibus to Kennedy, a State Department report noted that "unless there is a satisfactory multilateral arrangement, there will be increasing pressures within Germany for the development of a national nuclear deterrent, a development the Chancellor hopes can be forestalled."[61] Inequality might breed West German resentment, but it could still be acceptable if the allied defense of West German security interests was assured. Nevertheless, with uncertainty over the received security guarantee, submitting to an unequal arrangement like the one endorsed by the United States was an unattractive policy option.

Summary and Alternative Arguments

The evidence so far shows that West Germany's defensive alliance was insufficient for keeping the country from desiring nuclear weapons. Indeed, West German politicians linked the credibility of the American extended nuclear guarantee not only to nuclear weapons but also to in-theater conventional military deployments in a manner that appears to have driven West Germany's nuclear decision-making. Even American decision makers understood the value of those deployments for security assurances. But what about the alternative arguments?

The adversary thesis posits that Adenauer would have found the Soviet threat so alarming that he would have wanted nuclear weapons regardless of American actions. West German nuclear proliferation–related behavior was thus a function of West German decision makers' assessments of Soviet intentions. Yet two problems confront the adversary thesis. Most significantly, relations between Bonn and Moscow were *improving* in the years before 1958. The two countries restored diplomatic relations in 1955, and Adenauer even obtained a modest agreement with Khrushchev to return the remaining German prisoners of war from the Soviet Union.[62] During the so-called Khrushchev Thaw, the Soviet leader partially demobilized the Red Army and reduced troops in Central-Eastern Europe. He tried to signal his interest in demilitarizing the region to his American counterparts.[63] Nevertheless, diplomatic tensions did flare up in 1958, when Khrushchev issued his first ultimatum regarding the status of Berlin. In November, Khrushchev declared that the Western powers withdraw from Berlin within six months so as to make the city free and demilitarized. He also announced that East Germany would acquire control over all lines of communication with West Berlin, requiring the Western powers to negotiate with a state they refused to recognize. Khrushchev eventually canceled the deadline, but the controversy over the occupational status of Berlin lingered. However, Marc Trachtenberg argues persuasively that Khrushchev began the crisis not to bolster a weakening East Germany but in response to his fear that Bonn would gain access to nuclear weapons.[64] Soviet hostility was an effect, not a cause, of West Germany's behavior.

Adenauer acutely sensed the Soviet threat, but this threat mattered little to him as long as the United States deterred it. In a March 1953 meeting with his political party's national executive, he noted that "all our hopes and our salvation itself rest in American policies maintaining a constant course, and that Soviet Russia is aware that if it did anything, it would have the full force of American power at its throat."[65] According to official Adenauer biographer Hans-Peter Schwarz, the chancellor "staked everything on the United States."[66] Soviet actions in the Korean War and East Germany did not shake these beliefs. Indeed, the chancellor saw the Soviet Union as weakened by low living standards. Accentuating this vulnerability was its encirclement by the United States, American allies, and even China.[67] Adenauer continued holding these views despite other Soviet assertions of force in the Eastern Bloc, even seeing the Soviets as weak *because* they resorted to violence in quashing the Hungarian Revolution.[68] Thanks to American protection against Soviet aggression, West Germany was safe from harm.

Adenauer's threat perceptions heightened when American credibility became questionable. Adenauer began believing that his allies lacked resolve—a necessary condition for "encircling" the Soviet Union. The French and British appeared too keen on improving diplomatic relations with the Soviet Union, promoting disarmament in Europe, and alleviating the burden of their defense spending. These initiatives dismayed Adenauer. The United States, too, seemed to waver between containment and rapprochement.[69] Despite the Soviet Union's growing inability to expand westward, American abandonment worried Adenauer. In a fall 1956 letter, he wrote that "there can hardly be any doubt that in three, at the latest four years, American troops will have left Germany, even the whole of Europe. All good observers of US policies share this opinion."[70]

Of the domestic politics and prestige theses, the latter has the most support during this phase. Adenauer was outward looking insofar as he looked to the United States for support and the elevation of Strauss's role in West German defense policy reflected strategic considerations. Nevertheless, Adenauer and other West German decision makers like Strauss did perceive the status value of nuclear weapons. Invocations of rebus sic stantibus reflected a concern that West Germany was at risk of having a subordinate status within NATO, especially if three fellow allies had nuclear weapons of their own. Consider a 1962 State Department report on what animated Adenauer:

> The consensus in the Department of State is that the Chancellor's citing of the *rebus sic stantibus* doctrine reflects a deep-seated German concern about the implications of national British and French nuclear deterrents. The Germans are anxious to assure for themselves a leading position in European arrangements and at this juncture tend to view the nuclear diffusion problem more in political than [in] strategic terms. The immediate problem for the Germans, of course, is the discussion of the non-diffusion problem in the contexts of the Geneva disarmament talks and the Berlin proposals. In both cases, they have made it clear they would not subscribe to proposals which [sic] they felt discriminated against them. In the Department's view, there is an even more important long-range problem for the Germans—that is, the establishment of acceptable multilateral nuclear arrangements. The Chancellor, they believe, feels that unless there is a satisfactory multilateral arrangement, there will be increasing pressures within Germany for the development of a national nuclear deterrent, a development the Chancellor hopes can be forestalled. . . . Bonn will not acquiesce in an arrangement which subordinates it to Britain and France, or to Britain and France in a tripartite directorate with the U.S.[71]

At least from the American perspective, West German leaders saw status as contingent on nuclear weapons possession. However, this point should not be overstated: inequality might have been tolerable had security guarantees been more credible.

Alliance Coercion and West Germany

Curbing West Germany's nuclear behavior reflected a strong strategic rationale for neighboring states and the rival major powers. Moreover, a West German nuclear arsenal was objectionable for many decision makers due to their collective historical experience of the interwar period. A revisionist and remilitarizing West Germany conjured unpleasant memories, thereby behooving the United States to use its levers to ensure its nonproliferation status. Indeed, standard accounts of West Germany's nuclear proliferation–related behavior—at least those put forward by American scholars—agree that alliance coercion was decisive.[72]

I argue against this view and claim that alliance considerations at best had an indirect influence on West Germany's decision not to seek nuclear weapons. For one, hamstringing American coercive diplomacy were the crosscutting pressures to retain a military presence in Europe and to assure Bonn credibly. The security environment was such that an American withdrawal would have undermined deterrence and, by extension, promises of support to regional allies. Nevertheless, the United States faced mounting economic pressures to reduce its troop presence and their associated effects on the balance-of-payments crisis. The alliance itself was becoming an obstacle to any active counterproliferation effort. For another, West Germany was quickly becoming an economic powerhouse on the European continent, thereby lowering its sensitivity to possible American sanctions. In the next section I offer evidence that the United States experienced severe challenges in addressing West German nuclear interest. Its initial proposals for an alliance-based solution created a backlash despite (or perhaps due to) the support received from West Germany. Nonmilitary coercion also enjoyed limited effectiveness. Accordingly, West Germany finally agreed to renounce nuclear weapons when such a gesture served other interests, *independent of* American preferences.

THE ALLIANCE AS AN OBSTACLE

An alliance like NATO can be hard for a guarantor to manage. Aside from having to consider a wider spectrum of interests, establishing such an alliance can require the guarantor to sacrifice some of its foreign policy autonomy so as to gain the consent of its weaker allies.[73] It thus cannot change the institutional parameters of the alliance at will. When the guarantor tries to adjust the alliance with the goal of shaping the behavior of a particular member, it must generate consensus first. However, this endeavor risks backlash if fellow allies dislike it. Such dynamics unfolded when American decision makers first sought an alliance solution to resolve West German nuclear ambiguity.

To begin with, the United States identified a possible solution in the MLF, an institutional upgrade to NATO that would take seriously allies' preferences. This arrangement was to improve the participation of NATO members like West Germany in the alliance's nuclear decision-making and to reduce the incentives for nuclear proliferation. Although the MLF served to accommodate the interests of allies, its reception was lukewarm. London was somewhat willing to consider membership in the MLF, but it demanded clarification on its operational details following the Nassau Agreement (which gave Great Britain a supply of nuclear-capable Polaris missiles).[74] Italy expressed an early interest in participating in the MLF.[75] Turkey and Greece also supported the MLF, while Belgium and the Netherlands indicated their desire to follow the British approach.[76] Despite indicating that France was unlikely to join, even de Gaulle "thought it good for the Germans to do so as a way of preventing them from developing their own force."[77] The tepid support that greeted the MLF was unsurprising, and Kennedy acknowledged that "it was his impression that the British were not for it; the French were clearly against it; and the Italians did not have a deep-seated interest in it. The Germans reportedly were interested, but once they realized how little they were getting for their money, they might look at it differently." Kennedy advised that the United States should not "stick to the MLF too long if it seemed to be a losing proposition."[78] Still, that the MLF would fail was not inevitable. NATO members did not greet the initiative with hostility.

And yet the MLF failed spectacularly, almost tearing the alliance apart during its consideration. The Johnson administration—having inherited the initiative from Kennedy—had to abandon the proposal. Why did the MLF fail?

At least three factors produced the MLF's demise. The first factor was that the United States could not obtain British or French support. British decision makers resented their treatment by the United States during the Skybolt affair and the negotiations for the Nassau Agreement. The Skybolt affair erupted when the United States canceled the provision of a weapons system that the British needed to maintain their independent nuclear deterrent. Several weeks after Nassau, when British decision makers were still interpreting the significance of the MLF for their nuclear policy, de Gaulle announced his intention to veto British entry into the EEC.

As much as relations between all three nuclear NATO allies were acrimonious, London and Paris had their own reasons to find the MLF objectionable. For the British, the Nassau Agreement did not assure them of access to the much-wanted Polaris missiles. Instead, it aggravated their suspicions regarding American reliability. Moreover, their desire to preserve an independent nuclear deterrent was inconsistent with the mixed-manned operational form of the MLF.[79] For de Gaulle, the MLF was inimical to his grandiose conception of France's role in international affairs. It also would have further tethered Western Europe to the United States—a distasteful idea for Gaullism.[80] Distinguishing Great Britain from France was that the need to maintain at minimum the fiction of an independent nuclear deterrent had important electoral consequences for British prime minister Harold Macmillan.[81] By contrast, de Gaulle wanted the actual substance of independence. Given the importance that the British and the French attached to their positions, Washington could not elicit their approval.

The second factor was the propagandistic effort by communist states to link the MLF with West German nuclearization. Poland and East Germany feared that nuclear-sharing arrangements offered Bonn unfettered access to nuclear weapons. Indeed, Polish leader Władysław Gomułka opposed early Soviet draft proposals for a nonproliferation treaty that accepted NATO's use of nuclear-sharing arrangements.[82] For him, "the creation of multilateral nuclear forces would greatly increase the role of West Germany in NATO, [and] enable it to apply more forceful pressure . . . upon the policy of the USA and the entire NATO bloc towards the adoption of uncompromising and more aggressive positions with regard to the socialist states."[83] The Soviet politburo agreed and, after ousting Khrushchev from power, emphasized nuclear-sharing arrangements in subsequent treaty negotiations. Over time the Soviet Union's anti-MLF position hardened, rejecting any nonproliferation treaty that allowed any nuclear-sharing arrangement. The Soviet anti-MLF campaign might have even influenced popular attitudes toward the American-led initiative, as indicated in British public opinion polls.[84] Consequently, the United States could not have both the MLF and the NPT.[85]

The third factor was that other American allies simply came to dislike the MLF. Canada withdrew its support, while Greece and Turkey were lukewarm to the initiative.[86] The Benelux countries worried over the implications of the MLF for European integration. Domestic considerations made Italian politicians disinclined to endorse the MLF. De Gaulle began to argue intensely against the project and West Germany's participation in it.[87] An internal State Department memorandum observed that European governments interpreted the MLF as "a direct American challenge to de Gaulle's ambition to use a Franco-German entente as the basis for France's predominance in Europe," since the "launching of the MLF could provoke [de Gaulle] to lash out in some destructive act aimed at NATO and/or European Communities." Moreover, European governments believed that the financial burden associated with the MLF failed to justify the marginal improvement to the deterrent that the alliance already possessed.[88]

West Germany was the lone supporter for the MLF. Its commitment to the project is unsurprising, since it saw "the MLF as an instrument for keeping US nuclear power inextricably tied to the defense of Europe."[89] Failing to endorse the MLF also risked signaling that West Germany was contemplating an independent nuclear arsenal. Supporting the MLF might have still produced these fears, but such was the corner in which Bonn found itself. Moreover, it could not renounce nuclear weapons altogether, lest this action invite Soviet blackmail or consign West Germany to second-tier status within the alliance. Privately, West German leaders assured their American counterparts of their lack of intent to seek nuclear weapons.[90] Their public stance remained ambiguous, however. West German foreign and defense ministers claimed that the MLF would "strengthen moderate leadership in Germany, and by acting forehandedly will help prevent nationalistic adventures." Leading West German politicians echoed these sentiments, insinuating that the MLF's failure could galvanize nationalism in West Germany.[91] But if a multilateral solution like the MLF was infeasible, then neither was a bilateral one. Indeed, adding to the problem for Washington was that it could not strike a bilateral deal with Bonn. The United States was contemplating making cooperative arrangements with Great Britain and France by 1964, but these countries already had a nuclear weapons capability. Extending similar treatment to West Germany risked alienating allies like France and further antagonizing the Soviet Union.[92] Thus, between late 1964 and early

1965, the United States quietly abandoned the idea that nuclear-sharing arrangements were a viable solution for West Germany.[93] As described in the next section, so-called software solutions emerged to take their place in 1966.[94]

Because a NATO solution proved so hard to develop, could the United States not have applied unilateral nonmilitary pressure on West Germany so as to coerce a desirable outcome? At this time, the United States occupied a privileged status in the global economy due to its market size and the role of the greenback as the international reserve currency. Washington should have been able to use this clout to force Bonn into adopting credible pledges not to acquire nuclear weapons. However, with a deepening balance-of-payments crisis, the United States experienced difficulties in using such leverage to force West Germany into behaving more congruently with American interests.

The United States incurred large balance-of-payments deficits throughout the 1950s and 1960s. Resolving this issue became urgent for the Kennedy and Johnson administrations. Because six American divisions were stationed on its territory, West Germany received large amounts of American dollars and became the focus of efforts to reduce the deficit. According to one briefing document, by 1963 "expenditures in Germany by the US forces entering the international balance of payments [sic] run to about $675 million a year at current rates."[95] Moreover, American troops would use dollars to buy deutschmarks in order to purchase local goods and services. The foreign exchange costs of American troops grew from $345 million in 1956 to $749 million in 1962. During this period, West German gold reserves expanded by about 135 percent.[96]

Two options were available to American decision makers for addressing West Germany and the balance-of-payments problem. One involved reducing defense expenditures overseas unilaterally. Like its predecessor, the Kennedy administration felt the economic strain of large defense outlays spent abroad. Consequently, the Defense Department tried to cut spending under Robert McNamara's leadership.[97] Yet the State Department pleaded caution so as not to alarm allies or to show weakness to the Soviet Union. Indeed, the Berlin crisis forestalled any austere budgetary measures in the early 1960s.[98] Another option involved Bonn and Washington negotiating the extent to which the former would cover the American military presence. These types of agreements began in the early 1950s when West Germany paid so-called occupation costs in the amount of six hundred million deutschmarks a month alongside support-cost agreements with the United States, Great Britain, and other NATO members.[99] By the 1960s, negotiations tackled the issue of "offsets," the principle by which "every dollar spent in Germany defending Europe should be used by the Federal Republic to purchase American military equipment." This policy provoked resentment in West Germany, because it at once stoked abandonment fears and encouraged West German dependency on the American arms industry to develop conventional capabilities exclusively.[100]

Despite having concluded a series of support cost agreements in the 1950s, negotiating a new offset agreement with West Germany in 1960 and 1961 proved difficult. The United States wanted West Germany to purchase American weapons, but West Germany resisted on the grounds that American weapon systems were technologically outdated. Moreover, Adenauer and Minister of Defense Strauss expressed concern over Kennedy's views favoring flexible response and nuclear nonproliferation. As Zimmermann notes, gaining a "more direct influence over the use of nuclear weapons on its territory . . . became one of Strauss's conditions for agreeing to the gigantic amount of military purchases that the Americans demanded."[101] An agreement did emerge, but largely because the newly built Berlin Wall prompted West Germany to increase its own defense budget and buy American weapons. Still, in a subsequent letter exchange between the two governments, Bonn asserted that it could not promise certain budgetary decisions beyond the US fiscal year 1962. It also sought assurances of American support should the agreement upset relations with other NATO allies.[102]

The resulting Strauss-Gilpatric agreement eventually unraveled. Gold losses in the American economy continued, and the balance-of-payments deficit worsened. The first six months of 1962 saw gold losses of $420 million.[103] The American gold stock had fallen by almost a third between 1958 and 1962 with losses increasing in volume each year.[104] Meanwhile, the West German economy slowed. Though negotiations for a second offset agreement in early 1962 proved straightforward, West Germany sought additional conditions so that offset payments be made "subject to the availability of funds" in light of economic circumstances.[105] Washington initially succeeded in quashing early West German efforts to cut the defense budget and military procurement. Yet this sort of acquiescence by Bonn was brief. Budgetary constraints grew, and the West German Defense Ministry emphasized that it could not offer more than $1 billion of payments despite the second offset agreement. American pressure could elicit agreements, but not the budgetary decisions that satisfied American interests.[106]

American leaders thus reconsidered the first strategy described above—that of reducing troop levels in West Germany and Europe. Kennedy saw American troops in Europe as an indispensable tool for reassuring allies and preventing Soviet aggression.[107] However, the balance-of-payments crisis made him frustrated with West Germany's uncooperativeness. As one NSC meeting in January 1963 recorded, "The President said that we must not permit a situation to develop in which we should have to seek economic favors from Europe. . . . He thought we should be prepared to reduce quickly, if we so decided, our military forces in Germany."[108] This consideration of undertaking troop withdrawals was momentary. News that Washington was exploring the issue was leaked to the media, prompting outcry from Bonn. Eventually, Rusk publicly assured Bonn in October 1963 that the United States would maintain its six divisions in West Germany "as long as there is need for them—and under present circumstances, there is no doubt that they will continue to be needed."[109] Just one day before issuing this statement, however, Rusk privately stipulated to the West German minister of defense that West Germany had to meet the offset payments to maintain the American military presence.[110]

The United States did succeed in extracting the West German signature to the partial test ban treaty in 1963. Banning aboveground test detonations of nuclear weapons, the United States, the Soviet Union, and Great Britain first negotiated this treaty before the United States opened it to agreement by all states. Due to alliance considerations, West Germany accepted, but its leaders were dismayed, since one motivation behind this treaty was to prevent West German and Chinese proliferation.[111] For West Germany, though, the true cost of the treaty was not that it had to renounce testing nuclear weapons that it did not have. Rather, what alarmed West German decision makers was the concern that because the treaty was now open to all states, the United States and other participating states would have to recognize East Germany diplomatically should it sign the treaty. The treaty threatened to undo West Germany's efforts to deny East Germany the diplomatic recognition it had long coveted.[112]

In October 1963, Ludwig Erhard replaced Adenauer as chancellor, thereby creating new opportunities for the United States to negotiate favorable offset arrangements. Unlike Adenauer, Erhard wished to deepen American–West German relations.[113] Accordingly, the United States secured pledges from him to provide a full offset during his visit to Texas in December 1963. Yet obtaining such pledges did not translate to action. Tepid economic growth made West Germany unwilling to spend more on defense. Budget plans belied Erhard's private assurances that "[West Germany] would do everything that is possible to fulfill these offset commitments which have been approved by the Cabinet." Erhard's cabinet even agreed to freeze defense spending in favor of increasing public wages.[114]

The Johnson administration needed additional sources of leverage. To augment its bargaining position, it emphasized the link between offsets and troop levels. In meeting with his West German counterpart, "[McNamara] wished to make clear that he was making no threats, but it would be absolutely impossible for the United States to accept the gold drain caused by the US forces in Germany if Germany did not assist through continuation of the Offset Agreements."[115] Such exchanges might have pushed the Erhard government to agree to maintain its commitments, but their practical effects of these discussions on budgetary policy were still limited. Offset payments remained behind schedule. Rather than spending more on defense, the Erhard government lowered taxes and expanded social welfare programs in 1965 and 1966.[116] And yet West German officials highlighted budget difficulties to their American interlocutors, even invoking the Weimar Republic's experience of hyperinflation to suggest that increases in defense spending would be destabilizing.[117] Erhard himself suggested that the "stability of Germany was at stake." The gap between actual and promised payments widened over time with culminating effects. With respect to the 1964 offset agreement, the West German government paid only $267 million of $1.14 billion during the first year the agreement was in effect (with the expectation that $687 million would be paid by December).[118] The implicit threat behind the offset-troop linkage had little success. Some American officials found the strategy counterproductive amid Erhard's growing unpopularity at home and the emerging "German malaise over growing difference with the U.S. on offset and NATO issues."[119]

Eventually, the United States reached an agreement with West Germany (and Great Britain) over offsets through the 1967 Trilateral Negotiations. This initiative arose out of concern that because Great Britain could not maintain the value of the sterling, it would have to withdraw militarily from West Germany.[120] Although this action would save Great Britain from further foreign exchange losses, American leaders feared that it would jeopardize the Western alliance and rekindle abandonment fears in West Germany. The Trilateral Negotiations were acrimonious—even their organization proved difficult.[121] To avert a diplomatic breakdown, the three countries reached an agreement out of "mutual interest in the preservation of the European security structure and a series of concessions by all sides."[122] The agreement enabled the United States and Great Britain to withdraw thirty-five thousand and five thousand military personnel, respectively. West Germany agreed to additional offsets when the United States offered greater flexibility over the purchase of American Treasury bonds. Still, the American economy continued to hemorrhage gold and suffer inflation because of the Vietnam War and the Great Society program.[123] The agreement notwithstanding, maintaining the peg of thirty-five American dollars to an ounce of gold became more challenging. Embarrassingly for Erhard, his government collapsed one week into the negotiations. A disastrous visit that year to the United States to meet with Johnson further damaged Erhard's political prospects. Consequently, German Gaullists gained politically, further complicating the offset negotiations that still needed to occur. The sourness of this experience for all involved led future decision makers Nixon and Kissinger to abandon such an aggressive strategy and adopt a more congenial attitude toward West Germany.[124]

Because it received major inflows of American dollars and gold, West Germany was economically dependent on the United States and so should have been more compliant in meeting offset demands. However, West Germany's status as a frontline state in Cold War Europe partly inoculated American leverage. As Jonathan Kirshner writes of this period in transatlantic relations, "the reform of the [international monetary system] would not be dictated by the United States to grateful dependents, but negotiated with increasingly assertive allies."[125] American decision makers might have threatened to pull out of West Germany (and Europe), but they risked stoking abandonment fears in so doing. Concerns over German neutralism and nuclearization in the face of a significant land-based Soviet threat also meant that withdrawal would have been politically difficult to achieve. Its unique circumstances freed Bonn from being at the complete economic mercy of Washington.

OTHER CHANNELS OF AMERICAN COERCION?

American scholars have put forward two other mechanisms through which coercion compelled West Germany to abandon its nuclear interest. Aside from obliging West Germany to sign the partial test ban treaty—an interpretation questioned above—Trachtenberg argues that the United States exerted strong pressure on Adenauer to make way for Erhard to become chancellor, especially after Adenauer had made overtures to de Gaulle in going about the January 1963 Franco-German Élysée Treaty. In Trachtenberg's words, "the new tough line led to a major American intervention in internal German politics" to ensure a pro-American direction such that "the issue [of the Élysée treaty] became tied up with the question of how long Adenauer would continue in office and who would succeed him."[126] This reading misunderstands West German domestic politics. The CDU had already agreed after the autumn 1961 election that the octogenarian Adenauer would step down in exchange for the coalition participation of the Free Democratic Party (FDP).[127] After all, he had drawn criticism for his authoritarian leadership style and the Spiegel affair—a controversy regarding the publication of sensitive defense documents in the West German weekly magazine that resulted in Strauss's resignation as defense minister.[128] Erhard was a much more appealing politician thanks to his management of West Germany's economic recovery (*Wirtschaftswunder*) as economics minister since 1949. Erhard's accession might have suited American interests, but it did not result from American meddling.[129]

Gene Gerzhoy proposes another way in which the United States coerced West Germany into making strong nonproliferation pledges. He argues that threats of military abandonment were decisive in getting West German leaders to sign the NPT. His argument hinges on a February 1968 meeting between National Security Adviser Walt W. Rostow and Chancellor Kurt Kiesinger's envoy and chairman of the CDU/CSU parliamentary group, Rainer Barzel. The American transcript of this conversation records Rostow as saying that "the simple fact is that Germany depends and must depend on collective security. If you would not sign [the NPT] and decided to defend yourself with your own nuclear weapons, you would a) tear apart the Alliance; b) face a very difficult period during which you might well be destroyed."[130] Thereafter, according to Gerzhoy, West German leaders faced "unsustainable pressure . . . to sign the treaty."[131] Leaving aside how Kiesinger did not sign the NPT, this interpretation has several weaknesses. First, West German decision makers had already decided against acquiring an independent nuclear capability, thus making a key condition of Rostow's warning moot. Second, as Jonas Schneider and Makreeta Lahti point out, the Johnson administration decided against a ruthless approach to West Germany in favor of "patience, explanation and friendly persuasion."[132] Third, Barzel evidently did not inform Kiesinger of Rostow's threat in a memorandum summarizing their conversation, opting instead to discuss how he communicated Bonn's demands regarding the NPT.[133] To be sure, Gerzhoy notes that Kiesinger changed his rhetoric on the NPT over the course of 1967, from being a seemingly hostile critic to someone who privately reassured his American interlocutors that the West Germany would not stand in the way.[134] Gerzhoy attributes this change to "heavy US pressure," but another possibility is that such outspoken language was a bargaining tool in negotiations over the treaty itself.[135] To these negotiations we now turn.

Committing West Germany to Nonproliferation

Absent favorable circumstances for the guarantor, the decision to renounce nuclear weapons would reflect other factors, including the ally's own security interests that are independent of the guarantor's preferences. In the following section I argue that Washington (and Moscow) made various concessions to Bonn so as to gain West Germany's signature on the NPT. Yet these concessions still were insufficient. Ultimately, West Germany's signature on the NPT emerged from domestic political changes.

SOVIET-AMERICAN AGREEMENT ON A COUNTERPROLIFERATION STRATEGY

Ensuring West German nuclear abstention gained urgency with China's first nuclear detonation in October 1964. Johnson reacted to this development by forming a panel to identify potential proliferators and reconsider American counterproliferation strategy. This panel, called the Gilpatric Committee, released its report in January 1965.[136] Among its policy recommendations, the report asserted that nonproliferation should receive top priority in Johnson's foreign policy, adding that the United States "must acknowledge the importance of participation by the Soviet Union in efforts to stop proliferation."[137] Because the report emphasized the need for a global nondiffusion agreement, it advised that any nuclear-sharing arrangement should require nonnuclear participants to pledge not to acquire nuclear weapons. Johnson did not immediately adopt the Gilpaltric Committee's suggestions, partly to avoid giving West Germany the impression that a Soviet-American agreement would be made at West Germany's expense.[138] Nevertheless, by late 1965 and early 1966, the administration adopted a nonproliferation strategy that resembled what the Gilpatric Committee prescribed. The Soviet Union enabled this policy change.[139] Similarly alarmed by the prospects of wider nuclear proliferation in East Asia, the Soviet Union eased its rhetoric regarding nuclear-sharing arrangements. The softening of the Soviet position allowed the United States to disavow MLF finally. With this quid pro quo, the two adversaries converged in their positions regarding the NPT and West Germany.

Johnson still did not want the United States to appear willing to sacrifice West Germany's security interests in order to obtain Soviet agreement. Such an action would not only reignite abandonment fears but also stoke German nationalism. Accordingly, Bonn continued to seek new security assurances. As "hardware" solutions (i.e., nuclear-sharing arrangements) fell out of favor with Washington, a "software" solution that would address West German concerns became appealing. London had already been insisting on a software arrangement that centered on military consultations and nuclear planning involving allies.[140] In 1966, McNamara recommended that consideration of a Nuclear Planning Group (NPG) be given priority in order to meet West German demands for a greater role in nuclear decision-making in NATO.[141]

The formation of the NPG was nevertheless the death knell for nuclear-sharing arrangements within NATO, thereby representing a defeat for Bonn. The NPG was only a consultative body in which nonnuclear powers like West Germany could gain access to nuclear information and discuss issues relating to nuclear security. It was not a decision-making body.[142] That West Germany agreed to this outcome was admittedly a reflection of its limited influence within the alliance. France had by this time withdrawn militarily from NATO, Great Britain disliked nuclear-sharing arrangements of any sort, and the United States repudiated the MLF so as to pursue superpower cooperation.

Participation in the NPG thus did not eliminate West German insecurity, especially since uncertainty remained over how the NPT might affect West Germany's participation in the NPG.[143] The unease was palpable. At a January 1968 meeting of the West German National Defense Council, the "atmosphere . . . was heavy and despondent." With his top cabinet officials in attendance, Chancellor Kiesinger complained that the "inflexibility" that characterized existing drafts of the NPT "represented a real danger for [West Germany]'s security interests in the long term."[144] As Brandt explained in a letter to Rusk, greater flexibility would have entailed changes to the "procedural provisions on duration and extension, withdrawal, amendments, and review of the operation of the treaty."[145] If the treaty were to be even more flexible, Kiesinger asserted, then West Germany might be among the first to sign it.[146] One reason for this specific demand was that West German decision makers did not know the treaty's significance for West Germany's civilian nuclear industry. By this time, it was among the most advanced in the world. Participating in the treaty risked jeopardizing its success, especially if international monitoring would facilitate industrial espionage and the Soviets could use the treaty to curtail access to key nuclear materials for countries like West Germany. Accordingly, West German officials of various partisan stripes disagreed with international negotiators on what sort of safeguards should apply to their nuclear facilities. They preferred EURATOM safeguards, partly because IAEA safeguards would have enabled Soviet inspectors to collect sensitive information on West German facilities.[147]

Geopolitics was another consideration for Bonn. As one American embassy telegram noted, "there were important additional concerns, for instance as regards nuclear blackmail: for there was a growing number in the [West German Foreign Office] deeply worried that further Western troop withdrawals were inevitable and that possible safeguards against Soviet pressures should be obtained."[148] Recognizing these concerns, the superpowers accommodated West Germany by allowing EURATOM inspectors to enforce IAEA controls. They also agreed that the NPT would be in force for a fixed term of twenty-five years rather than lasting indefinitely. Washington addressed other, lesser demands made by Bonn. For instance, the United States also accepted (unilaterally) that a federal European force, should one ever appear, would be permitted to have a nuclear arsenal under the NPT, provided that Britain or France was a member.[149] Yet all these additional compromises did not determine West Germany's NPT signature. What brought about West Germany's signature, and what made it credible?

A major obstacle for West Germany's signature was rooted in domestic politics. The NPT was controversial and faced opposition from Gaullists in both the CDU and the CSU—the two political parties that formed the Grand Coalition (a governing coalition that contains the two biggest parties in the Bundestag) alongside the SDP between 1966 and 1969. Though Gaullism was ideologically flexible, it meant in West Germany closer alignment with France rather than with the United States. By proposing to institutionalize a global division of nuclear haves and have-nots, the NPT privileged a small coterie of states at the expense of emerging powers like West Germany. The rhetoric adopted by the Gaullist opponents of the NPT was impassioned. Adenauer, Strauss, and Kiesinger publicly decried the NPT as a "superpower diktat," "worse than the Morgenthau Plan," "a Versailles of cosmic dimension," and "another Yalta."[150] Politicians and government officials alike echoed earlier statements by Erhard and others that nuclear discrimination would fuel West German militarism, sometimes alleging that the NPT would mean electoral gains for the neo-Nazi National Democratic Party.[151] Moreover, the treaty exacerbated internal discord within the Grand Coalition. CSU leader Strauss had threatened to resign from his post as finance minister and cause the governing coalition to collapse if West Germany agreed to it. Kiesinger thus had a domestic incentive to forestall progress on the treaty.[152] Simply put, as long as this array of political interests within West Germany existed, Bonn's position toward the NPT would remain dubious.

MAKING OSTPOLITIK CREDIBLE

Yet another cleavage within the governing coalition had implications for West German foreign policy–making. Though the chancellor was the Christian Democrat Kiesinger, the vice chancellor and foreign minister in the Grand Coalition was former West Berlin mayor and SDP leader Brandt.

Both Brandt and Kiesinger believed that West Germany's diplomacy toward Eastern Europe was unsustainable. Since the mid-1950s, the Hallstein Doctrine was the centerpiece of its foreign policy. The doctrine stipulated that because West Germany held an exclusive right to govern the German nation, it would not pursue diplomatic relations with countries that recognized East Germany. Brandt had for some time believed that the Hallstein Doctrine needed to be abandoned. Having developed the intellectual basis of the policy as mayor of West Berlin, Brandt saw *Neue Ostpolitik* (New Eastern Policy) as a means to encourage the Cold War blocs to coexist peacefully as well as to deepen cooperation between Eastern Europe and the West.[153] Eliciting such cooperation meant using "economic, technical, scientific, cultural, and—wherever possible—political contacts with the peoples and states of Eastern Europe."[154] Under Kiesinger's leadership, Ostpolitik slowly emerged as a guiding principle of West German foreign policy. This early application of Ostpolitik enjoyed some diplomatic success, but it faced limits under Kiesinger. After all, it contradicted long-standing West German policy, thus drawing skepticism from the CDU and CSU members of the Grand Coalition as well as the members of the Soviet bloc.

For the Soviet bloc, Ostpolitik would gain credibility if West Germany undertook three actions: recognize the Oder-Neisse line as the border between East Germany and Poland, agree to the NPT, and renounce the Hallstein Doctrine.[155] However, such measures were risky. The East German government had just imposed new travel restrictions on, and denied access rights to, West Berlin citizens. Soviet leaders reiterated their right to intervene in German affairs by appealing to Articles 53 and 107 of the UN Charter.[156] Most alarmingly, the Soviets mobilized the Warsaw Pact so as to quash the reform-oriented Prague Spring in neighboring Czechoslovakia in October 1968. In this context, members of the CDU and CSU hardened their opposition to Ostpolitik.[157]

Breaking this logjam was the accession to power of a new coalition government forged between the SDP and the FDP following national elections in late October 1969. Now Brandt was chancellor, and one of his first post-election pledges was for West Germany to sign the NPT. On November 28, 1969, West Germany finally did so. The Nixon administration generally stood aloof at this juncture. Indeed, one document argues that progress was finally achieved because an "absence of pressure . . . has substantially decreased emotional resistance in Germany."[158] Brandt also opened negotiations with the Soviet Union and Poland over the recognition of the Oder-Neisse Line shortly thereafter.[159] To be sure, this change in how Bonn approached these issues was not abrupt. Kiesinger had made progress toward defining West Germany's position on the NPT throughout 1969, with Brandt and his Soviet interlocutors addressing such outstanding issues as the nonuse of force in Central Europe and Soviet rhetoric over Articles 53 and 107.[160] Still, Kiesinger could achieve only so much, admitting to Nixon that "the NPT situation is still difficult; there is division in my country and *in my party*, but we now should be discussing it on a higher level."[161] Without having to contend with CDU and CSU dissent, Brandt could now implement his vision of Ostpolitik. He did, and the resulting improvement in East-West relations solidified détente in Europe.

The benefits of Ostpolitik were not automatic in 1969. Many contemporary decision makers were unsure of how to interpret Brandt's foreign policy, and Soviet leaders remained skeptical of West German intentions as of December 1969.[162] Some NATO allies had their own reservations.[163] Nixon and Kissinger were wary of Brandt. Kissinger feared two possibilities: one in which German reunification would be made impossible and another in which German reunification would be possible but with the result being an independent Germany behaving much like it did during the interwar period.[164] The French were worried because they preferred to see Germany divided rather than reunited. French president Georges Pompidou even feared that intra-German reconciliation would lead to American troop withdrawals from Europe and a German-Soviet accord.[165] Still, despite harboring doubts about American security guarantees in a time of nuclear parity, Brandt did not believe Ostpolitik was anti-NATO. He instead felt that strong alliance ties were necessary for Ostpolitik and détente to flourish.[166] These observations suggest that when West Germany did finally renounce nuclear weapons, it did so in a way of its own choosing that departed from the interests of its allies.

Some critical readers might claim that my analysis overemphasizes Ostpolitik. After all, the Bundestag finally ratified the NPT in 1975, something that some scholars see as driven by attitudinal changes among CDU politicians toward their country's international status.[167] In the meantime, West Germany still undertook centrifuge research amid other efforts to develop its civilian nuclear industry. Nevertheless, I argue that the international political dimension of West Germany's nuclear proliferation–related behavior had largely run its course by 1970 thanks to Brandt's foreign policy.[168] Still, the fact that Bonn persisted so long in deflecting international calls to clarify its intentions only reinforces my broader point: West Germany was not so beholden to American pressure as to have a counterproliferation settlement imposed on it.

That said, the alliance with the United States did in fact pose limits on how far West Germany can resist calls to sign the NPT. Brandt recognized that Bonn risked international isolation by not signing the treaty: "No one will be prepared to show solidarity with us and defend us. We remain alone." His main political adviser, Egon Bahr, agreed. In an undated memorandum, Bahr recorded in mid-1968, "The question is, can the German government [resist] the combined pressure from East and West . . . and afford going it alone not just without, but against the allies? Only one answer should be possible here if one gauges the Federal Republic's political weight realistically." He added that "straining our relationship with our protector, the United States, is much more serious," while "at the same time, we will become isolated from our other allies once they sign the treaty." Even Kiesinger admitted as early as 1966, "We cannot reject a Nuclear Nonproliferation Treaty," acknowledging three years later that "in the end, there is of course nothing you can do against a superpower and you will have to sign [the NPT]."[169] Simply put, alliance politics did inhibit what West Germany could achieve in its nuclear policy, but this pressure was much more diffuse and cannot be measured in terms of concrete coercive actions undertaken by the United States, be they interventions in West German domestic politics or specific threats designed to coerce treaty agreements.

Summary and Alternative Arguments

Throughout the 1960s, the United States sought to avert the possibility of a nuclear-armed West Germany by getting it to make credible nonproliferation commitments. This effort faced major challenges. First, alliance dynamics with NATO thwarted attempts to advance an institutional solution, such as a nuclear-sharing arrangement similar to MLF. Second, American struggles with obtaining West German offset payments highlighted the limits of economic leverage. Bonn eventually signed the NPT, but only after extracting treaty concessions from the two superpowers and key changes in domestic politics that made a new foreign policy vision, Ostpolitik, practical. Nevertheless, signing the NPT largely served to make Ostpolitik a bona fide policy to placate Moscow rather than to gain relief from active American pressure. That is not to say that the alliance had no role in shaping West Germany's nuclear trajectory; key decision makers recognized that international isolation from the United States and other partners was so intolerable that signing the treaty was necessary. Still, the bottom line is that forcing West Germany to accept strong nonproliferation commitments was immensely difficult for the United States to undertake, much more so than suggested by some scholars.

The alternative arguments have mixed success in accounting for West Germany's choices. According to the adversary thesis, Bonn had no reason to renounce nuclear weapons credibly because the Soviet threat persisted throughout the 1960s. Khrushchev issued another ultimatum in June 1961 at the Vienna Summit when he indicated that he would sign a separate peace treaty with East Germany unless Western armed forces left Berlin. The Berlin Wall ended this crisis, but Khrushchev continued to practice nuclear brinkmanship when he placed nuclear-armed missiles in Cuba and sparked the Cuban missile crisis. This onslaught of crisis behavior eventually ceased, and the Soviet politburo replaced Khrushchev with Leonid Brezhnev. However, Brezhnev's emergence as the Soviet leader did not immediately produce détente with the United States. Though calmer than his predecessor, Brezhnev reversed some of Khrushchev's liberalizing reforms and sharply criticized the United States on such issues as Vietnam and the MLF. He undertook several provocative actions that directly affected West Germany's security, such as asserting the right to intervene directly in West German politics and deploying the Warsaw Pact to quash the Prague Spring in Czechoslovakia.

These two actions occurred when the Grand Coalition, under Kiesinger and Brandt, was attempting to implement Ostpolitik. Brandt's becoming chancellor and implementing Ostpolitik more consistently than before helped improve East-West relations in Europe. As William Glenn Gray concludes, "détente in the 1960s had skirted the German Question; détente in the 1970s was achieved precisely because of agreements on Germany."[170] Similarly, Trachtenberg observes that Ostpolitik was a response to the Soviet military buildup at a time when American security guarantees remained suspect. Brandt realized that Bonn had to accommodate Moscow somewhat.[171] Tensions with the Soviet Union were more a function of West Germany's stance toward nuclear weapons, not vice versa as the adversary thesis suggests.

The domestic politics thesis provides crucial insights into the timing, if not the substance, of West Germany's decisions. Kiesinger may have come to the view that signing the NPT was unavoidable, but hamstringing his leadership was the need for the CDU, the CSU and the SDP to work together in the Grand Coalition. Intraparty cleavages and coalition politics undermined the coherence of West German foreign policy. As such, the increasing power of Brandt and the left-of-center SDP within West German politics and society made at least the signing of the NPT possible. As long as there were politically influential CDU and CSU politicians suspicious of Ostpolitik, Soviet intentions, and American credibility, West Germany's signature would have had to occur under different circumstances. Accordingly, the domestic politics thesis may have greater applicability than what Etel Solingen realizes in light of her decision to restrict her argument to the post-1968 period.[172] Such an analytical move may have been unnecessary on her part: Kiesinger and Brandt believed that abstaining from the NPT would mean international isolation and lost opportunities in East-West cooperation. Simply put, West Germany became more outward looking than not with Ostpolitik.

The prestige thesis also receives empirical support. Discussions of nuclear weapons and the NPT were imbued with emotional language that reflected status anxiety. As indicated earlier in this chapter, West German leaders seemed to worry that they would be consigned to an inferior status within NATO if they had no nuclear weapons when the United States, Great Britain, and France had them. CDU and CSU politicians decried the NPT as a "superpower diktat."[173] Even when Kiesinger privately conceded that West Germany had no choice but to sign the treaty, he bemoaned his own country as "a virtual protectorate of the USA." Much as what would be expected according to the prestige thesis, Kiesinger still refrained from ceasing West Germany's nuclear proliferation–related behavior. Nevertheless, his reasons for being persistent owed more to domestic politics than to his ability to pursue what he wanted. The prestige thesis also can partly illuminate the timing of the NPT signature. Thomas Berger contends that a culture of antimilitarism was decisive in inhibiting West Germany's nuclear interest. After all, the forces associated with antimilitarism might have helped elevate Brandt to the chancellorship. Although "there was a general consensus that development of an independent national nuclear force would needlessly provoke the Soviet Union and alienate Germany's Western allies," Berger writes that "the presence of large, virulently antimilitary coalitions of social and political forces, supported by widespread public antipathy toward the new military [establishment] . . . arguably tipped the balance."[174] Still, as a policy of partial accommodation, Brandt's Ostpolitik served as a rationale that can be understood in its international context without reference to West German domestic politics.

Mostly landlocked and vulnerable to massive Soviet conventional military power, West Germany had much at stake in the protection offered by the United States. Distrust in the American security guarantee prompted West Germany's nuclear interest amid rumors that the United States was cutting its conventional forces. Yet the decision to adopt a clear nonproliferation stance through the NPT resulted from a confluence of multiple factors. Specifically, Bonn obtained treaty concessions from the two superpowers and evinced significant domestic political changes against an international context, whereby the Soviet Union and the United States were at rough nuclear parity. To the degree that alliance coercion took place, it was more psychic than actual: West German leaders feared international isolation given their geopolitical position. Even so, West Germany managed to develop impressive nuclear capabilities in reprocessing and enrichment during this time period.

Japan, 1952–1980

Postwar Japan had less room to maneuver than West Germany in determining its foreign policy. Article 9 of the Japanese Constitution and the so-called Yoshida Doctrine explicitly disavow the threat and the use of force to resolve international disputes. Hiroshima and Nagasaki were the only cities ever to experience nuclear devastation when the United States bombed them in August 1945. Following the 1954 *Daigo Fukuryu Maru* incident, in which the crew of a Japanese fishing trawler was exposed to radiation fallout from American nuclear weapons tests, an antinuclear movement emerged as a major force in Japanese domestic politics. This movement protested what it saw to be the overbearing presence of the United States in Japanese affairs. The military alliance was robust thanks to a formal security guarantee as well as the local presence of many American troops and nuclear weapons. Japan thus constitutes a most-likely case where the alliance should not only help deter a nuclear weapons program but also curb any nuclear interest in the unlikely event that such interest arises.

Yet closer investigation of this case reveals that as much as the alliance with the United States did obviate a Japanese nuclear weapons program, concern over redeployments of American conventional forces in East Asia and the direction of American foreign policy seems to have spurred some nuclear interest. Despite the limited nature of this interest, the United States still experienced difficulties in getting Japan to make firm nonproliferation commitments throughout the 1960s and the 1970s. Specifically, China's 1964 nuclear weapon detonation disturbed Japan's sense of security, leading Japan's decision makers to scrutinize more closely the quality of the American security guarantee. Abandonment fears intensified toward the late 1960s when the United States sought to lessen its involvement in the Vietnam War and East Asia. In response, Japan adopted a policy of nuclear hedging— buying time so as to develop a latent nuclear capability even if its leaders had no desire for nuclear weapons at the time. American decision makers were aware of these developments, but they felt unable to act fully on their concerns. Though Japan needed its alliance with the United States, domestic politics and its growing economic power inoculated it against American co-ercion. Largely on its own initiative, Japan ratified the nonproliferation treaty (NPT) in 1976. Still, some doubts over Japanese nuclear intentions lingered thereafter in light of the reprocessing activities at a nuclear facility in Tokai. Japan has since become "the most salient example of nuclear hedging" that "illustrates how a state signatory to the NPT and a champion of nonproliferation and disarmament can legitimately maintain a nuclear fuel-cycle capability and possess huge quantities of weapons-grade fissile material."[1] To be sure, Japan's nuclear activities very likely had in mind energy security as well, but the geostrategic dimension cannot be discounted altogether.

My framework illuminates how Japan went about its nuclear proliferation–related behavior. First, the alliance with the United States did not fully inhibit Japan's nuclear ambitions, since Japan ratcheted up its interest in enrichment and reprocessing technologies in the late 1960s. Second, Japan paid attention to in-theater conventional forces and doctrine in evaluating the strength of its received commitments. As such, American disengagement from Vietnam and the Nixon Doctrine helped intensify abandonment fears. Third, although the alliance did discourage some level of interest in nuclear weapons, the United States was reluctant to coerce Japan directly on this issue. Fourth, and finally, although the United States shaped Japan's nuclear choices through various nuclear agreements during the 1950s and the 1960s, Japan was *not* very susceptible to American economic pressure. American decision makers recognized that pushing Japan too much would be counterproductive. Though these alternative explanations have their own shortcomings in accounting for this case, domestic politics and, to a lesser extent, prestige considerations were arguably a greater influence on Japan's nuclear decision-making in the 1970s than alliance-related ones.

Before analyzing the case, I review the strategic and domestic circumstances that Japanese decision makers faced, thereby identifying what the alternative arguments would predict from this case.

The Strategic Context

The bilateral alliance between the United States and Japan had its roots in the American postwar occupation of Japan. The 1952 Treaty of San Francisco formalized the political commitment of Washington to Tokyo and was later amended in the 1960 Treaty of Mutual Cooperation and Security between the United States and Japan. Unlike landlocked West Germany, Japan is an archipelago state with islands located in close proximity to eastern frontiers of the former Soviet Union and China. However, Soviet naval forces became capable of projecting military power against Japanese territory only in the 1970s, whereas China would have still experienced difficulties in launching offensive operations against Taiwan by then. Because Japan had thus less use for American land power than did West Germany, the New Look should have had little practical significance for Tokyo. Indeed, by emphasizing air power and missile capabilities, the New Look was better aligned with Japan's strategic needs.

The political threat confronting Tokyo was still real. Communist China fought the Korean War on the side of the North and initiated multiple crises over the status of Taiwan, an island ruled by anticommunist nationalists who fled the Chinese mainland following their defeat in the Chinese Civil War. China also began constructing uranium-enrichment plants in 1958. Although American decision makers knew of Chinese nuclear efforts in 1960 and 1961, what Japanese decision makers knew exactly before 1964 remains unclear. The mystery ended when China first detonated a nuclear device on October 16, 1964. Taking place about one week into the Summer Olympic Games in Tokyo, the timing of this event was likely deliberate. This Olympiad was the first ever held in Asia and symbolized Japan's rehabilitated status in international politics. Moreover, Beijing was developing ballistic missile capabilities, making it even less likely to submit to American nuclear threats than in the past.[2] Japanese decision makers subsequently had greater reason to scrutinize their received security guarantees.

China showcased its nuclear capabilities when the Johnson administration was deliberating over whether to escalate the military involvement of the United States in Vietnam. American decision makers—including Johnson himself—believed that this decision would shape perceptions of American credibility to security partners around the world, especially those in Asia. Deploying manpower and resources in supporting the anticommunist regime in South Vietnam should attenuate abandonment fears but generate entrapment fears, though much less so with anticommunists. Of course, the Vietnam War did not widen into a major power conflict, becoming instead a military debacle for the United States. Given its geopolitical position, Japanese abandonment fears should intensify amid American efforts to disengage from East Asia upon losing a war in Vietnam.

The adversary thesis differs from my theory by arguing that sensitivity to Chinese and Soviet military threats alone would drive Japanese nuclear interests. American efforts to reassure Japan should not matter, since security guarantees are inherently unbelievable.

The Domestic Context

For much of the period under review, the Liberal Democratic Party (LDP) ruled Japan. This party emerged as the dominant political force following the 1955 merger of Shigeru Yoshida's Liberal Party and Ichiro Hatoyama's Japan Democratic Party. Yoshida is famous for being the namesake of the Yoshida Doctrine—the notion that Japan should focus primarily on economic growth while depending on American security guarantees. Hatoyama was a nationalist who sought to advance Japan's foreign policy autonomy. The LDP's main electoral competition was the Japan Socialist Party (JSP). Though the JSP usually held half of the seats as the LDP under the 1955 system, the JSP's popularity still generated concerns over Japan's internal order and potential neutralism among Japanese and American officials.[3]

Its dominance in Japanese politics notwithstanding, the LDP was internally divided, with factions that influenced candidate recruitment and personnel decisions. One conservative faction of the LDP was Kochikai and comprised followers of Yoshida such as Prime Minister Hayato Ikeda (1960–1964). Another faction, led by the self-made and entrepreneurial Kakuei Tanaka, became known as Heisei Kenkyukai; it generally favored international cooperation with China and South Korea. Prime ministers associated with this faction included the anticommunist Eisaku Sato (1964–1972) and Tanaka himself (1972–1974). Career bureaucrat Takeo Fukuda led another faction that originally bore the name of Tofu Sasshin Renmei before becoming known as Seiwa Seisaku Kenkyukai. It was more nationalist and economically liberal than the Tanaka-led faction but did not produce prime ministers during the period examined later in this chapter. Nevertheless, Nobusuke Kishi had already been prime minister (1957–1960) by the time Fukuda formed this faction in 1962.

Given these differences in the ruling coalitions that governed Japan, what would the predictions of the domestic politics and prestige theses be for this case? The domestic politics thesis predicts no nuclear weapons–related behavior since the Yoshida Doctrine postulated that the political survival of the new postwar regime hinged on Japan's ability to deliver growth through global economic integration. Etel Solingen notes in her rich, multicausal account of Japan's nuclear choices that the Yoshida Doctrine required "a strong economic infrastructure, manufacturing capabilities . . . and swimming with (not against) the great tide of market forces."[4] The Yoshida Doctrine, "as the heart of Japan's favored model of political survival, provided the glue that kept the anti-nuclear package together."[5] The prestige thesis offers a slightly different hypothesis, highlighting how antimilitarist and antinuclear attitudes in Japanese society became more salient over time and should discourage politicians of all stripes from considering nuclear weapons. Even Solingen admits that "the nuclear allergy appears to have grown stronger in more recent times than it was during the first two decades of the postwar era."[6] Indeed, some analysts claim that "having experienced Hiroshima and Nagasaki . . . Japan's political structures and national psyche have engendered a deeply enshrined cultural taboo . . . against even the public discussion."[7]

Nuclear Proliferation–Related Behavior: Hedging after a Period of Disinterest

The documentary record suggests that Japanese leaders exhibited little interest, if any, in nuclear weapons throughout the 1950s. As in West Germany, rearmament dominated Japanese-American security relations during this decade. For many Japanese politicians, the constitutionality of rearmament was a major subject of debate since article 9 of the Japanese Constitution renounced war, forbade the use or threat of force to resolve international disputes, and abjured the development of an armed force that had "war potential." Whether such arrangements could accommodate nuclear weapons was also unclear. Akira Kodaki, the director of the National Defense Agency, suggested that the Japanese military possess "nuclear weapons to [a] minimum extent necessary for sake of defense."[8] At a Diet committee meeting on May 7, 1957, Japanese prime minister Nobusuke Kishi interjected: "I do not think so-called nuclear weapons are prohibited entirely by constitution. In view of progress of science, we must have effective power to carry out modern warfare within scope self-defense [sic]."[9] Kishi later added that he did not intend to arm the Self-Defense Forces with nuclear weapons or to accept the placement of American nuclear units in Japan. Some American officials took note of these statements. A background paper on Japan's military observed that "the Japanese Government appears to be interested in acquiring eventually tactical nuclear weapons for its own forces." The paper argued that Kishi's evolving stance on nuclear weapons "represent[ed] a major modification in previous Japanese Government opposition to any form of nuclear weapons, offensive or defensive." The psychological impact of Hiroshima and Nagasaki mattered insofar as it fueled domestic opposition to any positioning of American nuclear weapons in Japan.[10] Nevertheless, American decision makers neither accorded much significance to these statements nor inferred that Japan wanted nuclear weapons.

Following China's first detonation of a nuclear device in October 1964, Japan began reconsidering its stance toward nuclear weapons. The Japanese government commissioned a report by the Cabinet Research Office entitled "Security of Japan and the Nuclear Test of the CCP" in December 1964. Written by Kei Wakaizumi and presented to the intelligence office of the cabinet, this report called for the development of a latent nuclear capacity by way of investing in satellite and missile technology and nuclear power plants.[11] As Toshimitsu Kishi concludes in analyzing how Tokyo reacted to the Chinese nuclear test, "many reports expressed the opinion that Japan should not be armed with nuclear weapons, but should develop its nuclear capabilities."[12] Thereafter, Tokyo adopted an ambivalent position toward the NPT just as it was still being negotiated. It endorsed universal nuclear disarmament but decried the political inequality that the treaty threatened to enshrine.[13] In January 1968, Prime Minister Eisaku Sato made a speech to the Japanese Diet that, according to Yuri Kase, sought to "challenge the prevalence of 'nuclear taboo' that existed among the population at the time . . . especially among the idealist left."[14] Though Japan signed the treaty in 1970, its leaders argued that its ratification would be conditional on the promotion of international nuclear disarmament by the great powers, the provision of security guarantees for nonnuclear weapons states, and assurances that nonnuclear weapons states would have equal access to atomic energy for peaceful use.

Accompanying this legal equivocation was the technological progress that Japan was striving to make in the nuclear domain. Its nuclear proliferation–related behavior was discreet: the Japanese government bolstered its centrifuge program in 1969 and intensified its civilian nuclear activities in the early 1970s, presumably to develop a virtual capability. According to Matthew Fuhrmann and Benjamin Tkach, Japan had its enrichment and reprocessing plants operational in 1968.[15] In 1969, the Atomic Energy Commission Expert Committee determined that the development of a centrifuge program was a national priority. It allocated a billion yen ($12 million in 2008 dollars) to an underfunded group of nuclear scientists who were already attempting to manufacture their own designs. Following some success, their budget saw a tenfold increase, allowing them to produce quickly several machine cascades.[16] In 1973, a new centrifuge program entered into existence.[17] These increases in both spending and activity in the nuclear sector mostly *preceded* the global energy crisis that began in 1973.[18]

A report commissioned by Sato also reflected Japan's nuclear ambivalence. Written by four nongovernmental university scholars, this two-volume report was not an official government report. The first volume appeared in 1968 and assessed the costs and benefits of a Japanese nuclear weapons program on technical, economic, and organizational grounds. It withheld judgment as to whether Japan should pursue a nuclear weapons program. However, it did aver that for the "time being" Japan should "keep the economic and technical potential for the production of nuclear weapons, while seeing to it that Japan not be interfered with in this regard."[19] Published in 1970, the second volume evaluated the strategic, political, and diplomatic implications of Japan acquiring nuclear weapons. It advised against an independent nuclear deterrent because of the lack of strategic depth as well as the costs associated with provoking communist adversaries and Washington. This two-volume report saw very limited circulation within the Japanese government bureaucracy, making its impact on actual decision-making unclear. This report may have helped Tokyo identify arguments to use in allaying international concerns over its nuclear intentions. Nevertheless, the production of this report indicates that Japan was at least weighing the merits of having nuclear weapons.[20]

And so ambiguity characterized their public stance even if Japanese leaders might have found nuclear weapons unnecessary or distasteful. For example, Tokyo partly objected to ratifying the NPT because the recommended safeguards were inadequate for preventing industrial espionage. However, as American diplomatic officials argued, the Japanese government itself could have themselves implemented the appropriate safeguards through domestic legislation rather than through international agreements.[21] American officials saw ulterior motives at play. As one embassy official wrote, "Reading between the lines, with liberal application of imagination, I would surmise that there is a political problem for the GOJ [Government of Japan] concerning the NPT which is more basic than their objection to the safeguards article, and which is related to the attitudes of a small but influential minority who wish at least to keep Japan's nuclear options open. I would guess that the Foreign Ministry and the LDP leadership, while aware of the broad consensus of feeling against nuclear armaments, nevertheless do not wish to antagonize this small influential minority by appearing to move too fast."[22] A conservative nationalist faction certainly delayed treaty ratification when legislation for it appeared in 1974. Yet Tokyo had its own reasons for desiring flexibility in international negotiations.

Consider Sato's three nonnuclear principles. In 1969, he vowed not to manufacture, possess, or even allow the introduction of nuclear weapons in Japan—the latter of which would impair Washington's ability to extend nuclear deterrence. These principles might have expressed a policy of nuclear denial, but Sato really wanted them to "stimulate debate on how Japan should defend itself in the nuclear era, rather than to express his support for the principles."[23] Unfortunately for him, it constrained later negotiations over the reversion of the island of Okinawa. The United States wanted to retain basing access and rights to deploy conventional forces to Korea, Taiwan, and Vietnam, as well as to keep nuclear weapons on the island. However, the JSP proposed a "nonnuclear" resolution in the Diet. Caught in this dilemma, Sato decried his rhetorical pledge as "unnecessary" because it complicated his efforts to strike a balance between American demands and the sensibilities of Japanese society.[24] He agreed to violate the third principle by granting Washington the ability to place and to install nuclear weapons in Japan.[25]

Two episodes from the 1970s further illustrate Japan's nuclear ambiguity. The first is a March 1973 interpellation between Prime Minister Tanaka and members of the Diet. On March 13, Tanaka asserted that "nuclear weapons are offensive weapons and against the Constitution." But on the next day the Japanese government issued a statement claiming that tactical nuclear weapons *were* constitutional. Asked to clarify his original statement several days later, Tanaka noted that "(1) if within the scope of self-defense, nuclear weapons will not run counter to the Constitution, (2) however, since nuclear weapons are considered to be offensive weapons, generally, they run counter to the Constitution, and (3) the Government will firmly maintain the Three Non-Nuclear Principles and will not carry out nuclear weapons." However, on March 20, Tanaka noted, "We will firmly maintain the policy based on the three non-nuclear principles. . . . We will not be able to hold offensive nuclear weapons, but it does not mean that we will not hold nuclear weapons at all."[26] Several months later, Tanaka told Nixon twice that "Japan would not possess nuclear or military power because of its constitutional restrictions."[27]

The second is an exchange between Nixon and Japanese foreign minister Masayoshi Ohira. Following India's "peaceful nuclear explosion" in 1974, Nixon inquired as to how Japan would react. After Ohira assured him that "Japan is in no way thinking of going nuclear," Nixon responded vaguely, "I would not indicate what Japan should do, but I would just point out the increasing likelihood of nuclear war as more states acquire these devices. Of course, the answer is to look to working even harder to strengthen a structure of peace . . . so that states will reject the option of force, nuclear or otherwise. It sounds idealistic but there is no other way to approach the problem."[28] At a minimum, he was signaling that the United States did not tolerate nuclear proliferation. Yet he did not request Japanese reassurances not to acquire an independent nuclear capability. To be sure, National Security Decision Memorandum 13 did not register as a goal of American foreign policy the clarification and credible renunciation of nuclear weapons by Japan.[29] Still, his coded language suggests that the ambiguity of Japan's nuclear policy bothered him. Several months later, Kissinger told Soviet foreign minister Andrei Gromyko, "The line between weapons and peaceful uses is vague. . . . The Japanese have a big nuclear program but have not done any explosion yet. If they moved this way, they would go like India and could be a big power very quickly."[30]

Japan's nuclear ambiguity disturbed other states. In his meeting with Kissinger ahead of Nixon's visit to China, Zhou Enlai opined that "the only thing lacking [for Japan] is the nuclear warhead" and that Japan was "bound to demand outward expansion."[31] For him, Japan's "feathers have grown on its wings and it is about to take off," meaning that it would soon convert its economic power into military power. Nixon tried to assuage Zhou's concerns, remarking that "we oppose a nuclear rearmed Japan no matter what some officials might suggest to the contrary."[32] American decision makers were even aware of Japanese nuclear blackmail against Moscow. Prime Minister Tanaka informed Nixon that he "told Brezhnev that he should not give the Japanese too rough a time because they were quite capable of nuclear weapons."[33]

This persistent ambiguity bought the Japanese government enough time to develop a latent nuclear capability. The success of the centrifuge program in the late 1970s gave Japan access to fissile materials—a necessary component for a nuclear bomb.[34] Nevertheless, political challenges aside, this so-called latent nuclear capability faced serious technical constraints that included an insufficient stockpile of weapons-grade plutonium, no ballistic missile deployment capability, and the need to divert nuclear power activity toward military purposes despite IAEA regulations.[35]

Explaining Japan's Behavior: Disinterest and Nuclear Hedging

What explains Japan's nuclear hedging after 1964? To what extent did concerns regarding American extended deterrence drive Japanese nuclear interest? According to my theoretical framework, Japanese decision makers should have attended to their received security guarantees in formulating their nuclear choices, with special reference to in-theater deployments and American doctrine. As such, Japanese decision makers should be satisfied with the military alliance until military defeats in the Vietnam War began straining American alliance commitments to East Asia. Such is what we see.

Throughout the 1950s, Japan benefited from being an archipelago state that faced no direct military threat. Its leaders were thus unfazed by the diminished role of conventional military power that the New Look embodied. Indeed, Japanese leaders wanted to reduce the American army presence in their efforts to revise the 1951 Security Treaty.[36] They sought a more equitable mutual defense treaty that contained provisions for limiting American use rights of bases located in Japan and stipulating the withdrawal of American ground forces.[37] After all, members of Japanese society regarded the US Army as an occupying force that had little deterrent value against potential adversaries, since Japan required a military presence based primarily on air and naval power.[38] Accordingly, the Radford Plan was desirable from the perspective of Japanese decision makers. The secretary general of the LDP, and later prime minister, Nobusuke Kishi, noted that a "major source of friction" between the two countries "[arose] from the existence of numerous United States bases and the presence of large numbers of American troops in Japan."[39] Still, Japanese leaders valued the presence of American naval and air forces. Reflecting this view, the Japanese proposal for a mutual defense treaty requested that the removal of such forces would take place "at the latest six years after completion of the withdrawal of the ground forces."[40]

Other factors shaped Japanese perceptions of American regional credibility. To begin with, American diplomatic exchanges included many expressions of commitment to containing local communist ambitions partly because American decision makers found East Asia more volatile, so as to require a more assertive presence. Whereas one communist state—the Soviet Union—threatened American allies in Europe, three threatened—the Soviet Union, China, and North Korea—American allies in East Asia. Consequently,

American-led containment efforts faced a greater challenge in this region.[41] Yet the challenges of deterring multiple communist adversaries also created opportunities to reassure local allies. When China bombarded offshore islands in the Taiwan Straits in 1955, for example, the United States signaled its resolve in defending Taiwan by threatening nuclear weapons use to force China to back down.[42]

Another factor was the unique care invested by American decision makers in fostering a strong Japan. In their view, what rendered the security environment more precarious was that Japan was politically and economically isolated from potential allies in the region. The American ambassador in Tokyo saw the country in a "semi-isolated" position within its region. It "had neither the leavening influence of close association with dependable free world neighbors which Germany has had nor Germany's first hand exposure to Soviet brutality."[43] Whatever Japan's own threat perceptions, American decision makers viewed the security environment in East Asia as volatile enough to require a robust American response and an indefinite regional presence. Even NSC 162/2 (which formulated the New Look) projected different levels of American military assistance to Western Europe and East Asia. It asserted that in Western Europe "the United States must continue to assist in creating and maintaining mutually agreed European forces, but should reduce such assistance as rapidly as United States interests permit." By contrast, it "should maintain the security of the offshore island chain and continue to develop the defensive capacity of Korea and Southeast Asia in accordance with existing commitments."[44] Moreover, because East Asia was not as economically developed as Western Europe, American leaders recognized that a military presence in the former region might have to last longer. Since Japan's economy exhibited uneven growth during the 1950s, American leaders were cautious about pressuring Japan into boosting defense spending. Secretary of State John Foster Dulles admitted that they "had tended to push the Japanese too hard" on such issues.[45] Finally, for Japanese leaders, the Korean War indicated that the United States was committed to curbing communism in the region. The American-led coalition not only repelled the North's bid to reunify the peninsula under communist control but also prevented communist forces from using the South to project military power against Japan.[46]

That the United States was tightening its alliances in East Asia should have inspired fears of entrapment and not abandonment. Indeed, Eisenhower's use of nuclear threats unsettled local actors. A March 1955 National Intelligence Estimate (NIE) surmised that in response to nuclear use, the "general reaction of non-Communist Asians would be emotional and would be extremely critical of the US. . . . The [Japanese] Government would probably attempt to steer a more neutral course." The NIE added that the United States should contain communist China without war or nuclear weapons so that "US prestige and the confidence of the non-Communist world in US leadership would be enhanced."[47] A dilemma for Eisenhower thus arose. He recognized that "if [a 'small war'] grew to anything like Korea proportions, the action would become one for atomic weapons."[48] Nevertheless, he noted that with respect to South Korea and Taiwan, "this business of arguing that you are going to defend these countries through recourse to nuclear weapons isn't very convincing. In point of fact, these countries do not wish to be defended by nuclear weapons. They all regard these weapons as essentially offensive in character, and our allies are absolutely scared to death that we will use such weapons."[49]

This sensitivity to nuclear strategy in East Asia indicates that the United States—and not Japan—feared abandonment. American decision makers doubted whether Tokyo was committed to the bilateral security partnership and whether it was able or willing to respond to regional communist threats over the long term. The so-called Yoshida Doctrine and its stated emphasis on American protection mattered little. After all, impassioned debate unfolded in Japan over the extent to which it should align itself with the United States and which American military assets could be stationed on Japanese territory. Indeed, ground forces notwithstanding, American decision makers wanted to maintain a general military presence in Japan "indefinitely."[50] For them, the security of Japan and that of the entire region were at stake. Dulles told British foreign secretary Harold Macmillan that "with Russia and China allied and Japan inert and lacking power, the United States had to maintain more military power in the Pacific area than it would otherwise choose. Were we to withdraw, one could look for a substantial expansion of Communist power throughout the Far East."[51] And so Washington beseeched Tokyo to accept a major military presence. One American official advised that the Japanese government should recognize that the "United States must retain air, naval, and ground-logistical bases in Japan on a long-term basis."[52]

Two unfavorable features of Japanese politics worried American decision makers. First, two factions were advocating policies that were inimical to American security objectives. The conservatives were pro-American but internally divided and anxious for foreign policy autonomy. Worse were the Socialists. They were "essentially neutralist and to an extent anti-American."[53] American influence over Japanese politics seemed to be rapidly diminishing. Second, American decision makers believed that Japanese lawmakers were naively optimistic regarding the communist threat and that Japanese trade with China would "substantially increase China's war potential" because of such Japanese exports as machine tools and electronic equipment.[54] Moreover, in advocating for American military withdrawal, Kishi dismissed the severity of the Soviet threat.[55] Although American leaders approved of Kishi, they were unsure that he would be a reliable ally should he become prime minister. One presidential adviser recommended that Kishi be disabused of the "'Alice-in-Wonderland Dream World' frame of mind" by having the Chair of the Joint Chiefs "[impress] Mr. Kishi with the exposed position which Japan would occupy if United States forces were to be entirely withdrawn at this time."[56]

Divergent threat perceptions and domestic controversies over the partnership shaped the context in which the two allies renegotiated their security treaty in the late 1950s.[57] Unlike West German leaders, who demanded from the United States a continuing military presence in Europe and greater say in military arrangements, Japanese leaders wanted American ground troops to withdraw. Hawkish and nationalist leaders like Hatoyama and Kishi needed convincing that the presence of American air and naval forces was necessary. These leaders desired a more equitable security treaty. Whereas the 1951 treaty did not specify the terms under which the United States could maintain its military presence and bases, the 1960 revision obliged the United States to consult with Japan over their use and nuclear storage. The treaty revision also gave the Japanese government's consent to the American use of Okinawa for military basing.[58] But these negotiations rattled both sides: Prime Minister Kishi resigned after violent demonstrations rocked Tokyo, and Eisenhower had to cancel a state visit to Japan. The experience demonstrated how intensely the Japanese left opposed the alliance.[59]

These controversies soon subsided. Tranquility characterized the alliance during Kennedy's presidency. Michael Schaller describes the first three years of the 1960s as "unusually convivial."[60] Roger Buckley characterizes this decade as the "quietest decade of the postwar relationship," observing that memoirs written by American government officials hardly mention Japan during this time.[61] Following the spectacular crisis that erupted over the treaty revisions, neither ally wanted controversy. For the LDP, the 1960 protests revealed the divisive and dangerous character that public debates over the alliance could take. As Buckley writes, "memories of 1960 acted as a powerful constraint from pressing matters too hard and too far."[62] For Washington, the protests exposed the risks of alliance adjustment. And so both sides managed any intermittent disagreements over such issues as Okinawa and trade with China with little fanfare. However, this tranquil period was possible because Japan still enjoyed a favorable geopolitical position. Without a direct military threat, Japanese leaders could avoid asking difficult questions regarding their defense policy.

This situation soon changed when China detonated a nuclear weapon on October 16, 1964, shattering Japanese insouciance regarding the communist threat. The Japanese government's public reaction appeared muted because it did not want the event to overshadow the 1964 Summer Olympic Games that had just started in Tokyo.[63] Privately, it was alarmed. Upon becoming prime minister, Sato held closed cabinet-level discussions to determine the desirability of starting a nuclear weapons program. Consideration of nuclear weapons did not yet progress beyond these discussions.[64]

Sato began seeking assurances from Washington. Just as the United States was increasing its military involvement in Vietnam, he was probing American resolve to defend anticommunist interests in East Asia. On January 12, 1965, he met with President Johnson, expressed his support for American actions in Vietnam, and advised that "the United States must hold out and be patient." After Johnson described his intent to fight in Vietnam, Sato "applauded the United States' determination to maintain a firm stand in Viet-Nam and reiterated his desire that [the United States] hold out." When later asked how the United States should proceed in Vietnam, Sato argued that "utmost patience and forbearance were required. Neither an advance north nor American withdrawal was desirable. The latter would provoke a 'falling domino' situation. The United States should hold on." Sato returned the favor with his own reassurances: when asked by Rusk for his thoughts on China's nuclear test, Sato reiterated his country's antinuclear stance.[65] However, Sato remarked to Johnson that "if the [Chinese communists] had nuclear weapons, the Japanese should have them."[66] This murkiness aside, Johnson and Sato issued a communiqué emphasizing commitment of each country to the other's security.[67] Japanese pledges of support continued as the United States increased its military involvement in Vietnam. Still, Japan was not entirely satisfied with its received assurances. In 1967, Sato beseeched Johnson to reiterate his pledge to defend Japan "against any form of attack."[68]

The Japanese government under Sato privately and cautiously supported the Vietnam War, a reasonable interpretation considering how it would react to later American military failures.[69] On March 31, 1968, following poor results in the New Hampshire Democratic primary, Johnson made two related announcements. First, he vowed to unilaterally de-escalate hostilities toward North Vietnam. Second, he declared that he would not run for reelection as president.[70] American ambassador to Japan Alexis Johnson noted that Johnson's speech "has been widely misinterpreted here as admission of defeat and reversal of US policy on Vietnam, foreshadowing US withdrawal from Asia," "as pulling the rug out from Sato," and portending closer alignment with China. Consequently, even the most pro-American members of the Japanese government began recommending that Japan "loosen its ties with [the] US including security relationship and adopt a more independent foreign policy."[71] He later reported that President Johnson's speech had political repercussions for Sato, since Sato was now "under heavy attack not only by opposition but within his own party for having tied himself too closely to us and then allegedly being left out on a limb by 'reversal' of our policy in Vietnam."[72]

President Johnson's speech made some Japanese government officials suspicious of the United States. In April 1968, a member of the Foreign Office noted that Japan now had to increase its defense expenditures, because "in view of worldwide US commitments it is 'dangerous' to place excessive reliance on US assistance in the conventional area."[73] An embassy telegram from Tokyo observed that the "Tet offensive and what was interpreted as an abrupt shift into de-escalation and negotiations with Hanoi have thrown doubt on US firmness and invincibility." It also noted how the "Arab-Israeli war, balance-of-payments difficulties, 'protectionism' scare, etc." were also fueling doubt among Japanese political elites.[74] Notwithstanding the additional indicators that appear to signify declining commitment, this document expressly linked the unilateral de-escalation of hostilities with American resolve and credibility. Other concerns had already started to animate Japanese politicians. The year before, Sato fretted over the Soviet-American détente. Specifically, "they are concerned that relations between the two 'super powers,' the US and the U.S.S.R., not 'improve' to the extent that we and the Soviets face Japan with fait accompli in matters concerning Japanese interests."[75] Though Japanese leaders regarded the Soviet Union as the primary threat, Alexis Johnson claimed that they held similar fears about the United States aligning itself too closely with China.[76]

These concerns intensified when Nixon became president. The Nixon Doctrine and the subsequent troop withdrawals in East Asia amplified the unease. Furthermore, North Korean provocations against the South—which predated Nixon—and China's antagonism toward Japan over its pro-Taiwan policy added significance to this announced redirection in American foreign policy.[77] How Japan, with its constitutional constraints and domestic politics, could adjust to the changing security environment was unclear. Foreign Minister Kiichi Aichi wrote in a 1969 *Foreign Affairs* article that "it is reasonable to assume that for some time to come there will be no substitute for the continuing presence of American deterrent power to counter effectively any designs for large-scale military adventures in the area."[78] The conservative columnist Takeshi Muramatsu highlighted various actions and statements made by American leaders as signifying declining credibility.[79] For example, the former commander of the Strategic Air Command said that Washington might not always aid Western Europe militarily. This statement served as an omen for the American alliance support that Japan could expect.[80] In the early 1970s, public opinion polls found that respondents were reporting increasingly unfavorable—if not mixed—feelings toward the United States.[81] By the end of the Vietnam War in 1975, survey respondents reported little confidence in American security guarantees despite expressing support for the Security Treaty.[82]

Such was the context when Sato's government commissioned studies regarding the feasibility and desirability of nuclear weapons before making a centrifuge program a national priority in 1969.[83] Abandonment fears were pronounced. Defense Agency director-general Yasuhiro Nakasone advised his American interlocutors not to engage in troop withdrawals that were "undertaken drastically and in an all-out fashion without coordination with the Japanese side."[84] Policy statements emanating from Tokyo declared the need to reconsider Japanese foreign policy. The Japan Defense Agency, for example, released a Defense White Paper in October 1970 announcing the need for a reconsideration of Japan's security relationship with the United States. Budgetary decisions accompanied such rhetoric: the 1970 budget included a 17.7 percent increase in defense spending. The reversion of Okinawa—partly intended to remove the last vestiges of American postwar occupation—was dealt in a manner to ensure that the United States would not be limited in its regional ability to provide extended deterrence.[85] Indeed, Japan signed the NPT as part of a negotiating ploy over Okinawa. As Ayako Kusunoki conjectures, Sato "might have timed acceptance of the NPT so as to help gain Washington's acceptance of a nuclear-free Okinawa after its reversion to Japanese control."[86]

Summary and Alternative Arguments

The evidence presented earlier in this chapter indicates that Japan was relatively free of abandonment fears until the mid-to-late 1960s. When those very fears intensified following signs that the United States was seeking to exit Vietnam and possibly East Asia, the Japanese government began undertaking nuclear proliferation–related behavior. The alliance was insufficient in curbing this interest. And until then Tokyo saw in-theater conventional deployments more as symbols of occupation that had little military value for an archipelago state. But as the United States was looking to reduce its presence in East Asia, they became symbols of commitment.

The alternative arguments partially illuminate the case so far. Consider first the adversary thesis. Neither the Soviet Union nor China had the maritime or aerial capability to pose a direct military threat to Japan during the first half of the Cold War. Rocking Japan's relatively comfortable geostrategic position was China's 1964 detonation. Whereas Japan's sense of security in the late 1950s might have created a permissive environment that promoted the intense controversies surrounding the treaty negotiation, the loss of that security led Tokyo to scrutinize the quality of its received security guarantees. Still, my explanation for how unfavorable alliance adjustments—real or anticipated—prompted nuclear proliferation–related behavior assumes that a salient external threat exists. Indeed, a nationally prioritized centrifuge program came several years after 1964 when American military failures in East Asia were becoming much more apparent.

The domestic politics and prestige theses have some validity, but their empirical value should not be overstated. With its emphasis on the Yoshida Doctrine as the dominant political strategy, the domestic politics thesis cannot account for why Japanese leaders did not fully reject nuclear weapons proliferation–related behavior. At best it explains the level of discretion and secrecy that surrounded Japan's nuclear activities. After all, the backlash surrounding the 1960 Security Treaty negotiations exposed the limits to which Japanese governments could even convey distrust for the United States. That experience discouraged any effort by both governments to foment overt diplomatic discord and stir controversy. In the late 1960s, these constraints grew as the Vietnam War provoked large student protests in Japan. For LDP politicians to criticize the United States under such circumstances, through either diplomatic exchanges or foreign policy actions, the grievances of opposition groups like the JSP and the Japanese Communist Party would gain credibility. As Victor Cha writes, "If Tokyo fervently expressed concerns about the Nixon Doctrine, this would focus the public and political agenda on the defense buildup issues as a means of coping with this fear. This, in turn, would fuel antirearmament [sic] forces in Japan and reignite popular support for Japanese neutralism, resulting in an environment hardly conducive to easy renewal of the [American-Japanese security] treaty."[87] The circumspection and discretion practiced by Japanese leaders during this period highlight the importance of domestic political considerations. Nevertheless, regardless of its domestic politics, an ally has strategic incentives not to be open about its nuclear activities lest its adversaries attack it.

What of the prestige thesis? The so-called nuclear allergy was starting to develop thanks to a burgeoning social movement that opposed nuclear weapons and American nuclear weapons policy. Partly because of censorship during the American occupation, the experience of the Hiroshima and Nagasaki atomic bombings provided little impetus for the emergence of this antinuclear movement. Rather, the real catalyst was the exposure of several Japanese fishermen to radiation fallout from an American nuclear weapons test near Bikini Atoll in 1954. The *Daigo Fukuryu Maru* incident, and the initial American efforts to cover it up, stoked fears regarding food contamination and provoked backlash against American nuclear tests in the Pacific Ocean. These growing anxieties found artistic expression that same year with *Godzilla*—a film that featured a prehistoric dinosaur that had mutated because of nuclear radiation, likely caused by a weapons test. In the film, the eponymous creature emerges from Tokyo Bay and launches a devastating attack on the capital city before descending back into the bay. That the monster's main weapon is its atomic breath and that both its appearance and disappearance take place in Tokyo are politically significant. After all, these tropes referred symbolically to American nuclear policy and its influence on Japanese security as well as on public health and safety. Though the impact of this film should not be overstated, *Godzilla*'s popularity may have reflected emerging norms and attitudes toward the alliance and American nuclear policy. Indeed, after 1954, the antinuclear movement started to organize large protests whenever an American nuclear-powered submarine or aircraft would dock at a Japanese port.[88]

Yet the prestige thesis ultimately emphasizes the beliefs of leaders instead of domestic society. Although Thomas Berger and Peter Katzenstein correctly regard the 1950s as the time when antimilitarist values were starting to percolate in Japanese society, the extent to which popular sentiments influenced Japanese decision makers during the 1950s is unclear. For one thing, Kishi and other senior officials did not refrain from openly discussing the constitutionality of Japanese nuclear weapons in the late 1950s. For another, the prestige thesis can explain Sato's nuclear ruminations and decision to develop a centrifuge program only by taking the view that he was an oppositional nationalist. However, categorizing Sato in this way encounters several problems. To begin with, evidence exists that Sato drew, and acted on, advice from realist scholars who argued against acquiring tactical nuclear weapons on military and alliance grounds.[89] Despite having a reputation for being hawkish, he hardly fit the profile of a leader with an exaggerated sense of threat or of a national capacity in dealing with adversaries—that is, of a leader who was an oppositional nationalist. In part because of how he managed diplomacy toward both the United States and China, he gathered a reputation for being an "overcautious" politician who "quite deliberately and successfully chose the middle road."[90]

Alliance Coercion and Japan

Despite the growing domestic unpopularity of nuclear weapons, Japan commissioned several studies exploring the nuclear weapons option before making a centrifuge program a national priority. These covert actions notwithstanding, allies and adversaries alike became concerned about Japan's nuclear status. Even if Japan had no intention to acquire nuclear weapons, clarifying its ambiguous stance on nuclear weapons was important for the nascent nonproliferation regime and thus for the United States. But what role, if any, did Washington have in Tokyo's ultimate decision to abide by the NPT fully?

Some would argue that the United States played a significant role in Japan's nuclear decision-making simply because Tokyo had little autonomy in crafting its defense policy. I argue against this view. Japan ratified the NPT mostly for domestic political reasons. The alliance with the United States was an important factor in terms of providing a disincentive for full-blown nuclear proliferation, but this case is notable for the absence of coercion. Indeed, domestic politics in Japan was one reason why Washington felt like it could not push Tokyo too hard. Moreover, American decision makers did not believe they could impose a clear nonproliferation status on Japan without sacrificing other foreign policy goals. A combination of propitious domestic and international circumstances allowed Tokyo to develop a latent nuclear capability.

THE ALLIANCE AS A POSSIBLE
NONPROLIFERATION MECHANISM

One alliance solution for nuclear proliferation that was attempted in Western Europe saw very limited consideration with respect to East Asia. That is, no nuclear-sharing arrangement was proposed to American allies in East Asia. Nevertheless, documents reveal that while the United States began to abandon the MLF in Western Europe, some American decision makers contemplated whether a similar nuclear-sharing arrangement would be appropriate in East Asia. Rusk even "asked a committee" to "[give] consideration to a US-supplied Far Eastern nuclear stockpile."[91] In a 1965 memorandum, the Joint Chiefs of Staff noted that to curb nuclear proliferation, the United States "should not rule out the possibility of increased nuclear support including some form of nuclear sharing with our allies in Asia when such is required in the US national interests."[92] And yet, despite some interest in the State Department and the Joint Chiefs of Staff, this policy idea did not see further development. The absence of documents regarding this issue suggests that American decision makers gave this idea little consideration.

Several reasons illuminate why no Asian MLF emerged. First, the hub-and-spoke system that characterized the regional American-led security order itself likely made such an initiative impractical. Japan's potential allies in the region remained economically underdeveloped and politically unstable. Japan and South Korea might have overcome their historical grievances by normalizing their relations in 1965, but lingering disagreements between them might have made an Asian MLF unworkable. Second, the failures attending the MLF in Western Europe likely dissuaded policy makers from considering something similar in East Asia, even in the absence of stubborn nuclear-armed allies like France and Great Britain. Third, American leaders might have regarded non-European peoples as unworthy of nuclear-sharing arrangements. According to Christopher Hemmer and Peter Katzenstein, American decision makers held highly racialized views of Asian peoples.[93] Whereas they considered their European counterparts as equals, Asians were "inferior" so as to necessitate a paternalistic approach in East Asia. However, a more compelling explanation is that popular attitudes toward nuclear weapons were more hostile in East Asia due to their exclusive use in the Pacific Front. A nuclear-sharing arrangement might have rebutted criticisms that Anglo-Saxons would use nuclear weapons at the expense of Asian populations. Nevertheless, public aversion would have complicated the development of a political foundation for a nuclear-sharing arrangement that NATO seemed to provide. Indeed, this same factor helps illuminate why the United States relied on secret bilateral agreements for the transit and storage of its nuclear weapons in Japan.

Besides nuclear-sharing arrangements receiving barely any consideration, American decision makers were much less severe with Japan than with West

Germany despite their dislike for the former's nuclear ambiguity. During NPT negotiations, Rusk advised that Japan express its "adherence" to the treaty.[94] When Sato visited Washington, DC, in January 1965, Rusk sought Japanese reassurances regarding its commitment to abstain from nuclear weapons development. Nixon and Kissinger barely registered the same level of concern and refrained from demanding that Japan not pursue nuclear weapons development. Members of the intelligence community validated this nonchalance. One Central Intelligence Agency (CIA) report indicated that "Japan's capability to develop and produce nuclear weapons and modest delivery systems is not questioned. The industrial and technological backup is available. But going nuclear would be a political decision; it would not be made on the basis of technological capability but on an assessment of overriding national interests." Only in the event of breakdown in global stability or a major crisis in American-Japanese relations might Japan get nuclear weapons.[95] Yet other American foreign policy observers did not share such attitudes. In the early 1970s, amid widespread speculation in the American media regarding Japan's nuclear intentions, Senator Hubert Humphrey petitioned the Nixon administration to get clarification on Japan's nuclear policy.[96] One concerned member of an American study group on a safeguards agreement mentioned that when it came to the NPT and the IAEA, the United States should "not permit the Japanese to outwait us by using stalling tactics."[97]

One should not overstate American insouciance. Nixon asked Japanese foreign minister Masayoshi Ohira about his government's reaction to India's "peaceful nuclear explosion." Ohira assured Nixon that Japan would not acquire nuclear weapons. This exchange was where Nixon ambiguously responded that more nuclear weapons states would make nuclear war likelier.[98] With those cryptic remarks, he was at minimum signaling that Washington would not tolerate nuclear proliferation. The Ford administration had similar concerns. As one briefing memorandum prepared for President Ford notes, "Militarily, Japan possesses enormous potential power, but remains content to maintain only a modest defense establishment. The absence of immediate and palpable military threats and a host of political and diplomatic factors continue to inhibit the Japanese from developing long-range conventional capabilities, deploying forces overseas, extending military assistance, and exercising a 'nuclear option.'" Nevertheless, the same memorandum later added, "The Indian nuclear test has been profoundly unsettling to the Japanese, and if expanded international efforts to deal with the proliferation issues are not undertaken, events in time could propel the Japanese toward a serious reassessment of their own non-nuclear status. There are two issues for us. (1) What steps can we take to enhance the prospects of early Japanese ratification of [the] Non-Proliferation Treaty? (2) How can we engage the Japanese in a broader multilateral non-proliferation strategy, including the prospective conference of nuclear industrial states?"[99]

Furthermore, Kissinger recognized that "the Japanese [were] preoccupied with reconsidering their security policy in the fluid international environment of post-Vietnam."[100] Finally, another memorandum prepared for Ford ahead of his meeting with Prime Minister Takeo Miki notes, "We privately told the Miki Government last spring that we hoped Japan would ratify the NPT at an early date."[101] Aversion to Japanese nuclear proliferation was private and tacit.

Yet a puzzle emerges from this discussion: if Washington was able to obtain Tokyo's support for secret transit and storage arrangements, then why were American decision makers so shy about using the alliance as a conduit for pressuring Japan into credibly renouncing nuclear weapons? I take up this issue in the following section.

THE LIMITS OF NONMILITARY COERCION AGAINST JAPAN

Japan's economic growth empowered it to obtain greater economic and technological independence from the United States by the late 1960s. Consider the following attributes of Japan's economy. Like West Germany, Japan had a balance-of-payments surplus with the United States of approximately $300 million in 1966, benefiting from an additional $300 million to $350 million of American military expenditures in its territory.[102] Its accumulated growth also created dislocations within the American economy. For example, the American textiles industry lost significant market share to Japanese imports. Already in 1961, when Japanese penetration of the American clothing market was negligible and American merchandise trade with Japan had a $782 million surplus, unions demanded stronger trade restrictions against Japanese firms.[103] Partly due to the liberalization of American trade policy following the Dillon Round and Japan's export-oriented industrial policy, deficits began characterizing American merchandise trade with Japan in 1965.[104] Japan also benefited from the Vietnam War thanks to both direct and indirect procurement by the United States and other Asian countries during the late 1960s.[105] The volume of Japanese exports grew from $2.4 billion in 1965 to over $9 billion in 1972.[106]

In contrast, the American economy suffered stagflation in the 1970s. Inflation and the unemployment rate both rose amid sluggish growth. Tight monetary policies were ineffective at curbing inflation, whereas foreign competition posed a new but significant threat to the automobile, steel, and electronics industries. That Japan's economy relied on exports mattered little for fixing this issue. A member of the NSC observed that "in bilateral negotiations with Japan, Japan is clearly vulnerable to the United States, as it exports eight times as much of its production to us as we export to it." Yet he cautioned, "We should not conclude from it that our interests are served by bludgeoning the Japanese with a threat to restrict their imports to the United States." Since American total exports were the largest in the world, any trade conflict with Japan would have "severe implications for us as well."[107] Simply put, the American and Japanese economies had become so interdependent as to preclude any meaningful economic sanctions against Tokyo, whether to extract concessions on nuclear policy or other related issues.

Japan's growing economic power partly explains why the United States was reluctant to apply pressure through economic and technological channels. American sensitivity toward domestic backlash in Japan was another factor. As early as February 1963, American officials discussed the likelihood of Japan implementing measures that could attenuate the American balance-of-payments deficit. As with West Germany, one solution available to Japan was to increase its defense expenditures and thus to buy more American military hardware. However, two problems arose. First, "the increase in the Japanese defense budget to a level which would permit any large-scale purchasing of US equipment will take a period of years because of the necessity for creating political support by the Japanese people for a sharp acceleration of its defense buildup." Second, "Even were the necessary funds available to the Japanese defense authorities, there may not be a sufficient amount of US military hardware that the Japanese are likely to purchase to offset our total expenditures. Much of the materiel they need can be supplied out of indigenous production."[108] The alternative measures put forward by the deputy secretary of defense would have, by his own admission, either increased the American military budget or required undesirable changes in the American regional force posture.[109] These discussions found no resolution. Negotiating Japanese offsets also proved challenging, since American decision makers felt that too much pressure on Japan to increase military expenditures (as one means to redress the balance-of-payments problem) would be counterproductive.[110] And so gold losses and expanding balance-of-payments deficits ensured ongoing discussions within the American government over its military expenditures and commitments overseas. Still, such deliberations were never as intense with regard to Japan as they were with West Germany.

Nixon was frustrated with Japanese intransigence on economic issues. Washington did successfully extract trade concessions from Tokyo over textiles, but only after acrimonious negotiations.[111] In 1969, the United States demanded that Japan curb its exports of cheap textiles. Within two years Japan finally relented and imposed export controls in 1971. Secret accords to settle the dispute early went ignored or were conveniently forgotten.[112] Japanese trade liberalization proceeded slowly in spite of American pressure to hasten it.[113] Annoyed, in a February 1973 cabinet meeting, Nixon opined that Japan was not "being a good partner" and Prime Minister Tanaka was not "a good ally."[114] Nixon found him less congenial than his predecessor Sato, noting to a colleague that "Tanaka's a very cocky, jingoistic type, and Sato is the old-line, friendly guy, helping the US like Kishi."[115] Kissinger acknowledged that the trade deficit posed a "perennial problem."[116] Relations between the two allies became strained.

Though economic leverage was lacking, Washington had technological leverage over Tokyo. Japan wanted American cooperation on civilian nuclear technologies and enriched uranium.[117] About 90 percent of its imports of uranium and enrichment services came from the United Sates. This cooperation dated back to the Atoms for Peace program, thanks to which the United States and Japan negotiated an agreement in 1955 for the supply of enrichment uranium from the United States to Japan as long as Japan returned all the spent fuel.[118] At the time, the United States recognized that such agreements could create proliferation risks but decided that diplomatic considerations had priority. Japan was able to extract plutonium once the Atomic Energy Commission permitted the research of small quantities of nuclear waste in 1957. The 1955 agreement was amended in 1958 to allow for reprocessing in Japan. Ten years later Japan secured an agreement from the United States to exchange information regarding fast breeder technology, which would have enabled Japan to generate fissile material more efficiently.[119] In 1972, yet another amendment of the 1955 agreement was negotiated, allowing a new reprocessing facility on the provision that the United States could legally intervene in that project.[120] And so, according to one observer, "a [Japanese] nuclear weapons program could not be attempted by Japan without either (1) abrogation of existing US-Japanese Atomic Cooperation treaties or (2) full cooperation of the United States."[121] Still, having this leverage did not eliminate fears that Japan could divert nuclear energy toward military purposes. For one, as Motoya Kitamura writes, "the United States could not forcefully or directly stop Japan if it were to obtain nuclear bombs, since such an attitude would disgust Tokyo and poison the bilateral partnership."[122] For another, India's "peaceful nuclear explosion" in 1974 alarmed Washington precisely because the device used plutonium gleaned from a Canadian research reactor.[123] To be sure, one major study acknowledges that "there is no evidence that Japanese plutonium programs were developed to enhance the ability of Japan to build nuclear weapons."[124] Nevertheless, as even Japan decision makers had not yet precluded the nuclear option or ratified the NPT, their intentions remained suspect.

Committing Japan to Nonproliferation

Japan's technological dependence on the United States was the best inhibitor of any nuclear ambitions Japan might have. However, doubts over its commitment to nuclear nonproliferation remained throughout much of the 1970s. I argue that Japan signed the NPT in 1970 not to clarify its stance but to fulfill other policy objectives. It ultimately ratified the treaty in 1976 for domestic political reasons.

SIGNING THE NPT FOR NONNUCLEAR REASONS

As it had done with West Germany, the Johnson administration encouraged Japan to support the NPT. Like West Germany, Japan resisted such demands and objected to the treaty. One objection was how the treaty might legitimize a new international hierarchy that would consign nonnuclear powers to subordinate status despite their economical superiority. For Japan, this hierarchy was unacceptable while it was growing economically and the nuclear-armed Great Britain and France—"countries which they considered no more prestigious than themselves"—were declining.[125] Japan also worried about whether the NPT would damage its civilian nuclear industry. American decision makers noticed, and tried to understand, Japan's opposition to the NPT. In a March 1967 telegram (conveyed to President Johnson), ambassador Alexis Johnson described the "schizophrenia of Japan on the nuclear proliferation treaty." Aside from "military considerations," Japan—like West Germany—did not want to see a "'super-powers' club from which Japan will be forever excluded." He added that relegation to second-class status could "ultimately constitute a powerful incentive to go after an independent nuclear capability," as in the case of West Germany. Japan would likely sign the NPT, but he cautioned against taking its participation "for granted."[126]

Japan's "schizophrenia" regarding the NPT reflected a dilemma its government faced. The dilemma was as follows. Supporting the NPT meant legitimating the ability of a few states to have nuclear weapons and, by extension, Japan's own reliance on American extended nuclear deterrence. Japanese calls for international disarmament would look hypocritical. Still, opposing the NPT was costly. It weakened the nascent nonproliferation regime by withholding membership of a major industrial democracy that possessed a large civilian nuclear industry. It also made Japan's nuclear intentions suspect. To resolve this dilemma, Japan signed the treaty in 1970, but conditioned its future ratification on the promotion of nuclear disarmament, security guarantees for nonnuclear weapons states, and equality in the use of atomic energy for peaceful purposes. As George Quester observed at the time, "The signature in 1970 has instead been accompanied by statements that ratification will not come quickly at all, and that no decision indeed is to be implied in the mere signature of the treaty."[127]

The issue of NPT ratification became dormant afterward. In the meantime, incentives for nuclear hedging persisted from an alliance perspective. The United States withdrew a troop division from South Korea, stoking abandonment fears among that country's elites. This withdrawal took place as the United States sought to remove itself from Vietnam and shift the defense burden onto its East Asian allies under the Nixon Doctrine. Adding to regional anxieties was Nixon's 1972 trip to China. When Japanese leaders first learned of his overtures to China, they worried that a deal would be struck at their expense. Displeasing Nixon and Kissinger, who hoped to use Japan as a counterweight to China, Japanese leaders decided to regain the initiative by normalizing relations that same year.[128] Under such conditions, Japan expanded its national centrifuge program and deflected international calls to ratify the NPT. Yasuhiro Nakasone, a right-wing politician who served as director general of the Japanese Defense Agency and later became prime minister in 1982, oversaw yet another secret government working group to explore the desirability and feasibility of an independent nuclear deterrent.[129] Nixon himself was reluctant to push Japan too hard on the NPT. He had even supported the prospect of Japan arming itself with nuclear weapons as part of a larger effort to balance against communist adversaries in East Asia. Kissinger cared little for Japan.[130] Both of them were ambivalent about the treaty and nuclear proliferation.[131]

India's "peaceful nuclear explosion" resuscitated American interest in nonproliferation. A June 1974 review of the American nonproliferation policy noted that "Japan and [West Germany] are in a special category—they have the nuclear capability to build large numbers of weapons, but strong political inhibitions coupled with the U.S. security relationship make them unlikely proliferators in the near-time."[132] It went onto argue that "in Japan, early NPT ratification has suffered a setback, but political inhibitions and the interest in maintaining close ties with the U.S., as well as the large portion of its electric power industry that is dependent on continued U.S. fuel supplies, will tend to work against a nuclear weapons decision." Still, it took note of "indications of increasing opposition to ratification."[133] For its part, the intelligence community produced a special NIE that stated how some leading intelligence officials believed that "Japan would not embark on a program of nuclear weapons in the absence of a major adverse shift in great power relationships which presented a Japan with a clearcut [sic] threat to its security." Other intelligence officials saw "a strong chance that Japan's leaders will conclude that they must have nuclear weapons if they are to achieve their national objectives in the developing Asian power balance. Such a decision could come in the early 1980s." These more pessimistic observers added that proliferation risks could intensify in the short term amid "any concurrent deterioration of Japanese relations with the Communist powers or a further decline in the credibility of U.S. defense guarantees."[134]

BUILDING A DOMESTIC COALITION FOR NPT RATIFICATION

NPT ratification entered the Japanese Diet's legislative agenda in December 1974 when Miki—having just replaced Tanaka as prime minister—announced his intention to introduce a motion for treaty ratification. Nixon's visit to China and the Arab oil embargo presumably encouraged Miki's decision to reopen debate on this issue. NPT ratification might have even served the same purpose for Japan as it did for West Germany. Whereas Brandt used the NPT partly to demonstrate his commitment to Ostpolitik,

Japanese leaders might have believed that ratifying the treaty would help reassure China. Moreover, the oil embargo made Japan suffer energy short-ages, as three-fourths of its imported oil came from the Middle East, thus threatening Japan's ability to sustain economic growth.[135] This vulnerabil-ity gave additional impetus for Japan to develop its civilian nuclear indus-try and become more energy self-sufficient.[136]

Miki made his announcement at a peculiar moment in Japanese politics. The LDP had a comfortable majority in the Diet's lower house and a thin majority in the upper house, but it was under turmoil in the wake of the Lockheed bribery scandal. This scandal broke out following reports that the aerospace company used yakuza power brokers (that is, major figures in Japanese organized crime syndicates) to bribe LDP politicians and to secure contracts for the purchase of its aircraft. It resulted in the arrest of Miki's predecessor, Tanaka.[137] In ordinary circumstances, an LDP prime minister would still need to overcome the factionalism that characterized the party and to build sufficient support in undertaking any major legislative action. The scandal made Miki's position tenuous, something that risked getting worse given the elite discord over the NPT that had already existed. As one memorandum intended for Kissinger noted six months later, "Prime Minis-ter Miki's position in the LDP cannot be said to be very strong. This explains the difficulty Miki has had getting some of his major bills through the Diet."[138] Pro-ratification forces included his foreign minister Kiichi Miyazawa and more dovish elements of the LDP. Outside the LDP, the JSP and the centrist political party Komeito favored the treaty's ratification. The main opposi-tion was the conservative nationalist faction Seiwa Seisaku Kenkyuaki (Seiwa Political-analysis Council), with prominent critics being the LDP vice presi-dent, the executive board chairman, such Upper House members as the far-right Minoru Genda, and the LDP Foreign Affairs Research Council and the Security Affairs Research Council.

The story of Japan's NPT ratification thereby involves building domestic consensus in order to overcome such opposition. Pro-ratification forces gained momentum at various junctures when they acquired the support of the chairman of the Atomic Energy Commission and concurrent director of the Science and Technology Agency, the chairman of the Japanese Atomic Industry Forum, and the civilian energy industry. The signing of the safe-guards agreement with the IAEA in early 1975 allayed concerns over whether Japan would face undue restrictions on its peaceful use of atomic energy. This agreement allowed Japan to enjoy "parity with EURATOM countries in safeguard measures" such that Japan could partly inspect itself.[139] With these negotiations satisfactorily completed and the high-level bureaucratic endorsements received, Miki and other leading party officials personally took to rallying other Diet members into supporting the treaty. Boosting this cause was former prime minister Sato declaring that now was the time to ratify the NPT.[140]

The NPT was controversial within the LDP because of its significance for Japanese security. One may go so far as to claim that the issue of NPT ratification was really a referendum on Japan's alliance with the United States. Treaty skeptics argued that Japan should retain a "free hand on nuclear devices." Genda was perhaps the most vocal proponent of this view, contending that ratification would place Japan at the mercy of American security guarantees—a policy that was antithetical to Japanese national security.[141] Indeed, critics worried that consenting to nuclear forbearance for twenty-five years—as the 1975 NPT Review Conference enjoined—was irresponsible when the United States could terminate its alliance with Japan at one year's notice.[142] Miki dismissed such claims, arguing that having a "free hand" contradicted the spirit of the three nonnuclear principles.

Although Miki rejected these right-wing criticisms, his minister of foreign affairs Kiichi Miyazawa used his April 1975 trip to Washington, DC, to obtain new security pledges from the United States.[143] This trip was successful, as a three-point statement released in the Japanese media suggests: "(1) Both Japan and the US are of the judgment that the maintenance of the Security Treaty will be in the interests, when viewed from a long-range standpoint; (2) US nuclear war potential is an important deterrent power toward aggression against Japan from the outside; (3) the US attaches importance to its treaty obligations that it will take charge of the defense of Japan in the case of its being attacked by nuclear or conventional weapons, and Japan will also continue to carry out its obligations based on the Treaty."[144] Such reassurances were insufficient for pro-ratification legislators to overcome the suspicions and reservations of their more skeptical counterparts in the Diet. The most hawkish Diet members still insisted that Japan should negotiate new mechanisms with Washington relating to the introduction of nuclear weapons on Japanese territory.[145] Accordingly, they voted against the treaty's ratification, forcing debate on the issue to continue for about another year. Still, these reassurances helped solidify a general consensus that spurred further progress toward ratification. The Japanese Diet finally ratified the treaty on June 8, 1976.

The April 1975 assurances notwithstanding, the Nixon and Ford administrations generally stood on the sidelines while the debate over ratification unfolded in the Japanese Diet. Neither administration insisted on the NPT as forcefully as the Johnson administration had with respect to West Germany.[146] On the contrary, Nixon and Kissinger remained quiet and provided reassurances when asked for them. This subdued disposition reflected their awareness that nuclear policy in Japan needed to be handled delicately. To avoid any misunderstanding over this issue, Japanese decision makers even insisted that their American counterparts be discreet. In a November 1974 meeting with Ford and Kissinger, Prime Minister Kakuei Tanaka stated:

> The [Government of Japan] firmly supports the [Mutual Security Treaty], which is important not just to the peace and security of Japan, but also Asia.

There is one important problem, however, nuclear weapons. Japan and the United States began their discussions of this question originally in the context of strategic nuclear weapons, but now tactical nuclear weapons have proliferated, and perhaps we should discuss this matter from this new point of view. I can understand that the Americans and the Europeans think about this matter in terms of a different kind of perception, but the Japanese people have a special sensitivity to nuclear weapons, which is mobilized by certain political forces for their own political ends.[147]

Although Ford responded by saying that he understood the "special sensitivities of the Japanese people," the Japanese foreign minister reiterated Tanaka's request later in that same conversation. Kissinger agreed that "we won't refer to the nuclear question."[148]

Because of Japan's advanced industry, civilian nuclear capabilities, and history, its 1975 ratification of the NPT represented an important moment in the development of the emerging nonproliferation regime. Nevertheless, Japanese nuclear interest in proliferation-risky technologies continued. A controversy between the United States and Japan developed in 1977 when Japan failed to receive American concessions on Japanese plans for the reprocessing of spent nuclear fuel.[149] Japan began using French technology to develop a small, prototype reprocessing plant at Tokai where it wanted to conduct hot tests.[150] However, the 1972 agreement gave Washington a legal right to intervene in the reprocessing program.[151] The sticking point in negotiations was Japan's desire to develop fast breeder technology.[152] The ends were arguably peaceful: Japan wanted to master the full nuclear cycle as a step toward reducing its dependence on "imported oil *and* natural uranium" in an era of persistent energy shortages.[153] Prime Minister Fukuda even called the situation "a life or death issue."[154] Yet acquiring a nuclear reprocessing capability required "US consent as almost all its [Japan's] spent fuel is US-enriched."[155] Although the United States found these activities at Tokai objectionable, this issue was politically sensitive in Japan. Such capabilities seemed consistent with article 4 of the NPT, which declared that countries have a right to seek nuclear power for peaceful purposes. However, some far-right members of the ruling LDP saw national self-sufficiency at stake.[156] Moreover, European Community members were not subject to American veto rights over the use of fuels that had American origins. Japan did not wish to be subject to discrimination.[157]

The documentary record remains unclear as to what extent American decision makers feared that Japan represented a genuine proliferation risk in light of its interests in mastering the full nuclear cycle. One LDP Diet member who accompanied Fukuda on his trip to Washington in early 1977 warned that "Japan might require nuclear weapons in view of receding US power in Asia."[158] Though this politician had limited influence, the international context was not so harmless as to render this statement innocuous. The Soviet military buildup in Northeast Asia and Carter's plans for a full troop withdrawal from neighboring South Korea still made the American commitment to the region seem suspect.[159] What is clear is that American decision makers and diplomats saw the controversy emerge as the result of key gaps in the global nonproliferation regime, particularly with respect to plutonium storage and the use of spent fuels.[160] Similar nuclear-related issues vexed American relations with Pakistan, India, and other countries.[161] For relations with Japan, the potential ramifications were significant. As one memorandum intended for National Security Adviser Zbigniew Brzezinski reported, "if Japan were not allowed to proceed with reprocessing there would be bitter resentment among the Japanese people, grave difficulties in Diet efforts to get IAEA safeguards agreement approved, questions regarding the value of the NPT adherence and continuing adherence of NPT, and a serious problem of de facto discrimination against Japan in favor of European countries."[162] The issue was eventually resolved. In September 1977, the two allies negotiated a tentative agreement whereby Japan would operate the Tokai facility so as to reprocess uranium from existing light water reactors for a two-year trial period. As part of this deal, Japan agreed to postpone its plutonium breeder program.[163] According to one analysis, Tokyo got what it wanted mostly for geopolitical reasons: Washington did not wish to alienate it when the Soviet Union was building up military power in the region.[164] Another analysis holds that Carter was unwilling to risk the alliance with Japan over this issue.[165]

That Japan was able to maneuver between various domestic and international constraints in going about its nuclear activities does not mean its military alliance had no inhibiting effect whatsoever. To the contrary, the alliance with the United States was an important consideration that shaped Japan's nuclear decision-making even if active coercion was conspicuously absent in this case. Although the Yoshida doctrine was "the heart of Japan's favored model of political survival," as Solingen writes, it was predicated on American security guarantees being sufficiently robust.[166] Nevertheless, critics of the NPT argued that Japan should restrict its options in view of their doubts about American reliability, whereas even supporters of ratification sought reassurances from Washington. The United States had technological leverage over Japanese nuclear activities, but it desisted from actively using that leverage to reduce the proliferation risks associated with Japan's being able to reprocess plutonium.

Summary and Alternative Arguments

With the American military campaign in Vietnam failing, uncertainty regarding American alliance commitments pushed Japan to hedge on nuclear weapons. The resulting ambiguity bothered American decision makers, but they could not apply nonmilitary pressure—especially economic sanctions—

without inflicting harm on the American economy. Washington did have direct leverage over Japan's nuclear capabilities. However, as much as this leverage might have restricted Japan's freedom of maneuver, the United States was reluctant to use it actively in order to extract nonproliferation concessions. Consistent with my theory's explanations, Japan finally renounced nuclear weapons by ratifying the NPT when its leaders felt that it served Japan's interest, *independent* of American pressure. Simply put, alliance coercion was not a big part of this story, and the United States—whatever its leverage—appears to have refrained from using its policy levers for the sake of nonproliferation.

The alternative explanations vary in their ability to account for how Japan developed its nuclear capabilities before ratifying the NPT in 1976. To begin with, the adversary thesis fares poorly. Sino-Japanese relations did improve rather quickly in the early 1970s such that the two adversaries normalized their diplomatic ties in 1972.[167] Of course, such rapprochement need not automatically entail a cessation of nuclear hedging because, by its nature, the strategy serves to provide some insurance in case of unfavorable geopolitical events. However, from the perspective of the adversary thesis, the irony of the NPT ratification is that the Soviet threat to Japan intensified shortly thereafter. Moscow reasserted its claims over the disputed Northern Territories—a group of islands that the Soviet Union annexed after Japan surrendered in World War II—and threatened Japanese sea-lanes of communications. Responding to what it saw as an anti-Soviet triumvirate between the United States, Japan, and China, the Soviet Union undertook a massive military buildup in its far east. This buildup comprised thirty-one troop divisions, over two thousand warplanes, and about 750 military vessels, fifty of which were nuclear-powered submarines.[168] The buildup continued into 1978 with the added deployment of supersonic long-range bombers, an aircraft carrier, and the construction of a new port and a major airstrip. Diplomatic provocations accompanied this buildup: border transgressions became more frequent, and the Soviet Union garrisoned marines on the Northern Territories. The Soviet Union even practiced military maneuvers that included a mock island invasion only 125 kilometers north of the Japanese island of Hokkaido.[169]

Though Japanese leaders might not have anticipated these Soviet provocations before 1976, the adversary thesis might seem to explain why Japan sought proliferation-risky technologies with its reprocessing plant. Yet this initiative built on existing efforts by Tokyo to improve its nuclear activities. The extent to which Soviet behavior renewed interest in reprocessing among Japanese decision makers is unclear given the available documentary record. What nuclear activities transpired at this time already had their origins in the decisions made, and policies that began, in the late 1960s. The adversary thesis makes more sense of how Japan had begun investing in conventional military, with special attention to air and naval power, at this time.[170]

The domestic politics and prestige theses might not have as much utility as some might believe. To be sure, the former best accounts for the timing of the NPT ratification, since Japanese leaders believed that a domestic coalition backing the treaty was possible in the Diet. However, members of this would-be coalition needed first to see a special safeguards agreement with the IAEA and additional assurances from the United States before they could vote in favor of treaty ratification. Even though members of the Japanese public became more disapproving of nuclear weapons over time, the Yoshida Doctrine was hardly a settled manner among decision makers. After all, the Yoshida Doctrine is practicable only if American security guarantees are strong enough for Japan to depend militarily on the United States. For its part, the prestige thesis pulls in opposite directions: whereas a nuclear allergy might have developed within the Japanese body politic, Japanese decision makers sometimes did see nuclear technology as having intrinsic value, since they complained that the treaty would deny emerging great powers like Japan access to nuclear weapons when declining ones like Great Britain were allowed to keep theirs. This point should not be overstated: Japanese leaders have occasionally used their stated support for nuclear disarmament as a means to reduce the status of nuclear weapons. They also have believed that nuclear power would address Japan's energy needs. Still, Japanese attitudes toward nuclear weapons even in the 1970s were not unequivocally antinuclear. Almost half of respondents in a 1976 poll expressed discomfort regarding how Japan did *not* have nuclear weapons, prompting one observer to comment that Japan's nuclear allergy is a "flexible phenomenon."[171]

The biggest weakness of the domestic politics and prestige theses is that they treat Japan's latent nuclear capability either as the result of technological determinism or as some sort of deus ex machina. Rather, it was the outcome of a successful strategy that smacked of nuclear proliferation–related behavior—one that emphasized the development of enrichment and reprocessing capabilities. Unfortunately, analysts who have investigated Japan's nuclear history have underappreciated this key dimension to Japan's behavior in the late 1960s and the 1970s. In otherwise excellent studies of Sato's nuclear diplomacy, Ayako Kusunoki, Yukinori Komine, and Fintan Hoey overlook the nuclear capabilities that Japan was developing during that period in their various historiographical writings.[172] Similarly, Maria Rost Rublee understates Japanese nuclear capabilities despite reaching conclusions that approximate my own about Japan's complex decision to ratify the NPT.[173] And so Jennifer Lind's observation that many analysts have underestimated Japan's dexterity in the conventional military domain applies just as well as to the nuclear domain.[174]

American credibility in East Asia suffered in the late 1960s and the 1970s, thereby undermining Japan's sense of security. Two additional data points are worth considering: Taiwan and South Korea. Taiwan also moved toward nuclear weapons acquisition following the Chinese 1964 nuclear detonation. South Korea did not react to events in 1964 in the same way as Japan and Taiwan, but its leaders did act on their own assessments of American credibility during the late 1960s and the 1970s. Chapter 5 explores this case.

South Korea, 1968–1980

If Germany and Japan were highly dependent on the United States during the Cold War, as some scholars claim, then South Korea should have had even less free rein in determining its foreign and defense policies. It relied on American-led forces to expel North Korean forces from its territory in the Korean War. Thereafter it signed a defense pact with the United States and hosted American tactical nuclear weapons as well as over fifty thousand American troops during the 1960s. The United States even had command of South Korean forces in peacetime and in wartime during the Cold War. South Korea was also much poorer than West Germany and Japan. Having endured Japanese colonialism and devastation in the Korean War, South Korea only began to industrialize in the 1960s and so depended on the United States for its economic and technological needs.

Notwithstanding these conditions, South Korea was able to engage in nuclear proliferation–related behavior. It undertook feasibility studies to explore nuclear weapons development in 1970. Two years later, it began devoting resources toward their acquisition. This program lasted several years before its cancellation in 1975 and the accompanying decision to ratify the NPT. However, these actions did not mark the end of South Korea's proliferation-related behavior. Suspicions of a nuclear program reemerged in the late 1970s when a major domestic debate erupted briefly in South Korea over its defense policy. Even in the early 1980s South Korea violated safeguard agreements when it conducted plutonium research.

The South Korean case further validates my theoretical framework. First, the military alliance with the United States on its own did not deter South Korea from seeking nuclear weapons. Second, American troop deployments were integral in shaping perceptions of American security guarantees in South Korea. Whereas troop numbers fell by a third during the early 1970s, the number of American tactical nuclear weapons remained stable. Third, American coercion of South Korea resulted in the dismantling of much of the nuclear program, underdeveloped as it might have been, but uncertainty abounds as to whether the United States successfully suppressed *all* of its activities. Fourth, Washington managed the South Korean proliferation most effectively through nonmilitary instruments. Nevertheless, the application of such tools did not fully prevent unwanted proliferation-related behavior after the mid-1970s.

Before assessing the case evidence, I describe the strategic and domestic context that South Korean leaders faced to clarify the predictions of the alternative explanations. The analysis then proceeds in two parts so as to investigate separately why and how South Korea began and ended its nuclear activities.

The Strategic Context

Following the July 1953 armistice that ended the active stage of the Korean War, the United States signed a new alliance treaty with South Korea and established a large troop presence on its territory. Yet postwar South Korea was in a precarious economic condition. Relative to the North, it was poor and lacked industry. Recognizing this disparity, American decision makers recognized the need to develop South Korea economically and so coupled military support with economic aid.[1] Nevertheless, South Korea did not rely exclusively on American aid. Shortly after taking power through a coup in 1961, Park used his military dictatorship to commit his country to a statist, export-oriented program that generated rapid economic growth and industrialization.[2] South Korea's industrial capacity increased several-fold by the end of the 1960s.

Despite the alliance and the armistice, South Korea's geopolitical environment remained threatening. North Korea was conventionally superior and enjoyed the patronage of both the Soviet Union and China. A Chinese occupation force remained in North Korea until 1958, during which time North Korea repaired its economy. After the withdrawal of Chinese forces, Kim Il-sung signed mutual defense treaties with both communist powers before eventually siding with China in the Sino-Soviet split. This realignment was significant: not only did China pursue a confrontational foreign policy toward its neighbors, it also succeeded in acquiring nuclear weapons by 1964. By the late 1960s, North Korea resumed an aggressive foreign policy directed against American and South Korean interests. Hoping to undermine the anticommunist alliance and incite an insurgency in the South, North Korea initiated irregular warfare in the area around the Korean Demilitarized Zone (DMZ) in 1968. Aside from a series of border skirmishes that took place over three years, the North Korean government attempted to assassinate Park in an incident called the Blue House raid on January 17, 1968 whereby North Korean forces sneaked behind the American forces along the DMZ to make an attempt on his life in his residence. One week later, North Korean patrol boats captured the *USS Pueblo* and its American crew in international waters. Despite the close timing of these events, the Johnson administration believed that Pyongyang did not want war, preferring instead to harass American forces and challenge the American military presence in East Asia.[3] However, when North Korean fighter jets shot down an American EC-121 reconnaissance aircraft, some members of the Nixon administration believed that the retaliatory use of force was finally necessary.[4] Though Washington decided against a military response, its decision makers noted Seoul's heightened threat perceptions. Nixon observed that the mood in South Korea was "very jittery." Chairman of the Joint Chiefs of Staff General Earl Wheeler commented that "they are apprehensive we won't do anything."[5]

These North Korean provocations took place against the backdrop of the Vietnam War. South Korea provided significant military assistance to the United States in that conflict, having at one point about fifty thousand troops in Vietnam. Several reasons explain the magnitude of South Korea's military contributions. First, Johnson wanted South Korea to share the burden of fighting the war.[6] Second, for these contributions, Seoul received considerable increases in American economic and military assistance.[7] It also received assurances regarding its received security commitments.[8] Third, Park shared American concerns that the fates of East Asian states in the struggle against transnational communism were linked. American success in Vietnam would, after all, strengthen the anticommunist coalition in the region.

Because the North was still the more powerful of the two Koreas, the American military presence improved the local conventional balance of power in the South's favor. Reducing that military presence would have weakened the South's position vis-à-vis the North. Still, American tactical nuclear weapons were stationed so as to provide nuclear extended deterrence. My framework expects that changes to American conventional military deployments would animate Seoul's nuclear interest. The adversary thesis would look to North Korean aggression as being the main driver instead.

The Domestic Context

For the period I examine, Park led a repressive military dictatorship following a coup d'état in 1960. Under his leadership, South Korea became a "developmental" state, whereby government forges alliances with labor and industry, protects fledgling export industries, and establishes a large government bureaucracy to oversee the private sector. Though Chalmers Johnson describes neighboring Japan as an archetype of the developmental state, other observers have extended the label to South Korea.[9] This "Asian Tiger" maintained high growth rates between the 1960s and the 1990s largely by strengthening those industries that produced export goods intended for rich industrialized states.[10] According to the domestic politics thesis, South Korea should not engage in nuclear weapons activities at all so as not to compromise such export-dependent strategies. Because South Korea was an autocracy in an intense security environment, norms might have been permissive enough such that antinuclear or antimilitarist beliefs did not resonate among members of South Korean society. Consistent with the prestige thesis, Park was likely an oppositional nationalist who might see nuclear weapons as being inherently valuable.

Nuclear Proliferation–Related Behavior: Project 890

With its newfound nuclear interest, the South Korean government founded in the early 1970s two new defense agencies, the Agency for Defense Development (ADD) and the Weapons Exploitation Committee (WEC), to determine whether to develop nuclear weapons indigenously. In 1972, a nuclear weapons program began in earnest.[11]

By this time, South Korea had a nascent civilian nuclear program with very limited access to nuclear materials throughout the 1960s. As a beneficiary of Eisenhower's Atoms for Peace initiative, Seoul acquired a small nuclear reactor in 1956. This reactor could not generate civilian energy, let alone process materials necessary to produce a nuclear weapon. It was under surveillance by the IAEA when South Korea joined that organization in 1956. Instead, South Korea used the reactor for peaceful scientific research and creating radioisotopes for medical and agricultural purposes. Access to this technology also raised hopes for the future acquisition of civilian nuclear power.[12] To make further progress in nuclear research, South Korea established the Korean Atomic Energy Research Institute (KAERI) and the Office of Atomic Energy. With American assistance, South Korea built a General Dynamics–designed 250-kilowatt research reactor. In the late 1960s Seoul began a major initiative directed at mastering the nuclear fuel cycle. Its aim was to construct a 500-megawatt electric nuclear power plant (the Kori 1) and study nuclear fuel fabrication and reprocessing by 1976.[13] KAERI already had a twelve-year plan for achieving national energy autonomy thanks to a uranium enrichment factory and a reprocessing facility that would be operational by 1981. As in Japan, such initiatives arguably aimed to address South Korea's increasing energy needs to support economic growth. In fact, KAERI sought American support for its nuclear research.[14] However, the activities of the newly created WEC suggest a dramatic change in Seoul's nuclear intentions.

By 1972, South Korea started mobilizing military, academic, and industrial resources toward the production of nuclear weapons.[15] However, the program—called Project 890—soon encountered several technical challenges. One problem was South Korea's limited access to the sensitive nuclear materials needed to produce a weapon. For much of South Korea's history of nuclear research until then, the United States was a major source of nuclear technology and fuel. Because of expected American opposition to this new initiative, Seoul had to find alternative suppliers to acquire a reprocessing capability. To this end, it directed the minister of science and technology to enlist the technical cooperation of France and Great Britain in building a reprocessing facility. Furthermore, South Korea sent representatives to other nuclear-capable countries such as Canada and Israel. These initiatives were successful in procuring foreign assistance. By 1974, South Korea signed a contract with the French company Saint Gobain Technique Nouvelle to acquire the design of a reprocessing facility and another contract with the Belgian company Belgonucléaire for mixed nuclear fuel fabrication facilities.[16] South Korean scientists were also able to secure the import of the heavy water reactor (the NRX) from Canada. Having this type of reactor would enable South Korea to produce weapon-grade plutonium.[17] Still, the nuclear program remained largely aspirational in 1974.[18]

Explaining South Korea's Behavior: Initiation

Seoul acted on concerns over its received commitments. At this time, the situation facing the United States in Vietnam appeared increasingly futile. The attritional warfare produced high numbers of casualties on both sides of the conflict. Partly because the military relied on conscription to support the campaign, members of the American public became increasingly critical of their country's involvement in the war. Taking advantage of these sentiments, a signature aspect of Nixon's successful presidential election campaign in 1968 was his pledge to end the Vietnam War. As president, Nixon believed that an American withdrawal from Vietnam could be achieved only if a workable arrangement existed that guaranteed South Vietnam's security.[19] Amid faltering negotiations with the North Vietnamese and increasing domestic pressure, Nixon initiated a strategy of phased troop withdrawals and increased reliance on Vietnamese troops.[20] Such was the context of the Nixon Doctrine, which stated that although the United States would maintain its treaty commitments and continue to provide extended nuclear deterrence, it would ask its allies to contribute more toward their own security needs. Yet the Nixon Doctrine was arguably the culmination of a deeper trend in American defense policy toward South Korea. After all, Johnson had already commissioned an internal report to reevaluate the alliance. It suggested reducing the American presence to one division by 1973.[21]

To clarify the Nixon Doctrine, Nixon communicated with key decision makers in East Asia.[22] On August 21, 1969, Nixon met with President Park in San Francisco to discuss the American–South Korean relationship and "elaborate on my new policy toward Asia." Nixon told Park that "we will not retreat from the Pacific area and we will not reduce commitments." However, he noted that South Korean "efforts toward military and economic self-reliance are the correct road to take." Park reminded Nixon that the

American troop presence deterred Kim Il-sung from invading the South and argued that Kim Il-sung was provoking the United States to reduce its military presence. When Park asked about troop withdrawals from Korea, his remarks elicited no direct response from Nixon. Indeed, Nixon knew he was vague and imprecise in his conversation with Park. At one point he admitted to Park that his comment about American military commitments was a "general statement."[23] Still, within several months, Nixon alerted National Security Adviser Henry Kissinger that "the time has come to reduce our Korean presence" by "half." Nixon desired this change in policy for some time, but he had to wait some time after the shooting down of the EC-121.[24] A National Security Decision Memorandum in March 1970 noted the need to remove one of the two infantry divisions from South Korea by the middle of 1971.[25]

South Korea's insecurity subsequently deepened. It already faced a dangerous threat environment since the conventionally superior North was behaving provocatively under Chinese patronage. Hence Seoul was worried about the implications of the partial withdrawal.[26] Before implementing it, the Nixon administration made several consultations with South Korea. When Wheeler mentioned the possibility of these cuts to Park, the South Korean president expressed "concern at the prospect of a pull-out or substantial reduction in American troops in Korea" and commented that war would be "inevitable" following the withdrawal of American troops. Yet Wheeler noted that Park was also "contradictory" in adding that South Korea would have to provide its own deterrent and defense capability.[27] Interestingly, an examination of the discussions between representatives of the two governments reveals that South Korean leaders did not expect any troop withdrawals. According to Chae-jin Lee, "Park left San Francisco with the belief that Nixon, despite his plan for Vietnamization, would not withdraw US troops from South Korea so long as South Korean troops remained in Vietnam and that if he eventually decided to do so, it would only take place after full consultation with South Korea in advance."[28]

That Washington sent mixed signals is one possible reason for Seoul's apparent lack of foresight. That is, South Korean decision makers were not emotionally prepared for the troop withdrawal because they had received some indications that none were forthcoming. On the one hand, Secretary of Defense Melvin Laird noted to his South Korean interlocutors that "pressures for reduction of our forces in Korea are increasing," adding that "[South Korean] forces should be modernized before we withdraw any of our forces." The domestic pressures to which Laird referred emphasized the magnitude of the financial costs associated with maintaining such a large troop presence. On the other hand, Laird did not say that "decisions [about troop withdrawals] had been made or that there would be any immediate US troop withdrawals."[29] Moreover, Seoul might have believed that contributing more than two infantry divisions to the war in Vietnam would have spared it from unfavorable alliance adjustments. Park was already disappointed that he did not receive the military modernization assistance that the United States had promised in the so-called Brown Memorandum.[30] In the event that adjustments would take place, South Korean leaders appeared to believe that discussions about troop reductions from South Korea would take place after the Vietnam War was over.[31]

South Korean decision makers previously believed that their participation in the Vietnam War would ensure a sustained American military presence. As one Korean-language secondary source argues, "The government (of South Korea) was aware of the effects of the Nixon Doctrine, and calculated that any discussions leading to downsizing of the US troops would happen after the end of the Vietnam War.... The government thought by committing more than two infantry divisions to Vietnam (about the same size as the US forces in Korea), withdrawal of the US troops from South Korea would not occur."[32]

Confusing messages and dashed expectations clarify why Seoul reacted harshly when Nixon finally announced the withdrawal of one combat division. With a timetable set for June 1971, the withdrawal would effectively cut the number of American troops on the peninsula from sixty-one thousand to forty thousand. Park protested and claimed that this announcement came as a "profound shock."[33] To assuage concerns over American security guarantees to South Korea, Nixon wrote a personal letter to Park, promising to obtain congressional approval for greater military assistance to South Korea and its efforts to modernize its army. However, Park suggested to the American ambassador to South Korea William Porter that without knowing the "nature and extent of modernization he cannot agree to any withdrawals." Park further added that the uncertainty induced by even a partial withdrawal and the lack of a viable modernization program would weaken his domestic position. He then asked for the United States to delay its decision for another five years.[34]

Park repeated this argument for several months with other American officials. Some of these officials disliked his "hard line resistance" and his "lack of sensitivity to American domestic problems bearing on this matter."[35] Yet those officials also expressed a lack of understanding of the South Korean position. During one high-level meeting, Park argued that the troop withdrawal appeared inconsistent with earlier American assurances to South Korea. Ambassador Porter responded that "from our point of view [the South Korean government] seems to lack confidence in US intentions and our statements, and we do not understand why."[36] Even worse, some efforts to allay South Korean concerns backfired. In an August 1970 press conference held in Seoul, Vice President Spiro Agnew deepened the uncertainty when he declared his government's intention to withdraw *all* American troops from the peninsula within five years.[37] Thus, in December 1970, South Korean prime minister Jong Pil Kim told Kissinger that "everyone in Korea understood [the withdrawal] meant a detachment of the US commitment to support [South] Korea and in effect the reestablishment of an Asian defense system."[38]

The partial withdrawal was not the only reason why Seoul became apprehensive of American security guarantees. First, Washington was scaling down its military presence all across East Asia in light of its military failure in Indochina. Second, American efforts at pursuing rapprochement with China created further unease over the future role that the United States would play in East Asia. Due to growing cleavages over communist doctrine and foreign policy interests, relations between Moscow and Beijing deteriorated to the point where Mao saw the United States as a lesser threat than its erstwhile ally. The Sino-Soviet split afforded Washington an opportunity to tilt the balance of power further against the Soviet Union. Nixon recognized the growing need to reach out to the Chinese in a 1967 *Foreign Affairs* piece that he had written as a presidential candidate.[39] Shortly after becoming president, Nixon used secure diplomatic channels to advance this initiative.[40] Though this was a pragmatic policy change for the United States, South Korean leaders felt threatened by the prospect of American rapprochement with China.[41] Specifically, they were worried that Washington would grant Beijing greater leeway in East Asia and accept its request for the American withdrawal from Korea.[42] Indeed, the American partial withdrawal likely magnified South Korean unease over the Sino-American rapprochement.[43]

In the absence of direct evidence, some readers might be unsatisfied with the connection between American partial withdrawals and South Korean nuclear activities. Yet other aspects of South Korea's behavior at this time are worth considering, since South Korea could also respond to its concerns over American security guarantees with other actions that might seem retaliatory or vindictive.

Consider how Seoul tried to complicate American efforts to change its regional force posture. To begin with, the documentary record is replete with examples of South Korean leaders seeking new reassurances from the United States. These requests were particularly salient when officials representing South Korea and the United States discussed modernization programs for the South Korean military. Specifically, they desired greater American support for the modernization of the South Korean military and stronger assurances regarding American security commitments. Oftentimes these goals were explicitly linked: Park wanted American deployments to remain unchanged until the South Korean military was sufficiently modernized.[44] Yet these demands elicited a mixed response from the United States. Notwithstanding the finality of the troop withdrawal plans, American decision makers sent mixed signals about expanding military assistance to South Korea. For example, in a letter to Park intended to placate the South Korean leader's concerns about American security commitments, Nixon wrote of the significant domestic pressure he faced to reallocate burdens among allies. He noted that "the level of military assistance for Korea provided by the Congress [sic] under the last military assistance appropriation has been less than we considered desirable." This explanation did not deter Nixon from adding, "Subject to Congressional approval, I propose to provide substantially higher military assistance over the period 1971–75 for Korean modernization. Moreover provided your Government assumes a larger defense burden we are also prepared to consider some increased economic assistance."[45] In effect, Nixon was promising more than what he could provide. And so, unsurprisingly, Park later asked Ambassador Porter for greater clarification regarding the "nature and extent of modernization" of South Korean military forces.[46] Park even threatened noncooperation in reduction talks should negotiations over South Korean military modernization prove to be unsatisfactory.[47] The desire for stronger assurances constituted a major theme in South Korea's diplomacy toward the United States just as it began to consider nuclear weapons research.

South Korea's desire for stronger assurances persisted throughout the year. Interestingly, its diplomacy softened shortly after the establishment of ADD and WEC in August 1970.[48] The most palatable change occurred in early November, when, following a presentation by Porter on the status of troop withdrawals and the military modernization package, Park appeared "acquiescent."[49] He even "abandon[ed] efforts to obtain diplomatic assurances regarding US troop reductions." Rogers thus observed that "he has probably realized that there is no chance that we will reconsider our positions and that further adamancy on his part could cost him heavily with both our Congress and the Korean electorate. Whatever the reasons for Park's apparent acquiescence, the result is entirely favorable."[50] The explanations offered by members of the State Department seem plausible, but Park might have begun treating these troop withdrawals as inevitable.

This new understanding between the two allies did not ease their relations, however. With the date for implementing the troop withdrawals approaching in early 1971, American government officials complained of the South Korean government's "delaying tactics" in deploying replacement troops along the DMZ.[51] Ironically, South Korea began implementing its own troop withdrawals from South Vietnam. This action frustrated American officials for some of the same reasons expressed by the South Korean government in 1970. Ambassador Porter's successor stated that he "requested [the South Korean government] not move suddenly with decisions or announcements of further withdrawals. [Acting minister of foreign affairs Yun Sok-Hon] said that they had no intention of making known their plans at this time. I reminded him I had already seen articles in newspapers, sourced to officials, that his government was planning withdrawals in '72 and mentioning [the South Vietnamese government's] request for their retention. It struck me this kind of loose talk was not helpful. He agreed but did not leave with any assurance it would cease."[52] Furthermore, South Korea resumed its efforts to extract even more assurances from the United States.[53] Despite Park's alleged acquiescence in the fall of 1970, he remained a troublesome ally.

Summary and Alternative Arguments

South Korea's record of nuclear interest demonstrates the primacy of alliance politics. The alliance broke down so as to encourage South Korea to seek nuclear weapons. Specifically, the Nixon Doctrine entailed some shift of American conventional military assets away from East Asia. Its impact on South Korean security interests toward the region became manifest with Nixon's announced withdrawal of one troop division from the Korean peninsula. Documents show that the South Korean government reacted harshly to this change in American force posture, demonstrating the importance of in-theater conventional military deployments for extended nuclear security guarantees. South Korean leaders, especially Park, responded by adopting a set of measures: they repeatedly sought verbal reassurances from their American interlocutors, they threatened to unilaterally withdraw South Korean troops from Vietnam, they engaged in foot-dragging to slow American withdrawal from the region, and, more importantly, they established the WEC and the ADD to oversee an eventual nuclear weapons program.

The adversary thesis would argue that South Korea responded primarily to the threat posed by adversaries rather than to unfavorable changes in American security guarantees. At first blush, this counterargument seems to have some merit, since North Korea intensified its provocations in the late 1960s. However, it had long maintained a threatening posture under Kim Il-sung's leadership, and its patron, China, behaved aggressively throughout the decade, including border clashes with India and its 1964 nuclear detonation. The North Korean threat was necessary but insufficient for South Korea's nuclear interest; indeed, its salience made the announcement of American troop withdrawals even more alarming. Abandonment fears, rather than the threats alone, led South Korea to engage in nuclear proliferation–related behavior.[54]

An instructive irony exists in the case of South Korea. In the late 1960s, American conventional deterrence against North Korea might have prevented full-scale invasion, but it barely thwarted other provocations. After the Blue House raid, Park was unnerved by Johnson's reluctance to respond against the Pyongyang military. He voiced his frustrations to the former deputy secretary of defense Cyrus Vance. Writing to Johnson, Vance noted, "Highly emotional volatile, frustrated and introspective, Park wanted to obtain from me a pledge for the United States to join his Government in instant, punitive, and retaliatory actions against North Korea in the event of another Blue House raid or comparable attack on some other important South Korean economic, governmental, or military facility. He wanted my assurance of an 'automatic' US response in the event of another serious raid against the ROK [Republic of Korea]. I refused to give any such assurances." Park partially blamed the United States for the Blue House raid itself.[55]

Nevertheless, this record of deterrence failure was insufficient for pushing Park Chung-hee to start a nuclear weapons program. The real push came when the United States weakened its conventional deterrent even when the number of tactical nuclear weapons on the peninsula remained unchanged. The adversary thesis cannot explain why South Korea would seek nuclear weapons following conventional military reductions when the presence of tactical nuclear weapons remained stable.

The domestic politics thesis fares poorly in illuminating Seoul's decision to start a nuclear weapons program. Park should not have begun a nuclear weapons program at all, because his political survival depended on his export-oriented economic program. Although South Korea was very sensitive to positive and negative economic inducements, as we will see later in this chapter, Park was willing to compromise his own preferred model of economic development when alliance commitments appeared uncertain. Indeed, if Park valued economic development so much, why would he jeopardize it by having a nuclear weapons program in the first place? Although the program was secret, its usefulness as a deterrent required Seoul to reveal its nuclear activities eventually.

The prestige thesis is more valid. After all, the strategic benefit that Park was hoping to gain from nuclear weapons remains unclear. With Seoul located so close to the DMZ, South Korea lacks strategic depth and therefore would have not absorbed a retaliatory strike from at least one of North Korea's allies, the Soviet Union or China. If North Korea were to have matched South Korean nuclear efforts, then the South Korean nuclear threat would lose credibility. Also uncertain are the conditions under which they would have revealed the program. Much like the doomsday device in Stanley Kubrick's *Dr. Strangelove*, the utility of the arsenal would have been limited at best if adversaries were ignorant of it. Perhaps South Korea would have had what Vipin Narang describes as a catalytic nuclear posture, whereby Seoul would mobilize its nuclear forces so as to provoke an American intervention on its behalf in the event of a military crisis.[56] Yet such a hypothesis is highly speculative when Park otherwise fits the profile of an oppositional nationalist. One description of him alludes to "his revolutionary ideological vision of 'rich nation, strong army'"; describes his leadership style as "more Nietzschian"; calls him a patriotic "populist . . . critical of his people's alleged passivity."[57] That said, the prestige thesis cannot account for the timing of his interest in nuclear weapons. Park might have seen nuclear weapons as some sort of military cure-all without a clear understanding of the doctrinal and operational implications associated with the possession of these weapons. This naiveté could have reflected an overabundance of faith that nuclear weapons could resolve South Korea's strategic problems. Such a view is not about prestige per se, but it implies that nuclear weapons had some inherent value.

Alliance Coercion and South Korea

South Korea did not succeed in acquiring nuclear weapons. Why? Conventional accounts of this proliferation episode emphasize the degree to which South Korea was vulnerable to American coercion. As the following analysis demonstrates, notwithstanding the uncertain size of South Korea's nuclear program, this view is largely correct. Nevertheless, this instance of counterproliferation success should not be overstated. To begin with, the Ford administration executed a counterproliferation that combined reassurance and coercion. In acknowledging the importance of providing military commitments to South Korea, the Ford administration leveraged South Korea's economic and technological dependence on the United States to extract counterproliferation commitments. Unfortunately, the Carter administration risked jeopardizing this rather successful effort by one-upping the Nixon Doctrine with its proposal to withdraw fully from the Korean Peninsula. As such, mystery abounds as to whether South Korean nuclear activities really did end during the Ford administration.

THE FORD ADMINISTRATION'S MULTIFACETED
COUNTERPROLIFERATION EFFORT

The United States detected the nascent program by the end of 1974. In November 1974, it was aware that South Korea was acquiring a type of Canadian nuclear reactor that "was most vulnerable to clandestine diversion." Nevertheless, an NSC memorandum expressed satisfaction over the safeguards implemented on American- and Canadian-supplied nuclear facilities to South Korea.[58] An internal Department of State memorandum circulated in October 1974 on South Korea made no mention of a nuclear weapons program.[59] However, a telegram sent two months later from the American embassy in Seoul alerted the secretary of state to South Korea's nuclear activities.[60] It added that "evidence accumulated that the [South] Korean [government] has decided to proceed with the initial phases of a nuclear weapons program." On February 28, 1975, the NSC agreed with the embassy's assessment and asserted that South Korea's nuclear activities would have a "decidedly destabilizing effect in Northeast Asia."[61]

With knowledge of the nuclear program, the Ford administration directed a counterproliferation effort against South Korea. The strategy underpinning this effort focused on achieving four objectives. The first objective was to force the termination of the South Korean nuclear program "through unilateral US action and through the development of common supplier nation policies." The second objective was to resolve informational issues and force Seoul to become more transparent in its uses of nuclear material. Greater transparency helped to advance a third objective: ensuring that South Korea could not restart its nuclear weapons program at a future date when the current controversy subsided. The fourth objective concerned the very issue that prompted the nuclear program in the first place. Washington had to allay skepticism over the reliability of its security commitments.[62] What gave special impetus for this counterproliferation effort was the Indian "peaceful nuclear explosion," which a Canadian reactor and American heavy water allegedly made possible.[63] The nonproliferation regime—as embodied in the NPT—seemed toothless.

To obtain the first objective, the Ford administration threatened to cut off financing for the Kori 2 nuclear power plant and other planned nuclear facilities through the Export-Import Bank, the American export credit agency. Sneider reported that he had asked a South Korean official "whether Korea [is] prepared [to] jeopardize availability of technology and [the] largest financing capability which only [the] US could offer, as well as vital partnership with [the] US, not only in nuclear and scientific areas but in broad political and security areas."[64] Furthermore, the United States applied pressure to third-party states to stop them from lending sensitive nuclear assistance to South Korea. The Canadian government was attuned to the risk of proliferation following India's nuclear test and had already faced severe criticism for supplying a repressive state with nuclear technology. After some wrangling, France agreed to withdraw its assistance to South Korea's efforts in obtaining a reprocessing capability. Belgian company Belgonucléaire terminated its contract with South Korea in November 1977.[65]

As for the second objective, the United States pressured South Korea to participate in a multilateral initiative that would enable East Asian states to reprocess spent fuel from a shared regional facility. Later in October 1976, in a public speech outlining the proliferation risks of reprocessing, Ford identified South Korea and Taiwan as two countries in which the United States forced the cancellation of local reprocessing activities.[66] For the third (and related) objective, getting the South Korean government to ratify the NPT was a significant step in addressing the issue of making a credible commitment to eschew nuclear weapons acquisition.[67] Some Pentagon officials agreed with this assessment, observing that "President Park's fears of isolation and the possible withdrawal of American forces have led him to embark on a secret program to develop nuclear weapons."[68] Indeed, the American embassy in Seoul noted the importance of South Korean perceptions of American security commitments ahead of a visit by Vice President Nelson Rockefeller: "Existing danger to [South Korea] has been greatly increased by communist successes in sea. [South Korean] security rests heavily on deterrent effect US force presence and military assistance provide. Any indication of lessening of US commitment will encourage already dangerous North Korean belligerence. Decline of military assistance below levels earlier agreed and criticism in US on [South Korea] have already created concern over US intentions towards its commitments."[69] NSC member William R. Smyser even circulated an old internal memorandum to Kissinger that outlined the decision-making behind the 1949 American troop withdrawal from South Korea. In the letter explaining this document, Smyser noted that "it is worth reflecting on this, for the obvious reason that we might not have had the Korean War if we had not pulled all of our forces out."[70]

Such sensitivity regarding troop withdrawals now informed American policy-making toward South Korea and the region. For example, the Department of Defense considered additional restructuring of troop deployments on the peninsula. Yet members of the Department of State and the Ford administration resisted the Department of Defense's policy recommendations. In a memorandum to Ford, Kissinger advised that "this is the wrong time to make any of these changes, or even to continue planning already underway with [South Korea] for such changes. To proceed would give the wrong signal to both Seoul and Pyongyang."[71] Ford apparently agreed. In a note addressed to the secretary of defense, Kissinger stated that proposed changes to American force deployments and structure in South Korea were presently "inadvisable."[72] Ford reports in his memoirs that he assured Park that "our troops would stay where they were" in a November 1974 meeting.[73]

The Ford administration appears to have succeeded in curtailing South Korea's nuclear ambitions. Admittedly, that the program was at such an early stage of development made it relatively easy to cancel. A 1978 intelligence estimate that reviewed the program's history noted that "beginning in late 1972, physicists assisted by an explosives technician had worked on a nuclear weapon design at the [ADD], a semi-independent adjunct of the Ministry of National Defense."[74] The technical difficulties encountered early by these researchers indicate the massive challenges that South Korea confronted in seeking nuclear weapons. And so the United States had various nonmilitary tools at its disposal. As Etel Solingen notes, almost all of the foreign direct investment in South Korea came from the United States and Japan. The United States accounted for a majority of South Korea's debt and trade.[75] However, the threat of economic sanctions arguably mattered less than the specific targeting of South Korea's nascent civilian nuclear industry. South Korean energy dependency and the structure of the international nuclear industry at the time were other reasons for the rapid success of American counterproliferation efforts. Due to the quick pace of its industrialization, existing energy sources available to South Korea were increasingly unable to meet demand. South Korean coal imports and petroleum imports both grew twentyfold between 1960 and 1975. Accordingly, South Korea's dependence on imported energy grew from less than 10 percent to over 50 percent by the early 1970s.[76] Nuclear energy provided a solution. Still, the United States exercised a dominant role in the international nuclear industry. Its nuclear reactors were the most appropriate and cost efficient in light of South Korean needs. Because these reactors required low-enriched uranium, the United States supplied the vast majority of uranium on the world market, especially if one were to exclude the Soviet

Union and China.[77] This dependency meant that South Korea was extraordinarily sensitive to the possibility that its access to peaceful American nuclear technology during the 1970s would be denied. Simply put, South Korea was susceptible to American pressure.[78]

In compelling South Korea to behave more favorably, the United States still had to offer some concessions. After all, even though South Korea succumbed to American pressure to ratify the NPT, its leaders clarified that its future behavior would be contingent on American security commitments. Such statements imply that South Korea was willing to compromise on its economic objectives if its security needs would not be satisfactorily met. Thus, as already discussed, the Ford administration refrained from opening any discussions of further troop withdrawals. Key officials verbally communicated their commitment to South Korean security as well as offered sophisticated military hardware to strengthen the South Korean military.[79] An opportunity to demonstrate American military support came when North Korean soldiers killed two US Army officers who were cutting down an obstructive poplar tree in the DMZ. Operation Paul Bunyan, as this effort was called, consisted of a convoy of military vehicles (supported by nearby helicopters, bombers, and jet aircraft) entering the DMZ without warning in order to cut down the tree.[80]

To be sure, American decision makers expressed such reassurances at a time when American credibility in the region was otherwise at its nadir. On April 12, 1975, the United States airlifted its nationals and members of the military-led government out of Cambodia. The communist Khmer Rouge subsequently gained control of that country. At the very end of the month, the People's Army of Vietnam and the National Liberation Front captured Saigon, the South Vietnamese capital. Its capture not only prompted the evacuation of most American civilian and military personnel from the city but also enabled the Provisional Revolutionary Government to gain nominal authority in South Vietnam. American losses in the region did not stop there: communist forces began acquiring significant control in Laos, another country whose government received American support. With these losses occurring in rapid succession, American decision makers, such as Kissinger and Secretary of Defense James Schlesinger, recognized that the international stature of the United States was now diminished. Such concerns likely motivated the forceful but clumsy effort by the Ford administration to rescue the SS *Mayaguez* and its American crew from Khmer Rouge forces.[81]

Did the United States threaten to abandon South Korea completely? Don Oberdorfer writes that in May 1976 Secretary of Defense Donald Rumsfeld informed the South Korean minister of defense that there might be a "review of the entire spectrum of [the United States'] relations with the ROK."[82] Yet this threat is vague and does not contain explicit warnings that the alliance would be abrogated. Moreover, the citation for the Rumsfeld threat is a 1995 interview with a Korean source dated in the *Monthly Chosun*.[83] Again on the basis of interviews, Kissinger allegedly also "threatened the withdrawal of the US security commitment."[84] Similarly, Oberdorfer notes that in August 1975 Schlesinger informed Park that nuclear proliferation by South Korea would undermine the alliance, whereas Ambassador Sneider asked a high-ranking South Korean official "whether Korea [is] prepared [to] jeopardize availability of best technology and largest financing capacity which only U.S. could offer, as well as a vital partnership with U.S., not only in nuclear and scientific areas but in broad political and security arenas."[85] Yet Seung-Young Kim offers a slightly different version of events, namely, that "Habib said the United States would recalculate the entire security alliance including the withdrawal of the US nuclear umbrella," which seem to imply the withdrawal of American tactical nuclear weapons from the Korean Peninsula.[86] No direct documentary evidence shows that American decision makers ever delivered an unambiguous threat linking South Korean nuclear weapons activities to the termination of the alliance. However, in an undated note summarizing his conversation with Sneider, the British ambassador to Seoul recounted that "Mr Sneider said it had been a very tough battle. . . . He was under orders to go straight to the President [Park] and to make it clear that if the Koreans went through with their plans then the Americans would both cut off all economic assistance and withdraw their nuclear weapons from Korea."[87] Perhaps Sneider did not want to tell his British counterpart that the United States would willingly terminate the military alliance with South Korea. Nevertheless, this contemporary recounting of events squares better with the documentary record than interviews conducted decades after the fact. Both threats were credible, whereas the wholesale termination of the alliance would not have been because of the instability it would generate in the wider East Asian region.

A POTENTIAL UNRAVELING OF THE NONPROLIFERATION SETTLEMENT

Emerging developments in American politics threatened the Ford administration's success with South Korea's nuclear program. The economic crisis and continuing fallout from the Watergate scandal doomed Ford's presidential bid in the 1976 election. His Democratic replacement—Jimmy Carter—entered the White House with a new vision for foreign policy that centered on human rights advocacy. Consistent with this approach, Carter found American support for a repressive regime like Park's distasteful.[88] During the campaign, Carter had even promised the complete withdrawal of all American military forces from the Korean Peninsula. He wanted to reorient American foreign policy away from East Asia and back toward Europe in the wake of the Vietnam War.[89] Such campaign rhetoric turned out to reflect Carter's true intentions for South Korea.[90] About forty thousand American troops still remained in South Korea in 1977, but Carter sought to reduce that number to zero shortly after assuming the presidency. He directed the NSC to produce a feasibility report regarding the implementation of a complete troop withdrawal from South Korea. Being so committed to this initiative, the White House did not even wish for an analysis of its probable consequences.[91]

Carter's position provoked a backlash from leading officials in the military, the NSC, and the Department of State. The chief of staff of the UN Command in Seoul even spoke publicly against Carter's proposal. The senior American commander in South Korea and the American ambassador in Seoul were less explicit in their opposition. An official privy to these internal debates later wrote that the NSC sought to persuade Carter to modify his position. Apparently, Secretary of State Cyrus Vance and Secretary of Defense Harold Brown privately recommended a softer policy position. These efforts came to naught as Carter ignored the advice of other senior decision makers and proceeded to issue Presidential Decision 12 on May 5, 1977. This statement called for the complete withdrawal of all troops by 1982, starting with one brigade of the second division (at least six thousand troops) to be removed from South Korea by late 1978.[92]

International opposition toward the planned troop withdrawal grew during the summer of 1977. The Chinese vice foreign minister cryptically told Australian government officials that "there will be war" after the American troop withdrawal. Though this statement was most likely not a reflection of the official Chinese position, it nevertheless communicated their unease over the larger geopolitical implications of this change in the American military presence in East Asia.[93] After all, China saw the American military presence in East Asia as a desirable offset to Soviet encirclement, despite being forced to call for troop withdrawals as part of its ideological competition with the Soviet Union.[94] American East Asian allies also seemed concerned about the implications of the withdrawal for the "wellsprings of US foreign policy." NSC staff member Mark Armacost noted after his trip to Asia that "since no concessions are being sought from [North Korea], most Asians conclude that diplomatic considerations got short shrift." If military reasons did not account for the new policy, then only American "domestic politics" seemed to be the last remaining explanation that made sense for American allies.[95]

Given how negative were the international and administration reactions, what was the response of the South Korean government? Though Carter's plans for a complete withdrawal never bore fruit, his intent might have prompted South Korea to pursue nuclear weapons development more furtively than before. Seung-Young Kim writes that Park instructed his senior economic adviser "to pursue a full scale development of nuclear industry, without making much noise" in November 1976, the same month as Carter's presidential election.[96] The next month saw Park's government establish a new institute dedicated to the research of nuclear reprocessing and fuel fabrication technologies.[97] Seoul even accelerated its efforts in developing its missile capabilities. According to Jonathan Pollack and Mitchell Reiss, South Korea worked on managing the nuclear fuel cycle during this time.[98] Though any such weapons research and development would have been highly secret, the vice-premier and foreign minister mooted the possibility of South Korea pursuing its own nuclear capability. Indeed, the minister of science and technology—with the likely sanctioning of President Park—proclaimed the expansion of South Korea's nuclear industry so as to domestically produce a fuel supply.[99] One source claims that Park announced in January 1977 his intention for South Korea not to go nuclear. Still, around this time at a legislative committee meeting convened to discuss Carter's troop withdrawals, the South Korean foreign minister vaguely threatened that "if it is necessary for national security interests and people's safety, it is possible for Korea as a sovereign state to make its own judgment on the matter."[100] This statement echoed Park's earlier declarations that "if the US nuclear umbrella were to be removed, we have to start developing our nuclear capability to save ourselves" and that "there were and still are quite a number of Koreans doubting the commitment of the United States."[101]

Carter's plans for complete withdrawal renewed fears of alliance abandonment among South Korean leaders.[102] Interestingly, American officials anticipated such a response because they knew of Park's desire to maintain the status quo. As one telegram observed, "convinced of the necessity for a credible expression of continuing US support as a deterrent to the North, [Park] has told us directly he wants close relations with the US, high-lighted by continuation of present US ground and other force levels."[103] Nevertheless, within a few months, Ambassador Richard Sneider reported that Park and his government were "reconciled to ground troop withdrawal." The challenge, however, concerned the question of how "to prepare its public."[104] Sneider repeated this view two weeks later, adding that Park is "almost isolated" and "will press for satisfactory compensatory actions particularly on timing and availability of weapons." He "will not resist ground force withdrawal despite his grave misgivings." Still, the ambassador now recognized that many members of the South Korean government did not share Park's attitudes. Sneider noted that "to many, the ground force withdrawal connotes loss of US tripwire and with it loss of US military support in event of North Korean attack following withdrawal which is now broadly expected."[105]

The announced troop withdrawal provoked concern over whether South Korea would try to acquire nuclear weapons. Carter recommended that "Park should be told that any move to produce nuclear weapons would terminate our security relationship"—a threat that seemed vacuous, since his planned withdrawals would already be a dramatic alteration to the alliance.[106] However, South Korean attitudes toward the bomb were difficult to gauge. To the surprise of American diplomats, one worry expressed by their South Korean interlocutors touched on whether their country would still enjoy the benefits of American extended nuclear deterrence. As Sneider related,

> In response to these suggestions of embracing Korea under US nuclear umbrella, I pointed out that in fact Korea, as any ally, would be covered by US nuclear umbrella and I was surprised that there was any misunderstanding on that point. Both Korean sources pointed out that Koreans have considered assumed [*sic*] stationing of nuclear weapons in Korea as providing them with nuclear protection. US in past has not talked specifically of placing Korea under nuclear umbrella but this was not considered necessary. However, with possibility of withdrawal of at least ground force nuclear weapons, Koreans suggested that we take some public posture vis-à-vis Korea as we do Japan with respect to nuclear umbrella.[107]

The American embassy in Seoul thus became acutely aware of the need to reassure South Korea. Sneider anticipated that South Korea would search for a way to achieve security independently. He noted that "one specific evidence of this concern is a continuing dialogue and heightened interest in the possibility of [South Korean] acquisition, as a means of bolstering [South Korean] self-reliance."[108] A CIA report dated June 1978 states that "officials in the Korean nuclear research community believe that, even while bowing to US preferences on the line of work they pursue, certain activities can and should be undertaken to keep Seoul's nuclear option open."[109] That the South Korean government signed the NPT just two years before did not seem to allay these fears.[110] And with good reason: South Korea still committed safeguard violations throughout the 1980s due to experiments involving plutonium separation and uranium enrichment.[111] Nuclear misbehavior did not necessarily end with Park's assassination in October 1979.[112]

The Carter administration eventually decided against the troop withdrawals. Yet this controversial policy had already inflicted much damage. Leading Democratic congressmen such as Robert Byrd, Sam Nunn, and Tip O'Neill reproached the Carter administration for its handling of South Korea, not least because North Korean military forces appeared to be gathering strength.[113] The American military also had reservations. To the dismay of the NSC, the Department of Defense leaked politically sensitive Joint Chiefs of Staff cables to Congress in June 1977. The purpose of this action was likely to bolster congressional opposition to Carter's initiative.[114] The probable actions of the South Korean government during this period also suggest a deep-seated unease over Carter's foreign policy. At a minimum, South Korea became a more difficult ally. When Carter explored the possibility of having a trilateral meeting with the two Koreas, one NSC member cautioned that "Park would not go along. There is little in such a meeting for him, unless we agreed to stop troop withdrawals entirely."[115] Even the Japanese government seemed relieved when the issue was finally resolved.[116]

If South Korea did engage in nuclear activities in the late 1970s, then Carter's stated intentions for a complete withdrawal likely had much to do with it. Park's earlier warnings about the consequences of a removal of the American nuclear umbrella cast a shadow over this episode. American officials understood the implications of such an action for the American alliance with South Korea and regional stability in East Asia, not least for the counterproliferation settlement that the Ford administration was able to impose.

Summary and Alternative Explanations

Alliance politics played an important role in the demise of the program. Had it not been for American pressure on South Korea and its international suppliers of nuclear assistance, South Korea might not have terminated its program when and how it did. Of course, the Ford administration was as successful as it was because of how much the South Korean program depended on outside support. The United States had nonmilitary leverage over South Korea that it used. Nevertheless, it still had to reassure South Korea as to the dependability of the alliance. And so the success of the Ford administration was put in jeopardy when Carter advocated for a full troop withdrawal. The uncertainty regarding the exact nature of South Korea's nuclear activities in the late 1970s (and early 1980s) aside, the evidence at least shows that South Korea reacted negatively to Carter's planned troop withdrawal. As such, South Korea persisted, albeit intermittently, in proliferation-related behavior even in the early 1980s.

Changes in the threat environment cannot account for why Seoul renounced nuclear weapons, to the extent that it did. In fact, the threat environment facing South Korea remained intense. Direct evidence of how South Korean leaders understood the regional security environment is difficult to ascertain so as to evaluate the adversary thesis properly. Still, the available evidence highlights how the South Koreans were still anxious over the broader repercussions of communist successes in Indochina. They worried that the subsequent American withdrawal might even embolden regional adversaries. Crucially, North Korea retained an aggressive posture and even made preparations for war. Kim Il-sung even toured China and Eastern Europe to make weapons and fuel purchases. Accordingly, "President Park believed that war could break out at any time."[117] Making matters worse, relations between Seoul and Tokyo deteriorated after a North Korean sympathizer attempted to assassinate Park in August 1974, fatally injuring the South Korean president's wife in the process. Because the would-be assassin was Japanese and entered South Korea on a Japanese passport, Park demanded an apology and the disbandment of a pro–North Korean residents' association. Insensitive to anti-Japanese sentiments in South Korea, the Japanese foreign minister further antagonized South Korean leaders by refusing to accept any responsibility for the attack. Though this controversy eventually subsided, the strain on their diplomatic relations added to an already conflict-ridden regional environment.[118] Considered together, regional tensions remained sufficiently high to warrant the continuation of a nuclear weapons program.

The domestic politics thesis fares no better. Solingen argues that Park capitulated to American counterproliferation demands in order to protect the viability of his strategy for economic development. Specifically, because economic development directly affected his political survival, Park had to renounce the nuclear weapons project openly by making nonproliferation commitments. As Solingen writes, "suspicions about South Korea's nuclear intentions had to be put to rest if the export-led growth strategy was to have any chance."[119] The alliance with the United States mattered, but largely because it was the locus of South Korea's strategy for economic development.

Little evidence exists to show that economics motivated Park more than alliance considerations. To support the assertion that Park renounced nuclear weapons to protect his country's economic development, Solingen cites a quote by Park in which he argues in favor of "doing away with those activities that tend to drain or waste our natural resources in a broad sense."[120] She adds that "even after North Korea assassinated Park's wife in 1974, he continued to focus on the synergies between South Korea's economic vitality, regional stability, and a positive 'recognition in the world community.'"[121] These passages are problematic for several reasons. The problem with the first statement by Park is that the specific "activities" to which he is referring remain unclear. Wasteful activities could encompass anything from bureaucratic red tape to inefficient production. Moreover, even if he did refer to the nuclear weapons program, the statement might be an example of post facto rationalization. Park marshaled various sectors of the economy toward nuclear research, and his nuclear interest suggests that for several years he did not regard such activity as a "waste." The problem with the second statement regarding Park's behavior following his wife's murder is that it has no historical support. The assassination by a North Korean sympathizer from Japan led to a crisis between Seoul and Tokyo. Park even mobilized large anti-Japanese protests in Seoul to demonstrate his country's dissatisfaction with how Japan handled the controversy.[122] These actions were inconsistent with any desire to improve regional stability and to receive positive international recognition.

The domestic politics thesis—as conceptualized by Solingen—misconstrues the nationalist character of Park's decision to integrate with the global economy. From the perspective of the South Korean government, its understanding of self-reliance was that of technological advancement rather than of economic self-sufficiency implied by the term "autarchy."[123] However, Sheila Jasanoff and Sang-Hyun Kim take this argument further, claiming that South Korea's nuclear projects in the late 1960s and 1970s were part of a larger state-led initiative that aimed at "the modernization of the fatherland" and a "self-reliant economy." They point to the nationalist rhetoric that extolled the achievements of scientists and engineers working on nuclear energy.[124] Yet Seoul's nationalist rhetoric did not focus on defense matters until after North Korean provocations and Nixon's troop withdrawals from the peninsula. During the 1960s nationalist rhetoric was necessary for economic mobilization. Seung-Young Kim writes that Park promoted self-reliance "to defend South Korea and to keep national dignity in the face of American meddling in South Korea's domestic affairs."[125] Still, Nixon's policies arguably compromised Park's strategy for achieving national self-reliance. As Ambassador Habbib noted, "Park's view of self-reliance, paradoxically, includes a desire and an expressed need for the U.S. presence and assistance to continue—at least in the short run. His concern that we will reduce our aid program, withdraw our troops sooner than he would like, and his doubt over the firmness of our treaty commitment, come to the surface from time to time. Generally speaking, he wishes to hold on to these elements of strength for as long as he can, expecting they will diminish as time goes on."[126] Park continued this line of argument with Ford, asserting that "of course, we do not expect the US presence to remain indefinitely, given the mounting US public opinion and pressure in Congress. However, Korean self-reliance must be insured [sic] before US troop reductions take place."[127] Simply put, Park saw American protection as complementing, rather than constraining, self-reliance.

Issues of prestige do not surface so much with regard to the drawdown of South Korea's nuclear weapons interest. In contrast, alliance considerations appear to have had more of an effect on how South Korea toned down its proliferation-related behavior. Nevertheless, some speculate that the nuclear weapons program lasted as long as Park Chung Hee—an oppositional nationalist leader—lived. Rumors have even circulated that the CIA was behind the October 1979 assassination of Park Chung Hee in a bid to terminate the weapons program.[128] Whatever the veracity of such claims, safeguard violations did occur in the early 1980s, suggesting that the program cannot be reduced simply to one man and the beliefs he might have had about nuclear weapons. The role of prestige is indeterminate in accounting for this phase of South Korea's nuclear interest.

Like West Germany, South Korea was a frontline state in the Cold War that emerged out of a nation divided territorially by communism and anticommunism. And like West Germany, it saw American ground forces as necessary for bolstering its received security guarantees. Yet South Korea was both more forthright in its nuclear proliferation–related behavior and more vulnerable to American pressure. Washington used its leverage, but South Korea was still able to persist in questionable activities thereafter.

Nuclear Proliferation and Other American Alliances

Chapters 3, 4, and 5 examined three allies of the United States and argued that military alliances played less of a role in forestalling nuclear proliferation than often assumed. Yet some unconvinced readers might still argue that West Germany, Japan, and South Korea are somehow an unrepresentative sample of alliance politics more broadly. In anticipating this critique, this chapter widens the variation by considering additional cases in the order in which they transpired: Great Britain, France, Norway, Australia, and Taiwan. Though space constraints preclude an intensive analysis on them, these cases highlight at least some of the propositions derived from my theoretical account of the connection between alliances and nuclear proliferation. The United States treated NATO members Great Britain and France differently with regard to their nuclear weapons programs: only France was truly able to retain an independent nuclear capability. The other countries varied in the quality of their received security guarantees and the level of nuclear proliferation–related behavior they undertook. Norway was another NATO ally on the front line, but it had little interest in hosting in-theater American deployments or acquiring its own nuclear capabilities. Australia had a security pledge from the United States, but it coveted more military commitments and even attempted a nuclear weapons program. Taiwan was a formal treaty ally that hosted in-theater conventional forces. It sought to develop an independent nuclear arsenal as well.

This chapter examines each American security partner in turn. Several key findings emerge from this discussion. Though prestige was a major driver of Great Britain's interest in nuclear weapons, security concerns relating to American actions prompted both it and France to seek nuclear weapons. However, differences in economic and technological vulnerabilities account for why the British nuclear arsenal and not the French one became at least partially subordinated to the United States. Notwithstanding its frontline status, the combination of its Nordic geography and domestic politics reduced Norway's appetite for either in-theater deployments or nuclear capabilities.

Australia more clearly fits the pattern of a state that seeks nuclear weapons out of frustration with its received security commitments, only to renounce its interest for mostly domestic reasons. Although Taiwan is a case in which alliance coercion did suppress a nuclear weapons program, it also illustrates the difficulties of ending the nuclear interest of even a diplomatically isolated, economically dependent state that relies so much on the United States for its security.

Great Britain: A Partially Subordinated Nuclear-Armed Ally

British interest in nuclear weapons preceded the Cold War and thus any security partnership with the United States. In July 1940—the same month that the Battle of Britain began—the government-commissioned Maud Committee determined that Great Britain could and should develop a "uranium super bomb" so as to shorten the war. Technical difficulties hamstrung this project, and so Great Britain's nuclear ambitions had to wait until 1946 when the British government under Prime Minister Clement Attlee began a civilian nuclear program that was also intended to produce fissile material necessary for making a weapons stockpile. London decided finally to acquire the bomb in 1947. Great Britain detonated a nuclear weapon successfully in 1952, becoming the third nuclear weapons state after the United States and the Soviet Union.

Two factors drove London's interest in nuclear weapons. The first was the British experience in World War II. While the United States stood neutral, Great Britain confronted Nazi Germany alone following the spring 1940 defeat of France and withstood a sustained air attack called the Blitz during the Battle of Britain. A nuclear deterrent was now necessary for deterring a similar attack in the atomic age.[1] To be sure, London would have preferred developing nuclear weapons with Washington, but the McMahon Act—a law passed by Congress that forbade the sharing of atomic bomb information with all other countries under penalty of death or life imprisonment—and American concerns over espionage frustrated British attempts at cooperation.[2]

The second factor was prestige. Already during World War II, British leaders realized that great power status would soon require mastery over atomic technology. They saw the bomb as the "key to national power in the postwar world."[3] The chief scientist working on the British nuclear program noted that "the discriminative test for a first class power is whether it has made an atomic bomb and we have either got to pass the test or suffer a serious loss of prestige both inside the country and internationally."[4] The official historian of the British nuclear program concluded that driving the decision to acquire the bomb was "a feeling that Britain must possess so climacteric a weapon in order to deter an atomically armed enemy, a feeling that Britain as a Great Power must acquire all the major new weapons, a feeling that atomic weapons were a manifestation of the scientific and technological superiority on which Britain's strength, so deficient if measured in sheer numbers of men, must depend."[5]

Great Britain is a peculiar case because—unlike France—it held the status of being a nuclear weapons state while relying on the United States for extended deterrence. Indeed, to some extent, abandonment fears amplified London's interest in nuclear weapons.[6] However, Great Britain represents a case study of nuclear reversal insofar as the United States sought to curtail the independence of its nuclear weapons program. Consistent with one proposition of my argument, economic vulnerabilities and technological gaps gave Washington opportunities to subordinate British nuclear forces. Nevertheless, the United States only partially succeeded. Competing foreign policy priorities in Washington allowed London to claim operational independence of its nuclear arsenal despite its dependence on American technology.

To understand why a British nuclear reversal was conceivable even after 1952, consider the nature of Great Britain's nuclear deterrent itself. Already before embarking on a nuclear weapons program, London experienced difficulties with atomic energy. Technological challenges continued to mark the weapons program despite the successful 1952 detonation. Great Britain first relied on strategic bomber aircraft (the V-force) to deliver nuclear weapons against Soviet targets. However, toward the late 1950s, the V bombers faced obsolescence as the Soviet Union acquired intercontinental missile capabilities and effective antiaircraft missiles. The V bombers were so beset by difficulties that they eventually lost operational independence as a nuclear deterrent force.[7] Highlighting this inability to keep pace with technological developments was the economic weakness of postwar Great Britain. Following the American example, the British chiefs of staff wanted to implement "massive nuclear retaliation" so as to "allow reductions of the manpower goals" set for withdrawing British forces from Europe.[8]

To upgrade its deterrent in view of Soviet military advances, Great Britain recognized that delivering nuclear gravity bombs was becoming infeasible and that rocket-powered supersonic missiles carrying nuclear or thermonuclear warheads were more desirable. Such capabilities would take time to develop, and so Great Britain sought to deploy a U.S. Air Force–designed, liquid-fueled IRBM called Thor in the meantime. Yet London needed to overcome the injunctions of the McMahon Act in order to obtain American assistance. Three factors allowed Great Britain to reinvigorate Anglo-American nuclear cooperation and to receive sixty land-based Thors. First, because Eisenhower saw atomic energy as a diplomatic tool, he was more open to sharing it with allies, whether through Atoms for Peace or nuclear-sharing arrangements within NATO. Since Great Britain already had nuclear weapons, it was less of a proliferation threat than others.[9] Second, Anglo-American relations needed mending after the Suez crisis saw Eisenhower threaten to undermine the sterling so as to restrain Great Britain.[10] Atomic cooperation was useful for relieving alliance tensions.[11] Third, the Sputnik launching alarmed NATO capitals such that Western European allies sought not only more IRBM deployments on their territories but also a greater say in alliance nuclear decision-making. These propitious circumstances thus prompted agreement between London and Washington over the Thor deployment. Although British decision makers coveted this arrangement, it came at a cost. The dual-key formula meant that Great Britain "would own, man and operate the Thor missiles; the United States would retain ownership, custody and control of the missiles' nuclear warheads."[12] Indeed, domestic controversy ensued over the inability of London to veto the launch of nuclear weapons by the United States from British territory.[13] The Thor deployment signified greater integration of British nuclear forces into NATO.[14]

Great Britain tried to develop its own missile capability with the Blue Steel standoff missile and the Blue Streak intermediate-range ballistic missile, but neither proved satisfactory.[15] Consequently, London looked to Washington for access to the AGM-48 Skybolt system, which could be mounted on the Vulcan bomber and launched without the aircraft having to penetrate Soviet airspace. Excited by this technology, Prime Minister Harold Macmillan received authorization from Eisenhower to acquire the Skybolt and committed the British defense establishment to focus exclusively on integrating this weapon system. Nevertheless, British decision makers neglected a critical aspect of the agreement struck by Eisenhower and Macmillan: Washington saw the deal as contingent on the technological success of Polaris, the submarine-launched ballistic missile program.[16] Some members of the British defense establishment understood the implication. Quietly, they spoke of how "the time [had] come to consider giving up the concept of independent control of the British nuclear weapons and their delivery systems and that [they] should negotiate the best terms possible with the Americans in return or handing over control to them."[17]

Unfortunately for Great Britain, the Skybolt failed early tests amid improvements in silo-based and submarine-based missiles like the Polaris. When the Kennedy administration informed London that it was contemplating the cancellation of the program altogether, a crisis quickly engulfed Anglo-American relations. Yet the so-called Skybolt affair was not rooted in technical differences and bureaucratic misunderstandings, as one account suggests.[18] The controversy was political. Members of the Kennedy administration thought lowly of Great Britain and even less of the so-called special relationship. Dean Acheson once remarked that "Great Britain has lost an empire and has not yet found a role. The attempt to play a separate power role—that is, a role apart from Europe, a role based on a 'special relationship' with the United States . . . is about played out."[19] Moreover, the United States sought to integrate NATO allies into the MLF under its leadership. Without the Skybolt, London might have to join the MLF, thus fully subordinating its nuclear forces. British decision makers were unhappy. A parliamentarian opined that "some of us on this side, who want to see Britain retain a nuclear deterrent, are highly suspicious of some of the American motives."[20] To repair their relationship, both countries successfully negotiated the Nassau Agreement. It provided that London would obtain nuclear-capable Polaris missiles, whereas Washington would receive rights to use a nuclear submarine base located in Scotland. The Polaris missiles would also be fitted on British submarines that would go on to be *integrated* into the MLF. How to interpret and how to handle this specific provision preoccupied the British government for some time, but getting Macmillan to agree to consider the MLF was a major concession that the United States extracted.[21]

I have argued that in rolling back the nuclear weapons program of an ally, the best coercive of action available to the United States consists of exploiting economic and technological vulnerabilities, if not reassuring credibly. To this effect, Britain was susceptible to American pressure. Its postwar economy failed to exhibit the same dramatic growth as France's and West Germany's. Though London played a central role in the establishment of the Bretton Woods system, it was unable to meet the requirements of having the sterling be a reserve currency. The weaknesses of the postwar British economy created much stress on the sterling, sparking a run on the currency in 1947 and devaluation in 1949. A mixture of internal and external constraints inhibited British economic growth. Internal constraints included inefficient industrial production, shortage of credit, and management-union relations. External constraints included persistent balance-of-payments deficits in addition to more financial and economic commitments than London could bear.[22] Despite its postwar recovery and low unemployment, the British economy had to endure several major adjustments due to a costly nationalization program, the Labour Party's creation of the welfare state, and the opening of the British pound sterling bloc—specifically, members of the British Empire and Commonwealth that had pegged their currencies to the pound sterling—to international trade.[23] Pressure on the sterling continued, with another devaluation occurring in 1967.[24]

Could the United States have exploited British vulnerabilities for nonproliferation ends? To be sure, shutting down a program when it is still in its planning stages is easier than shutting down one that has successfully produced nuclear weapons devices and has already received substantial government and military investment. The costs associated with compelling a British nuclear reversal of this magnitude would have been high for the

United States. Nevertheless, some American decision makers did consider the possibility of using economic levers to reduce Great Britain's nuclear capabilities. Senior American diplomat George Ball tried to persuade Johnson to do as much ahead of the president's meeting with the recently elected prime minister, Harold Wilson. Ball argued that Great Britain "cannot afford the resources and foreign exchange that go into the construction of the present four nuclear submarines." Rusk believed that London would benefit from canceling the Polaris program and reaping the savings. Both believed that an independent British nuclear capability complicated NATO decision-making and American nonproliferation objectives.[25] Johnson ultimately decided against using such tactics.

Nevertheless, the British nuclear weapons program had already lost some degree of independence. By the early 1970s, the nuclear deterrent force consisted of four nuclear submarines, each armed with sixteen Polaris A-3 missiles. Only one submarine would reliably be operational at a given time owing to the demands of refitting and overhauling after long patrols. The nuclear warheads and the submarines were of British manufacture. The MIRVs used on the missiles were also of British design.[26] Still, nuclear cooperation with the United States ceased again on Nixon's orders, leaving the British to modify the Polaris system on their own in response to perceived advances in Soviet missile technology.[27] Accordingly, London retained the ability to destroy Moscow and other Soviet industrial centers on its own with high probability even if the United States supplied parts of navigation, fire-control, and communications systems for the missiles.[28] Such technological reliance continues to this day: Great Britain uses the ballistic missile Trident II as its delivery system—a technology that Prime Minister Margaret Thatcher had to request from the United States in the early 1980s.[29]

Whether Johnson could have pressed further against Great Britain is a difficult counterfactual to assess. He had good reasons not to. Consistent with one of my propositions, other foreign policy goals can arise that inhibit the nonproliferation mission. As David James Gill writes, "[Johnson] remained reluctant to push nuclear issues when they threatened to undermine cooperation in more important areas. The president instead desired the continuation of Britain's international defense commitments, in order to share some of the Cold War burden and thus help his own increasingly costly policies in Vietnam."[30] Further complicating any campaign is that the United States would have still had to address the political problem that produced British nuclear interest in the first place. Why would Great Britain voluntarily surrender even a technologically dependent (but operationally independent) nuclear capability if the American security guarantees to Europe remained problematic? And so the final outcome may have been the best of all possible worlds: Great Britain could have its nuclear weapons program, while the United States would retain its technological supremacy.

France: An Insubordinate Nuclear-Armed Ally

France's interest in nuclear energy predated the Cold War. After all, the lab of Pierre and Marie Curie was where radioactive isotopes were first isolated. Their son-in-law Frédéric Joliot-Curie also undertook atomic research and, thanks to an appointment by de Gaulle following the Liberation, became the high commissioner for atomic energy.[31] Under his supervision the first French atomic reactor was built.[32] However, French government outfits and working groups aimed at nuclear weapons production first appeared at the end of 1954.[33] The Centre Saharien d'Expérimentations Militaires—which would oversee French nuclear tests in central Algeria—was established in 1957.[34] In the same year, France entered into a trilateral project with Italy and Germany (the F-I-G initiative) to research and to develop nuclear weapons, but some French government officials still did not want to upset Washington, since they wanted (and expected) American assistance to their own national nuclear program.[35] French nuclear ambitions thus preceded de Gaulle's 1958 return to power and the establishment of the Fifth Republic. Yet his influence on the French nuclear weapons program was significant. Upon becoming president, he canceled the F-I-G initiative, since he believed that France should arm only itself and not its allies, especially a West Germany of dubious intent. The French nuclear program accelerated thereafter and had ceased to be clandestine with a memorandum dated September 17, 1958, sent to Washington. In February 1960, France detonated a 70-kiloton nuclear weapon (four times the power of the bomb dropped over Hiroshima) in the Algerian desert.

Security was a primary motivation for France's nuclear weapons interest. The change in military thinking embodied by the New Look impressed on French decision makers the military value of nuclear weapons. French military leaders noted "the fact that Europe cannot be defended against an attack from the east without the use of atomic weapons leads to the acceptance of the principle that this weapon will be used, first of all to discourage the aggressor, and if necessary to defeat him."[36] Yet the New Look had one startling implication for them. As the *chef d'état-major* (or the French equivalent of the chair of the Joint Chiefs of Staff) believed, "the determining importance of atomic weapons is that from now on only those countries that possess their own arsenals of this type will conserve some degree of autonomy in defense and would be able to have a real influence in the development of common (defense) plans."[37] A French diplomat concurred with this assessment, observing that "an army deprived of atomic means will no longer be an army. . . . National independence, the autonomy of our diplomacy . . . demand that France make its own atomic effort in the military domain."[38] Thus, when the French National Assembly considered a treaty regarding the European Defense Community (EDC), one area that drew heavy criticism was a clause stipulating that all member states would be forbidden to undertake an atomic military program. Though out of government, de Gaulle charged that this treaty would reduce France to a permanent state of dependency.[39] These criticisms smack of prestige concerns, but at this time French leaders were disappointed that communist aggression in Indochina failed to elicit a nuclear response from the Eisenhower administration despite the rhetoric of the New Look.[40] That Washington took a hard-line approach against Paris and London during the Suez crisis also left a deep impression.[41] While France was still developing its first nuclear weapons, de Gaulle famously asked Eisenhower in 1959, "Will they [Eisenhower's successors] take the risk of devastating American cities so that Berlin, Brussels and Paris might remain free?"[42]

In contrast to Great Britain, France succeeded in retaining the full independence of its nuclear forces. What explains this difference? Why did the French nuclear deterrent not become folded into NATO or reliant on American technology?

The standard response to these questions might echo the prestige thesis and emphasize de Gaulle's strong personality. Consistent with what Hymans describes of oppositional nationalists, de Gaulle had a vision for French grandeur and pursued whichever military policy was necessary for advancing that vision.[43] Not all of his policies were rooted in such motives; his approach to the question of British participation in the EEC seems driven by interest group demands.[44] Nevertheless, as the prestige thesis would hold, his acute need to preserve French political sovereignty and diplomatic status influenced his military policies. The bomb was the most visible and tangible manifestation of de Gaulle's strategic vision. It was beyond compromise.

My argument is that economic and technological levers represent the best option for the United States to curb nuclear proliferation to the extent that the ally is susceptible to their use. On this score, Paris did not share London's vulnerabilities, allowing de Gaulle to have it relatively easy when dealing with the United States. To begin with, the economic circumstances he faced were more favorable than those faced by his Fourth Republic predecessors, to say nothing of his British counterparts. In the immediate postwar period, France was indeed in a state of dependency. Describing the postwar economic relationship between the United States and France, Philip Nord writes that the "France that emerged from the war was different indeed from what it had been before, but the change was not a welcome one. France was reduced to an economic satellite of the United States."[45] And yet over time the leaders of the Fourth Republic used their cunning to extract more favorable bargains from the United States.[46] France's economic development proceeded rapidly. When de Gaulle returned to power, France had already enjoyed the beginning of what would be termed as *les trentes glorieuses*—a thirty-year period of high economic growth.

France prospered despite the damage it endured in the two world wars and the false economic starts of the immediate postwar years. It was steadily becoming an economic powerhouse that benefited its highly productive and well-salaried citizens with one of the best standards of living in the world. Its growth rates for the years between 1950 and 1973 were among the highest in Europe and about twice as much as Great Britain.[47] Not all was rosy, however: French balance-of-payments did weaken over the course of the 1950s as a result of persistent reserve losses. Fighting colonial wars in Indochina and Algeria drove these losses.[48] But even this situation soon changed to the advantage of Paris, since both London and Washington saw growing deficits in their balance-of-payments. By 1965 France was converting its balance-of-payments excesses into gold, thereby generating pressure on the American dollar.[49] France went from depending on American economic power to challenging American efforts to preserve the integrity of the international economic order.[50]

Paris was thus able to pivot its diplomatic power to support either a continental European or a transatlantic vision for defense cooperation. Amid deepening suspicions regarding American alliance reliability, France had allies in West Germany and Italy with which it could pursue a continental vision.[51] Those countries were not always receptive to de Gaulle's overtures: the relationship between de Gaulle and Adenauer was uneven, and de Gaulle found Erhard's Atlanticist tilt distasteful.[52] Yet de Gaulle was not entirely hostile to Washington.[53] The American military presence in West Germany, after all, posed a welcomed constraint on that country's foreign policy ambitions. Still, structural conditions were permissive for de Gaulle to pursue an independent and assertive foreign policy in the 1960s, thus allowing him to reject American proposals for nuclear-sharing arrangements like the MLF, to retain the autonomy of its force de frappe, and even to withdraw France from NATO's military command structure in 1966. Washington had little choice but to respect the strength of Paris, even going so far as seeking its cooperation in the area of nuclear weapons by the late 1960s.[54]

Norway: An Abstaining Frontline Ally

Great Britain and France were two NATO members that had acquired nuclear weapons, whereas West Germany was on the front line and so coveted greater nuclear decision-making befitting of its status. Yet Norway was also on the front line in Cold War, albeit farther north on more difficult terrain. Though Norway was among the first to commit to the NPT, its military leaders briefly contemplated in the early Cold War period whether an independent nuclear arsenal was worthwhile. With a civilian nuclear industry dating back to the 1940s, Norway engaged in enrichment and reprocessing activities over the course of the 1960s.[55] By the late 1960s, however, Oslo became an active proponent of stringent nuclear safeguards for the IAEA to oversee.[56] To what extent did alliance considerations shape Norway's nuclear choices?

Norway benefited from a combination of geography and American nuclear extended guarantees. To be sure, Astrid Forland argues that Norwegian decision makers in the 1940s saw a military nuclear program as too expensive for a country that was still relatively poor.[57] The defense establishment considered it to be more cost-effective for the country to rely on the American nuclear deterrent. Yet costs might be more tolerable if the security environment were more threatening. Despite its shared borders with the Soviet Union and wartime experience with Nazi occupation, Norway enjoyed a favorable geographical position among its NATO allies. After all, the Soviet Union would have experienced great difficulty in invading Norway in a purely conventional military conflict. To attack Norwegian population centers by land from the north would have required the Soviet Union to traverse difficult terrain in addition to attacking neutral Sweden.[58] From the south, Soviet forces would have first had to overrun West Germany and Denmark. That is not to say that Norway held no interest for the Soviet Union. US Secretary of the Navy James Forrestal noted that "the acquisition of a common frontier with [Norway] in the Far North and the proximity of Norwegian territory to Murmansk, Russia's only ice-free port opening directly on the high sea, give Norway a very special place in Russian eyes."[59] However, Oslo could afford to be selective about the sort of alliance commitment it desired from Washington.

Despite being a founding member of NATO, Norway did not receive many security goods. It never hosted American military bases, only agreeing to store oil and provide airfields for American use should a crisis develop. Admittedly, the growing vulnerability of forward air bases that the United States could use lowered their appeal.[60] And only in the 1980s did U.S. Marines pre-position weapons, ammunition, vehicles, and other equipment in climate-controlled caves and buildings in central Norway to support a task force of over thirteen thousand Marines.[61] Earlier in the Cold War, however, the American presence was very limited. The Norwegian government even regulated access rights to allied naval and aerial units operating in and around Norwegian territory. Prime Minister Einar Gerhardsen announced at a 1957 NATO summit meeting that Norway would not host nuclear weapons on its territory.[62] A greater military presence would have courted political controversy. For one, domestic politics constrained Norwegian decision makers because of the desire to achieve cross-party consensus on foreign and defense policy even when the ruling Labour Party commanded a parliamentary majority. For another, Gerhardsen wished to reassure the Soviet Union of NATO's defensive nature.[63] This policy of détente was typical of the Nordic experience in the Cold War: the Scandinavian countries would embrace disarmament and social democracy while holding both the United States and the Soviet Union at bay.[64]

The case of Norway illustrates the ambivalent connection between nuclear proliferation and military alliances. It was a frontline state on NATO's so-called northern flank, but it expressed only a limited interest in hosting in-theater conventional weapons and hardly any in acquiring its own nuclear weapon capability. The threat environment might have militated against desiring either strong military assurances or a robust independent defense policy. Domestic politics was certainly a key factor, since Prime Minister Gerhardsen wished to forge a cross-party consensus on defense and foreign policy. He did not have a moral aversion to nuclear energy, since his government did agree to provide a heavy water reactor for Israel to use at Dimona, to say nothing of Norwegian shipments of heavy water for France's thermonuclear arsenal.[65] However, if Norwegian leaders had more severe threat assessments early in the Cold War, then perhaps they would have demanded greater security goods from the United States. This counterfactual could involve a full-fledged interest in nuclear weapons if the United States failed either to provide or to sustain military deployments on Norwegian territory.

Australia: The Archetypal Nuclear Proliferating Ally

Unlike Norway, Australia clearly engaged in nuclear proliferation–related behavior. Between 1956 and 1963, it tried to procure tactical nuclear weapons from Great Britain. When this effort failed, Australia began trying to develop its own indigenous nuclear capability. By the late 1960s, Australia had a ten-megawatt heavy-water moderated, enriched-uranium research reactor and a smaller reactor for physics experiments.[66] Australia signed the NPT in 1969, but Prime Minister John Gorton declared that "the treaty is not binding on us until it is ratified."[67] Under his leadership the Australian government sought to find a way to work around the NPT in light of its plans to develop a five hundred–megawatt nuclear power reactor. It even signed a secret nuclear cooperation agreement with France.[68] Nevertheless, Canberra ratified the NPT in 1973.

Australia nicely embodies the dynamics that my theory expects of most alliances: it became interested in nuclear weapons because of perceived gaps in its received security commitments, but it ended that interest on its own accord. To begin with, unease over British imperial defense arrangements in Asia prompted Australian decision makers to reevaluate their national armament policies. At this time, too, they were probing the nature of American defense planning and commitment. Despite being party to a security treaty with New Zealand and the United States, Australia unsatisfactorily received only a pledge that the United States would support them in a military crisis, mostly likely resulting from a Chinese intervention in Indochina.[69] Washington did not couple its pledge with in-theater conventional deployments. And so starting in the mid-1960s when Canberra embraced the notion of developing an indigenous nuclear weapons program, its security partnerships became even more problematic. Despite China's nuclear weapons detonation in 1964, British prime minister Harold Wilson announced in January 1968 that Great Britain would be withdrawing its forces from Southeast Asia and the Middle East ("East of Suez") over the next several years.[70] Worsening the deteriorating security situation was how the United States began to contemplate a military disengagement from Vietnam. Such was the context when nuclear weapons advocate Gorton served as Australia's prime minister.[71]

Did alliance coercion play any part in Australia's ultimate decision to ratify the NPT four years after signing it? The available evidence suggests it did not. Signing the treaty became a more acceptable proposition once West Germany and Japan also signed.[72] Nevertheless, Gorton believed that signing the treaty did not by itself foreclose the nuclear option. Moreover, domestic politics intervened. A faction within Gorton's Liberal Party successfully launched a leadership challenge against him, only to lose power eventually to the pro-disarmament Labor Party. Putting an end to Australia's nuclear ambitions, the Labor Party ratified the NPT. After all, a nuclear weapons program was too expensive, especially when the Labor Party was intent on instituting universal health care and free university education.[73] Thus, as Jim Walsh argues, explanations highlighting the role of American coercion in obtaining Australian commitments to the NPT are probably exaggerated.[74] Indeed, the irony is that the security concerns that prompted Australia's nuclear proliferation–related behavior in the first place should have intensified instead of softening when the decision to renounce nuclear weapons was made. The United States was pulling out of Vietnam amid domestic turmoil and improved relations with China. Despite such circumstances, Australian leaders seem to have accepted American promises of extended nuclear deterrence.[75] Similarly, Hymans finds that some Australian leaders were more concerned about entrapment by the United States than abandonment.[76] Australia renounced nuclear weapons for its own reasons.

Taiwan: A Persistent Proliferation Risk

Though it received its first nuclear reactor from the United States via the Atoms for Peace program in 1956, Taiwan began its nuclear weapons program in 1967.[77] The Taiwanese Institute for Nuclear Energy Research (INER) purchased a forty-megawatt heavy water reactor from Canada. Taiwan also received from Canada heavy water and twenty-five metric tons of natural uranium fuel rods, thereby giving the small East Asian country the possibility of producing at least ten kilograms of weapon-grade plutonium a year.

Additionally, INER built a small reprocessing laboratory.[78] In 1973, the Taiwan Research Reactor (TRR) became operational. Despite these efforts, Taiwan never acquired nuclear weapons. It represents an archetypal case in which the United States suppressed the nuclear ambitions of an ally. To what extent did alliance considerations really shape Taiwan's nuclear trajectory? I argue that abandonment fears were a major driver of Taipei's nuclear interest, but Washington has had uneven success in curbing its activities.

Abandonment fears intensified among Taiwanese decision makers following China's 1964 nuclear test. After all, the previous decade saw China threaten to use force against Taiwan so as to destroy the anticommunist Nationalist government in Taipei and to conclude definitively the Chinese Civil War. Although China lacked the means to mount a cross-strait invasion, vague nuclear threats issued by Eisenhower during the Taiwan Straits Crises arguably made Mao de-escalate.[79] Having his own nuclear arsenal might embolden Mao against Taipei and inoculate him against American threats. China's military capabilities alarmed President Chiang Kai-shek. He described to American officials that Chinese communists "already have three very disturbing capabilities which they are reserving mainly for use against Taiwan, viz.: short range missiles, submarines capable of operating effectively in Taiwan Strait, and MIG-21s."[80] Moreover, although Taiwan had been an American treaty ally since 1954, Chiang Kai-shek was already anticipating some sort of rapprochement between Washington and Beijing in the 1960s. Indeed, American military and intelligence support to Taiwan started to wane by the end of that decade.[81] Nor did Chiang Kai-shek agree with other American allies in East Asia on the Vietnam War. He saw that conflict as futile and believed that Washington should leave the war for Asians to fight.[82] What strategic uses Chiang Kai-shek had for nuclear weapons are difficult to determine, but if Taiwan were to acquire ballistic missiles, then it might have hoped to hold Chinese military assets and population centers at risk so as to deter a cross-straits invasion.

The counterproliferation effort that the United States mounted against Taiwan might have seemed to result in a satisfactory outcome, but the process was arduous and oftentimes inconclusive. To begin with, credible reassurance would have been hard to achieve when the United States seemed intent on improving, and later normalizing, diplomatic relations with China.[83] Not helpful, either, was Nixon's declared policy that the United States was retracting its military commitments from East Asia more generally. Washington did resort to applying nonmilitary tools to curb Taiwan's nuclear activities, but with varying degrees of success. In fact, the United States had been observing suspiciously Taiwanese nuclear activities since at least 1966, when it learned of Taiwanese efforts to obtain nuclear materials from Israel and nuclear reactors from West Germany.[84] Little mystery seemed to swirl around Taiwan's intentions. As one embassy airgram from June 1966 notes,

"At the direction of President Chiang, the GRC Defense Ministry continues to try to develop an atomic weapon and delivery system, according to a source close to the effort. The President has overridden the advice of Lt. General T'ang Chun-po, Vice Minister of Defense who also heads up the defense scientific program; T'ang believes the attempt impractical and beyond ROC [Taiwan] resources. Thus far the GRC has been frustrated in its efforts to procure the necessary nuclear materials and has been similarly unsuccessful in its attempts to hire scientists from abroad to work on the project."[85] The local American embassy had no illusions as to what was afoot in Taiwan. Funny enough, in a case where the dog of alliance coercion did not bark, the United States could not prevent Taiwan from acquiring the West German nuclear reactor, since Bonn insisted that the reactor would have IAEA safeguards. Nevertheless, Taiwan did not receive the nuclear reactor, because its costs sparked too much bureaucratic controversy.[86]

Taiwan remained undaunted in its attempts to import nuclear technology. In 1972, Taiwanese government officials approached a West German firm to discuss the "delivery of *parts* to an ROC reprocessing plant (not a complete plant), as well as a contract for design and construction of such a plant."[87] Because Taiwan lost recognition of its sovereignty to China at the United Nations, any attempt to impose IAEA safeguards would be challenging, despite how "such a plant reprocesses spent reactor cores and also produces significant quantities of plutonium, an essential component of nuclear weapons."[88] The next year saw the State Department tussle with Taiwan over this potential purchase, having informed the Taiwanese foreign minister that the United States opposed it.[89] In a repeat of what happened before, Taiwan signed a contract with the West German firm UHDE to acquire the reprocessing plant only to see the purchase canceled. Washington had this time notified Taipei and Bonn of its objections. This time Bonn successfully pressured UHDE to terminate the deal, but Taipei insisted that its nuclear intentions were peaceful.[90]

As Taiwan persisted in its proliferation-related behavior, the United States sought to collect information, sometimes collaborating with Great Britain.[91] In 1973, the American embassy learned of a Canadian research reactor, which it deemed to be a "military secret," that Taiwan imported.[92] But despite the 1968 embassy airgram that plainly stated that Taiwan was seeking nuclear weapons, the State Department itself seemed hesitant to draw definitive conclusions. Its Bureau of Intelligence and Research found "at present no plans for proceeding to systematically undertake the development of nuclear weapons. We have no evidence of such plans, or of plans to acquire a nuclear delivery capability—the lack of which would substantially diminish the value of nuclear weapons to the ROC."[93] Suspicions abounded, and American officials were dismayed when they learned that Taiwan was intent on developing a nuclear reprocessing plant. The Atomic Energy Commission's international director warned that "it would be extremely imprudent for the ROC to begin planning for a reprocessing plant and that he wished to discourage the ROC from proceeding with any such plans."[94] Some diplomats became frustrated. William H. Gleysteen observed that "we cannot guarantee that certain people will not continue to nudge [Taiwan] into activities associated with a nuclear weapons program but short of a flat statement to Premier Chiang I think we have done everything possible to underscore the firmness of our position."[95] But uncertainty over Taiwan's intentions began to dissipate, and by late 1974, CIA analysts asserted that "Taipei conducts its small nuclear program with a weapon option clearly in mind, and it will be in a position to fabricate a nuclear device after five years or so."[96]

A cat-and-mouse game ensued despite Taiwan's alleged dependence on the United States. The Ford administration issued a demarche to Taiwan so that it would abandon its nuclear weapons program. Kissinger even cautioned the American ambassador in Taipei that "Fonmin Shen [the Taiwanese foreign minister] will reiterate assurances that ROC will not develop nuclear weapons and will not seek to acquire a national reprocessing facility. In that event you should refrain from expressing satisfaction with such assurances. . . . We do not wish to convey impression that matter is closed."[97] Kissinger's concerns were well founded. Within months of the demarche, more intelligence emerged that concerned Taiwan's nuclear activities.[98] Even during the Carter administration, unsafeguarded ports at TRR were discovered, prompting more assurances from Taipei as to its nuclear intentions. Washington subsequently demanded that Taipei "include all present and future ROC nuclear facilities and materials under the US/ROC bilateral agreement for cooperation . . . terminate all fuel cycle activities and reorient facilities involving or leading to weapons-usable materials" and "transfer all present holdings of plutonium to the US under appropriate compensatory arrangements."[99] Taiwan eventually acquiesced to these demands, in part because of extreme pressure that the United States put on it. Thereafter, Carter's national security adviser declared that "the American effort to crack down on this project clearly yielded its desired results."[100] Such optimism might have been premature: the United States discovered a secret uranium enrichment program that it later shut down in the summer of 1978. As President Chiang observed, the United States could handle Taiwan "in a fashion which few other countries would tolerate."[101]

The American intelligence community continued to monitor its actions, and for good reason: Taiwan's nuclear proliferation–related behavior did not really end in the 1970s. Taiwan experimented with plutonium separation in the early 1980s, and the INER began construction of a hot cell facility where scientists could perform reprocessing experiments.[102] Fortunately for the United States, its intelligence services had infiltrated the INER: American-trained deputy director Col. Chang Hsien-yi defected from Taiwan and revealed the scope of its illicit nuclear activities. The United States subsequently worked with the IAEA to shut down this new facility. Washington also forced Taipei to close its heavy water reactor after threatening to cease heavy water shipments.[103] Even with democratization and greater market liberalization, suspicion hangs over Taiwan's nuclear ambitions. In July 1995, shortly after China test-fired missiles that landed near the island, President Lee Teng-hui publicly suggested that Taiwan's nuclear weapons policy should be reconsidered, later proclaiming that Taiwan "has the ability to develop nuclear weapons but will not develop" them.[104]

Washington did apply coercive pressure on Taipei to curb its nuclear activities. Since Taiwan failed to acquire nuclear weapons, and has had to resort to much duplicity and secrecy in its proliferation-related behavior, such coercion appears to have been effective. However, the protracted character of this counterproliferation effort reveals the difficulties associated with suppressing a determined state's appetite for nuclear weapons, even when that state is as diplomatically isolated and as dependent on its guarantor for economic *and* security goods as Taiwan. These difficulties might have resulted from the uncertainty over how much the United States would punish nuclear proliferation at the time. Nicholas Miller claims that because the Symington Amendment—which banned American economic and military assistance to countries that do not comply with IAEA regulations and inspections with regard to enrichment technology—was only passed in June 1976 and went into effect in August 1977, Taiwanese officials were unsure as to "exactly how far the US government would go to enforce congressional dictates."[105] They halted their efforts once they learned of the stiff penalties that they would receive if they continued certain nuclear activities. The problem with his account is that only within a year of this uncertainty being resolved did the United States discover yet another secret uranium enrichment program, to say nothing of the secret reprocessing program disclosed by the CIA agent about a decade later. The real secret to success lies not with the economic sanctions that Taiwan wished to avoid, as Miller argues, but with the American intelligence efforts that detected those programs. William Burr is thus correct in observing that "the repeated U.S. interventions in Taipei's nuclear affairs show the great difficulty of imposing nonproliferation standards even on friendly client states."[106] And so Taiwan may have been so resilient precisely because its decision makers had judged that they had little to lose. It had lost its treaty alliance with the United States in 1979 and subsequently had to accept weaker, less committal measures such as arms sales through the 1979 Taiwan Relations Act and the 1982 Six Assurances despite the gathering strength of China.

The cases examined in this chapter further illustrate that the record of military alliances in curbing nuclear proliferation is more mixed and ambiguous than some accounts suggest. To be sure, perceptions of security commitments mattered for those states that did embark on proliferation-related behavior. France sensed its interests were diverging from those of the United States, Australia did not receive the military commitments it wanted, and Taiwan came to realize that its interests were becoming out of step with those of the United States as China became a potential balancer to the Soviet Union. For its part, Norway represents the least straightforward case. Its frontline status in the Cold War notwithstanding, Norwegian leaders had little interest in hosting in-theater American deployments (until the 1980s) or acquiring nuclear weapons.

These additional cases also demonstrate that alliance coercion has at best a spotty record. Australia gave up on nuclear weapons for domestic reasons, and Taiwan demonstrated a unique persistence in spite of the best efforts of the United States. Great Britain eventually saw its nuclear arsenal at least partially subordinated to the United States, especially when we consider its technological reliance. Yet this dependency arose less from an active American campaign to reverse Great Britain's nuclear status and more from Great Britain's economic and technological weaknesses early in the Cold War. France was so strong that it did not have those weaknesses that the United States could exploit. Put together, the cases highlight that the connection between military alliances and nuclear proliferation is not as clear-cut as many accounts suggest.

Conclusion

Understanding and Managing Alliances in the 21st Century

How do alliances curb potential or actual cases of nuclear proliferation, if at all? Many scholars argue that alliances are effective tools for bridling the nuclear ambitions of states. When allies do try to acquire nuclear weapons, their alliance relationships serve as conduits for the guarantor to coerce a nonproliferation outcome. In this book, I show that such optimism about the role military alliances play is overstated. Alliances can deter nuclear proliferation if they marry written pledges of support with compatible foreign policy and defense doctrines as well as in-theater conventional deployments. Yet alliances are prone to severe adjustments that can unsettle the ally. When guarantors make major unilateral changes to the security relationship, through undesirable doctrinal announcements or troop withdrawals, abandonment fears intensify. The affected ally becomes so doubtful of its received guarantees that it becomes more likely to engage in nuclear proliferation–related behavior. Unfortunately for the guarantor, curbing such behavior once it has started is very difficult. It requires fixing the broken security guarantee that prompted the nuclear interest in the first place. Nonmilitary tools like economic sanctions may be the best coercive instruments available, but their viability depends on the extent to which the ally relies on the guarantor. Simply put, alliances are better for deterring potential than for preventing actual nuclear proliferation.

The empirical cases support this argument. Table 2 summarizes the main findings. Fears of abandonment in West Germany intensified after July 1956 amid rumors that the Eisenhower administration would reduce the size of the US Army by a third. Shortly thereafter, West Germany joined France and Italy in a short-lived and unsuccessful effort to develop nuclear weapons. Throughout the subsequent decade, Bonn deflected calls for it to make clear nonproliferation pledges while obtaining enrichment and reprocessing capabilities. Its alliance with the United States certainly constrained its decision-making, but arguments that distinct coercion episodes prompted West

Table 2 Summary of the main cases

Explanation	Start	Stop	Start	Stop	Start	Stop
	West Germany		Japan		South Korea	
Alliance	✓	✗	✓	✗	✓	○
Adversary	✗	✗	✓	✗	✗	✗
Domestic	✗	✓	✗	○	✗	✗
Prestige	✓	✓	✓	○	✓	○

✓ denotes empirical support, ✗ little to no empirical support, and ○ inconclusiveness.

German leaders to renounce nuclear proliferation are overstated. Domestic politics and prestige considerations were important factors as well.

Japan followed a somewhat similar trajectory. It began evaluating the strength of its received security guarantees more fastidiously following China's nuclear device detonation in late 1964. Yet Japan did not begin making serious moves in investing in nuclear technology until the prospect of American withdrawal from Vietnam and even East Asia became highly likely at the end of the decade. Similarly to West Germany, Japan did not have an actual program dedicated to the production of an indigenous nuclear weapons capability. But like that of West Germany, Japan's stance toward nuclear nonproliferation remained dubious. When Japan finally ratified the NPT, it did so largely because of domestic politics. Ideational arguments about the inherent value of the bomb were also influential. The United States provided assurances when asked to do so but had largely refrained from efforts to compel Japan into making nonproliferation commitments. Nevertheless, some controversy ensued not long after NPT ratification regarding activities at a Japanese reprocessing plant.

South Korea had a clear intent to acquire nuclear weapons. Despite South Korea's weathering various provocations by North Korea, what triggered South Korea to seek nuclear weapons was Nixon's unexpected announcement that the United States would withdraw one US Army division from the peninsula. Thankfully for Washington, South Korea depended on the United States for economic and technological goods, thus rendering South Korea vulnerable to American efforts in suppressing the program in 1976. Still, South Korea's interest in nuclear weapons was not entirely snuffed out. Some speculate that the program went further underground. Whatever the truth, safeguard violations did occur in the 1980s.

Although I have not studied them at the same level of detail, the five smaller cases further corroborate the argument. Great Britain and France both sought nuclear weapons in part because of having to fight alone and without American support. What distinguishes Great Britain from France is that Great Britain came to depend on American technology for its nuclear deterrent. Great Britain still retains operational independence, but the French nuclear arsenal is fully autonomous from the United States. For its part, Norway remained satisfied with the security provided by the United States, so much so that it rejected having much of an American conventional military presence until the 1980s when it accepted pre-positioned gear from the US Marine Corps. Only very briefly at the beginning of the Cold War did Norwegian military leaders consider nuclear weapons. By contrast, Australia wanted more alliance goods but had no guarantor—whether the United States or Great Britain—that would supply them. On the basis of its security fears, Australia had a nuclear weapons program that it eventually renounced following a change in government. Alliance coercion arguably played no part. Finally, Taiwan began its attempt to produce nuclear weapons once it sensed that the geopolitical tide was turning against it. The United States gradually seemed more open to accommodating China, which had by that point come to possess nuclear weapons. What ensued was a cat-and-mouse game that spanned about two decades. The United States used different levers to ensure that Taiwan would not go nuclear, but its success in restraining Taiwan's ambitions appears to have had more to do with intelligence than with sanctions per se.

The takeaway of this book is that alliances are better for deterring states from engaging in nuclear proliferation–related behavior than for compelling states to give up their nuclear weapons programs. In this chapter, I address the implications for theory and policy. In so doing, I outline possible avenues for future research as well as how my analysis sheds light on contemporary policy problems.

Theoretical Implications

My argument has several theoretical implications for how we should think about key questions in international relations theory. First, I show that my analysis bears on a contemporary debate in international relations regarding how beliefs about credibility are formed. Second, I argue that scholars are wrong to divide the study of nuclear weapons from that of conventional military power. Third, I add to the growing scholarship on the effectiveness of coercion in international relations by considering the alliance politics of nuclear proliferation.

THE BASIS OF CREDIBILITY

One major debate among international relations scholars concerns the basis of credibility: what makes threats—and, for that matter, promises—believable? A dominant school of thought holds that assessments of credibility turn on situational considerations like the war-fighting capabilities and geopolitical stakes involved behind the threats or promises that states make to one another.[1] Policy makers are thus foolish to believe that they can develop reputations on the basis of their historical record for keeping or breaking commitments. This perspective has received criticism. For one, past actions communicate—intentionally or not—the interests that states have, whereas situational assessments depend partly on the historical record.[2] For another, this school of thought has mischaracterized the work of Thomas Schelling, which it has held responsible for the belief that commitments are so interdependent that reputations for keeping commitments are necessary for deterrence. Schelling instead argued that past actions matter in cases where states are continuously negotiating with each other, not in all coercive bargaining encounters.[3]

My findings further challenge the perspective that current, ahistorical calculations of power and interest determine credibility. I find that in attending to the foreign policy doctrines and conventional military deployments of their guarantors, allies accord importance to the local military effectiveness of their guarantors. Still, some actions undertaken by the guarantor can provide information as to its interests and foreign policy interests, especially if those actions include major and unfavorable military redeployments. In brief, my findings blur the distinction between reputation, on the one hand, and current calculations like power and interest, on the other hand. To be sure, I do not offer a systematic test as to the sources of alliance credibility. I examined narrowly how abandonment fears intensify so as to make states more likely to engage in nuclear proliferation–related behavior. Scholars should thus focus more on alliance credibility as a dependent variable.

NUCLEAR WEAPONS AND CONVENTIONAL MILITARY POWER

States form judgments about the security guarantees that they receive with reference to the conventional military capabilities that their guarantor could muster on their behalf for defense and deterrence purposes. The reason why allies look to the conventional capabilities of their guarantor is that they value deterrence-by-denial as much as they do deterrence-by-punishment, if not more. Indeed, from the perspective of allies like West Germany and especially South Korea, nuclear weapons are partly a means for offsetting the conventional superiority of adversaries, especially when those same adversaries possess nuclear weapons as well.

Unfortunately, scholars separate the study of nuclear weapons from that of conventional military power. Many studies of nuclear proliferation simply assume that nuclear weapons represent a special category, even though the factors that predict which states have nuclear weapons can also predict which states would have access to fifth-generation fighter jets, third-generation advanced tanks, ballistic missile capabilities, and so forth.[4] In social scientific parlance, these studies neglect an important endogeneity problem, whereby conventional and nuclear weapons systems are related to each other. States that experience unfavorable alterations in their received security guarantees might opt for nuclear weapons, because they cannot develop sufficient conventional military capabilities for deterring an adversary in time. Some states, like Great Britain and France, acquire nuclear weapons because they already have most leading military technologies. Interestingly, the best works on conventional deterrence and military power neglect the nuclear dimension altogether.[5] To take one example, excluding the role nuclear weapons have played in the Arab-Israeli conflict—as John Mearsheimer has done—could lead to mistaken understandings of how deterrence in general succeeds.[6]

THE EFFECTIVENESS OF COERCION

The core message of this book is that military alliances are better at preventing nuclear proliferation than stopping it once it has started. I have presented evidence that apparent success stories of alliance coercion are less than what they appear. What does this finding mean more generally for international relations scholarship?

Schelling famously wrote that compellence is harder than deterrence because the former seeks to change the status quo, whereas the latter seeks to maintain it. Much of the recent literature seems to support this maxim, notwithstanding the difficulties in empirically distinguishing deterrence from compellence.[7] Drawing on data regarding compellent threats, Todd Sechser observes that strong states have trouble compelling weaker states because those weaker states worry that capitulation would lead to new demands. Their very strength leads strong states to underappreciate these reputational concerns.[8] Using similar data, Todd Sechser and Matthew Fuhrmann show that nuclear weapons rarely confer any bargaining leverage on its possessors, since they are useless for territorial conquest and involve high costs as tools for punishment.[9] Dianne Chamberlain finds that because using military force has become less costly for the United States, weak adversaries discount its threats.[10] Dan Altman argues that states do not even bother with coercion at all in making territorial gains—they grab what they want rather than dispute a proposed territorial division in a crisis.[11] Some disagreement exists among scholars. Kyle Beardsley and Victor Asal write that "the possession of nuclear weapons helps states to succeed in their confrontations with other states even when they do not 'use' these weapons," whereas Matthew Kroenig argues that nuclear superiority confers an advantage in crisis bargaining.[12]

All these studies, however, focus on coercive bargaining between adversaries rather than between allies. When scholars examine military or nonmilitary threats that states make to their allies, the issue-area under dispute usually revolves around nuclear proliferation.[13] My case studies show that alliance coercion in this domain is often difficult for the United States to do effectively. That is not to say that alliance coercion is never effective. Such a view would be sorely mistaken. Rather, my argument is that its effect is more subtle and indirect than commonly presumed. Still, a more general or comparative study of intra-alliance coercion would benefit international relations scholarship—one that encompasses other issues such as wartime coalition participation and peacetime burden-sharing.[14] Many empirical questions still need an answer. For example, is alliance coercion more effective in some issue areas than in others? Why or why not?

THE NUCLEAR SOURCES OF AMERICAN PRIMACY

The case studies also suggest that to understand the preponderant role of the United States in international politics, we should not overlook the nuclear dimension. Unfortunately, many existing theories of hierarchy and hegemony often view the world in largely conventional military terms, as the books of David Lake and John Ikenberry do.[15] This oversight is problematic for the very reason that whatever one thinks of the global military presence of the United States, it is at least partly the product of a consistent desire to forestall nuclear proliferation. Daniel Deudney adds that "unipolarity, to the extent it still exists, is made much easier and more durable by nuclear weapons" because the deterrent effects they generate help stabilize interstate relations and inhibit encroachment and counterbalancing.[16] Nuclear proliferation undercuts hegemony because it negates American power projection capabilities.

Claiming that nonproliferation has been as much a goal of American grand strategy as openness and containment might be a slight overstatement, however.[17] Sometimes other foreign policy goals get in the way—the Kennedy administration discovered this tension when it came to value nuclear nonproliferation while voicing its frustrations with the defense and monetary policies of West Germany. On occasion foreign policy goals are complementary so as to reinforce each other: quashing Taiwan's nuclear ambitions was important for Sino-American relations. Moreover, the United States has good reason not to enshrine nuclear nonproliferation as an overriding priority that trumps all other foreign policy objectives: states would have an incentive to manipulate American interest in nonproliferation. Accordingly, despite what realists say about the lack of a central enforcer of rules in the international system, states would be able to "dial 911" for help by signaling some intent to acquire nuclear weapons.[18] But partly because the United States has conflicting foreign policy interests, this option remains problematic for allies to use.

The nuclear dimension of American global leadership might, then, be more complicated than what seems to be the case at first glance. If the United States views nonproliferation as a goal unto itself, then it might be an offensive realist: that is, it uses whatever means to secure regional—if not global—hegemony at the expense of other states.[19] In contrast, if nonproliferation is a goal that is either subordinate or complementary to other interests, then the United States might be a defensive realist. In other words, it might not see nuclear proliferation as problematic per se and can in fact be open to it, but it sometimes works hard to forestall it lest the spread of nuclear weapons would complicate other foreign policy objectives.[20]

GREAT POWER MANAGEMENT OF WEAKER STATES

This book addresses how American security guarantees can forestall nuclear proliferation. It does not investigate how the security guarantees of other major powers—namely, the Soviet Union and China—can affect the nuclear interest of their own security partners.

My argument has implications for understanding nuclear proliferation and nonproliferation within non-American alliance systems. Consider first the Soviet Union and its alliances.[21] Romania was the only Warsaw Pact member out of seven to covet nuclear weapons, whereas both East Asian allies—China and North Korea—made efforts to acquire nuclear weapons in the Cold War with varying degrees of success. Despite the contiguity of the Soviet Union with all those countries, its security guarantees to them varied in quality. For better or for worse, none of these countries held the Soviet geopolitical interest and hosted Soviet armed forces to the same extent, if at all, as the industrialized Northern Tier of the Warsaw Pact (Poland, East Germany, and Czechoslovakia).[22] Romania might have been a member of the Warsaw Pact, but it perceived a growing disconnect between its security interests and those of the Kremlin between the late 1950s and early 1960s. In particular, it did not wish to be consigned to being the soft agricultural underbelly of the Soviet bloc.[23] Moreover, the Soviet Union accorded so much significance to its holdings in Central and Eastern Europe that it cared less about developments in East Asia. Chinese and North Korean leaders might have reached this conclusion in the 1950s when the Soviet Union appeared disinterested in the fate of its communist partners during the Korean War.[24] Those countries thus discounted Soviet support early and decided to develop nuclear weapons. And so the dynamics outlined in this book could very well be applicable to the Soviet context.[25]

My argument bears insights for how China has managed the North Korean proliferation problem. Interestingly, North Korea began considering whether to acquire nuclear technologies shortly after China withdrew its forces from North Korea in 1958.[26] North Korea had good reason to discount Chinese security guarantees, formalized as they were with a 1961 mutual defense treaty. After all, China came to North Korea's aid in the Korean War only when American-led forces approached the Yalu River. As Jonathan Pollack writes, Pyongyang "faced four decades of continuous nuclear threat . . .

without a countervailing nuclear retaliatory threat of its own or allied nuclear deployments on its own territory."[27]

But what has China done about North Korea? A common refrain is that China can and should do more to curb its ally's destabilizing ambitions, especially since China is the main source of North Korea's trade, food, arms, and energy.[28] Despite how scholars sometimes argue that guarantors seek to prevent nuclear proliferation in order to preserve their standing and power projection capabilities, China appears exceptional in having shielded its ally from multilateral sanctions for the most part. One can argue that it has even free-ridden on American efforts to restrain Taiwan and South Korea without doing much of the same toward North Korea. However, my analysis yields two notes of caution. The first is that China might have perceived that reversing North Korea's nuclear program was not in China's interest, especially if China's worries about regime stability, refugee flows, and a reunified Korea are legitimate. The second is that experts might be overestimating China's ability to restrain its ally, especially when North Korea has by now developed certain missile capabilities and thermonuclear weapons. To be sure, Beijing could have at least forbidden North Korean citizens from receiving training in China—scientists who probably went on to participate in advanced weapons development in their native country.[29] Still, in the improbable event that North Korea renounces its nuclear weapons, it would likely do so for non-alliance reasons.

Policy Implications

The policy implications of this study seem grim. Not only does the denuclearization of North Korea seem fantastical, but also any move toward acquiring nuclear weapons on the part of an ally would be extraordinarily difficult for the United States to reverse. The policy community should take small comfort in how American decision makers have restrained the ambitions of South Korea, Taiwan, and West Germany. The successes of those decision makers were at best overstated.

Yet there are upsides. One is that the United States *can* deter nuclear weapons interest among its allies. Given how vital strong security guarantees are toward this end, American decision makers thankfully have a say. More specifically, they can recalibrate doctrines and deployments so as to shape perceptions of credibility. Ally leaders appear to refer to these metrics in their own nuclear decision-making. We should thus remember that it is of the utmost importance that American defense planners take the time to think about the effects of their moves from more than just a budgetary or rational perspective. Having Marines in Okinawa might make little tactical or operational sense, but shifting them thousands of miles away could still be destabilizing. Symbols matter, and they may matter more from the perspective of allies than from the perspective of Washington.[30] Nevertheless, the symbolic nature of such deployments should not be overstated. Allies value them because they believe such forces can put up a fight against an adversary should deterrence fail. In a world of anti-access and area denial (A2/AD) military technology, a United States that practices offshore balancing might experience overwhelming difficulties in entering a theater of operations so as to aid an ally under siege. An onshore presence makes the United States look more capable and resolved to allies and adversaries alike.[31] That said, withdrawing forces unilaterally might be counterproductive when it comes to having an ally bear a greater share of the collective defense burden. If the ally feels threatened by a nuclear-armed aggressor, then it might arm itself in ways that are to the detriment of the guarantor's own interests.

Another upside is that decoupling does not make nuclear proliferation inevitable.[32] Because North Korea is developing capabilities so that it could strike the continental United States with nuclear weapons, some observers fear that Washington would become less likely to defend South Korea and Japan in order to avoid being attacked. Accordingly, those two allies sense that their interests are becoming decoupled from that of the United States and so would strive to secure themselves nuclear weapons of their own. Yet this fear is overstated. For one, they have already endured decoupling throughout the Cold War and after the Soviet Union and China had acquired survivable second-strike capabilities. For another, my analysis suggests that decoupling need not translate to nuclear proliferation as long as those allies believe that the United States would fight on their behalf and deny adversaries battlefield success. Providing hostages for the sake of extended deterrence is insufficient. Having aligned doctrines and in-theater deployments capable of inflicting harm on the adversary can influence such beliefs in a positive direction.

Perceptions of credibility are malleable, but we must be careful not to overstate idiosyncratic factors. Many analysts and experts worry that President Donald Trump's unique style of communication can undercut deterrence and destabilize alliance relations. For example, in an excellent overview of his attitudes toward nuclear weapons, Jeffrey Michaels and Heather Williams caution that his use of social media could lead to misperceptions and miscalculations by friends and foes alike.[33] According to this argument, an errant tweet would undermine American credibility. My analysis suggests that such concerns may be slightly exaggerated. A tweet is but one signal among many. Allies like South Korea and Poland will pay more attention to the military basis of their received commitments than to Twitter accounts in going about their nuclear decision-making.

Allies that host large-scale American forward-deployed forces might learn the wrong lessons from this book. Specifically, they might feel that they would be unstoppable if they elect to seek nuclear weapons after determining that their received commitments are not as strong as they used to be.

That the United States would likely experience immense difficulties in suppressing their activities could even embolden them. Yet those allies should remember that most countries that flirted with nuclear proliferation ultimately decided against acquiring their own arsenals, not least because they reasoned that nuclear weapons did not serve their interests, political or military. Though Taiwan and Poland have dramatically different relationships with the United States, they would do well to heed this lesson. Poland has already begun investing in A2/AD to deter Russian aggression, whereas Taiwan should do the same thing with respect to China. In both cases, they have a special interest in bolstering their nonproliferation credentials. Any ambiguity might undermine the deterrent value of their conventional A2/AD capabilities if their adversary worries that an incoming cruise missile might be nuclear tipped. As such, Russia and China could escalate tensions when faced with the prospect of nuclear proliferation in their neighborhood—something that we have seen when fears of West German nuclearization led Khrushchev to harden his line over the status of Berlin.

Some security experts argue that a new, more dangerous age in international security is upon us. This gloomy vision holds that unlike in the Cold War, the prevention of nuclear wars no longer depends on the superpowers—the United States and the Soviet Union—managing their competition rationally. Rather, a multipolar nuclear order beckons as states in the Middle East, Asia, and even Europe may come to see nuclear weapons as essential for their security.[34] Much is at stake if growth in the number of nuclear weapons states means a greater risk of nuclear mishaps or even accidental nuclear war.

Perhaps such pessimism is warranted amid the Teutonic shifts in international politics that attend the rise of China and the apparent decline of the United States. Yet the view that the future is unlike the past is an overstatement. American security commitments will come under stress, just as they have in the past. The difference may well be that the United States would not have the same clout over its allies as before if predictions of its relative decline are correct. If the United States had trouble suppressing the nuclear interest of industrializing allies like South Korea and Taiwan in the 1970s, then future nonproliferation efforts will be much more hard-pressed to achieve success. Nevertheless, as in the past, the United States may well continue to hold sufficiently strong military and technological capabilities over adversaries.[35] As such, allies' behavior could reflect how the United States decides to allocate its strategic attention and military resources more so than deep structural trends. Nuclear proliferation among allies is not inevitable, but the choice is for the United States to make in order to prevent it from happening.

Notes

JSP	Japan Socialist Party
KAERI	Korean Atomic Energy Research Institute
LBJL	LBJ Presidential Library
LDP	Liberal Democratic Party
MAD	mutually assured destruction
MIRV	multiple independently targetable reentry vehicle
MLF	Multilateral Force
MRBM	medium-range ballistic missile
MX	Missile-eXperimental
NARA	National Archives and Records Administration
NATO	North Atlantic Treaty Organization
NIE	National Intelligence Estimate
NPG	Nuclear Planning Group
NPIHP	Nuclear Proliferation International History Project
NPT	nonproliferation treaty
NRX	heavy water nuclear reactor
NSA	National Security Archive
NSAM	National Security Action Memorandum
NSC	National Security Council
PNE	peaceful nuclear explosion
RAC	Remote Archives Capture
RG	Record Group
RMNL	Richard M. Nixon Library
ROC	Republic of China
ROK	Republic of Korea
SALT	Strategic Arms Limitation Treaty
SDP	Social Democratic Party
SEATO	Southeast Asia Treaty Organization
TRR	Taiwan Research Reactor
WEC	Weapons Exploitation Committee

Introduction

1. Telegram from Embassy in Seoul to the Department of State, June 13, 1977, Jimmy Carter Presidential Library, Atlantic, GA, Remote Archive Capture (RAC) Project Number NLC-16-11-2-17-2.

2. On alliances and moral hazard, see Brett V. Benson, *Constructing International Security: Alliance, Deterrence, and Moral Hazard* (New York: Cambridge University Press, 2012).

3. On the alliance dilemma, see Glenn Snyder, *Alliance Politics* (Ithaca, NY: Cornell University Press, 1997), 187–188. The alliance dilemma should not be confused with the alliance security dilemma, described in Glenn Snyder, "The Security Dilemma in Alliance Politics," *World Politics* 36, no. 4 (1984): 461–495.

4. James D. Morrow, "Alliances: Why Write Them Down?," *Annual Review of Political Science* 3 (2000): 63–83.

5. G. John Ikenberry, *After Victory: Institutions, Strategic Restraint, and the Rebuilding of Order after Major Wars* (Princeton, NJ: Princeton University Press, 2001).

6. Tongfi Kim, "Why Alliances Entangle but Seldom Entrap States," *Security Studies* 20, no. 3 (2011): 350–377; and Michael Beckley, "The Myth of Entangling Alliances: Reassessing the Security Risks of US Defense Pacts," *International Security* 39, no. 4 (2015): 7–48.

7. Scott D. Sagan, "Why Do States Build Nuclear Weapons? Three Models in Search of a Bomb," *International Security* 21, no. 3 (1996–1997): 54–86; Avery Goldstein, *Deterrence and Security in the 21st Century: China, Britain, France, and the Enduring Legacy of the Nuclear Revolution* (Stanford, CA: Stanford University Press, 2000); Nuno P. Monteiro and Alexandre Debs, "The Strategic Logic of Nuclear Proliferation," *International Security* 39, no. 2 (2014): 7–51; and T. V. Paul, *Power versus Prudence: Why Nations Forgo Nuclear Weapons* (Montreal: McGill-Queen's University Press, 2000).

8. Philipp C. Bleek, *When Did (and Didn't) States Proliferate: Chronicling the Spread of Nuclear Weapons* (Cambridge, MA: Belfer Center for Science and International Affairs, 2017).

9. Jacques E. C. Hymans, *The Psychology of Nuclear Proliferation: Identity, Emotions, and Foreign Policy* (New York: Cambridge University Press, 2006); and Etel Solingen, *Nuclear Logics: Contrasting Paths in East Asia and the Middle East* (Princeton, NJ: Princeton University Press, 2007).

10. Nicholas L. Miller, "The Secret Success of Nonproliferation Sanctions," *International Organization* 68, no. 4 (2014): 913–944.

11. Gene Gerzhoy, "Alliance Coercion and Nuclear Restraint: How the United States Thwarted West Germany's Nuclear Ambitions," *International Security* 39, no. 4 (2015): 91–129; and Francis J. Gavin, "Strategies of Inhibition: US Grand Strategy, the Nuclear Revolution, and Nonproliferation," *International Security* 40, no. 1 (2015): 9–46. See also Or Rabinowitz and Nicholas L. Miller, "Keeping the Bombs in the Basement: US Nonproliferation Policy toward Israel, South Africa, and Pakistan," *International Security* 40, no. 1 (2015): 47–86.

12. Michael A. Hunzeker and Alexander Lanoszka, "Landpower and American Credibility," *Parameters* 45, no. 4 (2015–2016): 17–26.

13. The ambiguity of the West German case—as indicated by how scholars as diverse as Gene Gerzhoy and Andreas Lutsch treat it—reflects a deeper controversy over how to conceptualize nuclear behavior more generally. See Itty Abraham, "The Ambivalence of Nuclear Histories," *Osiris* 21, no. 1 (2006): 49–65.

1. How Alliances (Mis)Manage Nuclear Proliferation

1. Michael N. Barnett and Jack S. Levy, "Domestic Sources of Alliances and Alignments: The Case of Egypt, 1962–1973," *International Organization* 45, no. 3 (1991): 370.

2. Sonali Singh and Christopher R. Way, "The Correlates of Nuclear Proliferation: A Quantitative Test," *Journal of Conflict Resolution* 48, no. 6 (2004): 866–867.

3. Alexander H. Montgomery and Scott D. Sagan, "The Perils of Predicting Proliferation," *Journal of Conflict Resolution* 53, no. 2 (2009): 302–328; and Todd C. Robinson, "What Do We Mean by Nuclear Proliferation," *Nonproliferation Review* 22, no. 1 (2015): 53–70.

4. Robert M. Cornejo, "When Sukarno Sought the Bomb: Indonesian Nuclear Aspirations in the Mid-1960s," *Nonproliferation Review* 7, no. 2 (2000): 35.

5. Vipin Narang, "Strategies of Nuclear Proliferation: How States Pursue the Bomb," *International Security* 41, no. 3 (2017): 110–140.

6. Gregory D. Miller, *Shadow of the Past: Reputation and Military Alliances before the First World War* (Ithaca, NY: Cornell University Press, 2012); and Mark J. C. Crescenzi, Jacob D. Kathman, Katja B. Kleinberg, and Reed M. Wood, "Reliability, Reputation, and Alliance Formation," *International Studies Quarterly* 56, no. 2 (2012): 259–274.

7. Many international relations theorists argue that democracies make stronger commitments than autocracies. For a critical review, see Alexander B. Downes and Todd S. Sechser, "The Illusion of Democratic Credibility," *International Organization* 66, no. 3 (2012): 457–489.

8. James D. Morrow, "Alliances: Why Write Them Down?," *Annual Review of Political Science* 3 (2000): 63–83.

9. Glenn Snyder, *Alliance Politics* (Ithaca, NY: Cornell University Press, 1997), 187–188.

10. See Tongfi Kim, "Why Alliances Entangle but Seldom Entrap States," *Security Studies* 20, no. 3 (2011): 350–377; and Brett V. Benson, *Constructing International Security: Alliance, Deterrence, and Moral Hazard* (New York: Cambridge University Press, 2012). For a general review of how entrapment risks arise, see Alexander Lanoszka, "Tangled Up in Rose? Theories of Alliance Entrapment and the 2008 Russo-Georgian War," *Contemporary Security Policy* 39, no. 2 (2018): 234–257.

11. Scott D. Sagan, "Why Do States Build Nuclear Weapons? Three Models in Search of a Bomb," *International Security* 21, no. 3 (1996–1997): 57–58.

12. Avery Goldstein, *Deterrence and Security in the 21st Century: China, Britain, France, and the Enduring Legacy of the Nuclear Proliferation* (Stanford, CA: Stanford University Press), 17–26.

13. Dan Reiter, "Security Commitments and Nuclear Proliferation," *Foreign Policy Analysis* 10, no. 1 (2013): 61–80.

14. Philipp C. Bleek and Eric B. Lorber, "Security Guarantees and Allied Nuclear Proliferation," *Journal of Conflict Resolution* 58, no. 3 (2014): 429–454.

15. Nuno P. Monteiro and Alexandre Debs, "The Strategic Logic of Nuclear Proliferation," *International Security* 39, no. 2 (2014): 7–51.

16. Singh and Way, "Correlates," 875–876; and Dong-Joon Jo and Erik Gartzke, "Determinants of Nuclear Weapons Proliferation," *Journal of Conflict Resolution* 51, no. 1 (2007): 186.

17. Mark S. Bell, "Examining Explanations for Nuclear Proliferation," *International Studies Quarterly* 60, no. 3 (2016): 520–529.

18. I use "nuclear interest," "nuclear proliferation," and "proliferation-related behavior" interchangeably for stylistic reasons.

19. James D. Morrow, "Arms versus Allies: Trade-Offs in the Search for Security," *International Organization* 47, no. 2 (1993): 207–233.

20. Paul. K. Huth, "Extended Deterrence and the Outbreak of War," *American Political Science Review* 82, no. 2 (1988): 424.

21. Brett Ashley Leeds and Michaela Mattes, "Alliance Politics during the Cold War: Aberration, New World Order, or Continuation of History?," *Conflict Management and Peace Science* 24, no. 3 (2007): 183–199; and Mira Rapp-Hooper, "Absolute Alliances: Extended Deterrence in International Politics" (PhD diss., Columbia University, 2014).

22. These interests might also align if allies share beliefs about the relative effectiveness of offensive military power over defensive military power. Chain-ganging—that is, a situation where allies feel obligated to honor an alliance commitment—could occur when states intervene in a war on an ally's behalf. Thomas J. Christensen and Jack Snyder, "Chain Gangs and Passed Bucks: Predicting Alliance Patterns in Multipolarity," *International Organization* 44, no. 2 (1990): 137–168.

23. Thomas J. Schelling, *Arms and Influence* (New Haven, CT: Yale University Press, 1966 [2008]), 47–48. On how hostages make credible commitments, see Oliver E. Williamson, "Credible Commitments: Using Hostages to Support Exchange," *American Economic Review* 73, no. 4 (1983): 519–540.

24. Foch quoted in Margaret Macmillan, *The War That Ended Peace: The Road to 1914* (New York: Random House, 2014), 376. On 'skin in the game,' see Michael A. Hunzeker and Alexander Lanoszka, "Landpower and American Credibility," *Parameters* 45, no. 4 (2015–2016): 17–26.

25. Robert Pape, *Bombing to Win: Air Power and Coercion in War* (Ithaca, NY: Cornell University Press, 1996); and John J. Mearsheimer, *Conventional Deterrence* (Ithaca, NY: Cornell University Press, 1983).

26. Huth, "Extended Deterrence," 435.

27. Earl C. Ravenal, "Counterforce and Alliance: The Ultimate Connection," *International Security* 6, no. 4 (1982): 26–43. On how nuclear superiority matters in crisis bargaining, see Matthew Kroenig "Nuclear Superiority and the Balance of Resolve: Explaining Nuclear Crisis Outcomes," *International Organization* 67, no. 1 (2013): 141–171. For a critical view, see Todd S. Sechser and Matthew Fuhrmann, "Crisis Bargaining and Nuclear Blackmail," *International Organization* 67, no. 1 (2013): 173–195.

28. Hence the argument that trying to escape mutually assured destruction is unwise. See Robert Jervis, "Why Nuclear Superiority Doesn't Matter," *Political Science Quarterly* 94, no. 4 (1979–1980): 617–633.

29. Matthew Fuhrmann and Todd S. Sechser, "Signaling Alliance Commitments: Hand-Tying and Sunk Costs in Extended Nuclear Deterrence," *American Journal of Political Science* 58, no. 4 (2014): 923–924.

30. Ironically, during the Berlin crisis, Soviet and American leaders sometimes believed that enhancing conventional military deterrence would weaken nuclear deterrence. See Craig Campbell, *Destroying the Village: Eisenhower and Thermonuclear War* (New York: Columbia University Press), 132. Obviously, nuclear crises very rarely occur. My general argument applies to those long intervals between them.

31. Military garrisons also assure "the security of resource flows" like oil. Kent E. Calder, *Embattled Garrisons: Comparative Base Politics and American Globalism* (Princeton, NJ: Princeton University Press, 2007), 33.

32. Sooyeon Yoon, "South Korea's Wartime Operational Control Transfer Debate: From an Organizational Perspective," *Journal of International and Area Studies* 22, no. 2 (2015): 89–108.

33. Michael Herman, *Intelligence Power in Peace and War* (Cambridge: Cambridge University Press, 1999 [1996]), 69.

34. Herman, *Intelligence Power in Peace and War*, 206.

35. Alexander Cooley and Daniel H. Nexon, "'The Empire Will Compensate You': The Structural Dynamics of the U.S. Overseas Basing Network," *Perspectives on Politics* 11, no. 4 (2013): 1038.

36. Alexander Cooley and Hendrik Spruyt, *Contracting States: Sovereign Transfers in International Relations* (Princeton, NJ: Princeton University Press, 2009).

37. Herman, *Intelligence Power*, 185.

38. American military bases have grown in number since the end of the Cold War. A 2015 estimate pegs the cost of maintaining overseas bases and military personnel (excluding those in Afghanistan and Iraq) to be between $72 billion and $120 billion each year. See David Vine, *Base Nation: How U.S. Military Bases Abroad Harm America and the World* (New York: Metropolitan, 2015), 9.

39. Aaron L. Friedberg, *In the Shadow of the Garrison State: America's Anti-Statism and Its Cold War Strategy* (Princeton, NJ: Princeton University Press, 2000), 130. The purported economic benefits of the New Look complemented the strategic benefits. See Marc Trachtenberg, *History and Strategy* (Princeton, NJ: Princeton University Press, 1991), 153–167.

40. My theory accords much importance to the troop withdrawals being significant, unforeseen, or unilateral. Note also that I assume the existence of a major threat posed by an adversary (one that is nuclear armed). Otherwise, my theory would predict too many false positives, since we observe many instances of troop withdrawals but relative few cases of proliferation-related behavior. Indeed, the United States withdrew its forces from the territory of its allies without adverse proliferation consequences. Such cases include South Korea and Europe in the early 1990s. In those cases, however, those allies no longer faced such hostile threat environments that made certain troop numbers so desirable.

41. On nuclear deterrence theory, see Robert Powell, *Nuclear Deterrence Theory: The Search for Credibility* (Cambridge: Cambridge University Press, 1990). On middle powers and deterrence theory, see Goldstein, *Deterrence*.

42. Joseph M. Parent and Sebastian Rosato, "Balancing in Neorealism," *International Security* 40, no. 2 (2015): 57.

43. Tristan A. Volpe, "Atomic Leverage: Compellence with Nuclear Latency," *Security Studies* 26, no. 3 (2017): 517–544. Alternatively, see Rupal N. Mehta and Rachel Elizabeth Whitlark, "The Benefits and Burdens of Nuclear Latency," *International Studies Quarterly* 61, no. 3 (2017): 517–528.

44. James D. Fearon, "Rationalist Explanations for War," *International Organization* 49, no. 3 (1995): 381.

45. On the difficulties of nuclear signaling, see Scott D. Sagan and Jeremi Suri, "The Madman Nuclear Alert: Secrecy, Signaling, and Safety in October 1969," *International Security* 27, no. 4 (2003): 150–183.

46. Matthew Kroenig, *Exporting the Bomb: Technology Transfer and the Spread of Nuclear Weapons* (Ithaca, NY: Cornell University Press, 2010), 3; and Or Rabinowitz and Nicholas L. Miller,

"Keeping the Bombs in the Basement: US Nonproliferation Policy toward Israel, South Africa, and Pakistan," *International Security* 40, no. 1 (2015): 47–86.

47. Robert Jervis, "Cooperation under the Security Dilemma," *World Politics* 30, no. 2 (1978): 167–214. On how guarantors can manage security dilemmas, see Thomas J. Christensen, "China, the U.S.-Japan Alliance, and the Security Dilemma in East Asia," *International Security* 23, no. 4 (2014): 49–80.

48. Schelling, *Arms and Influence*, 100.

49. States are more likely to attack or to threaten militarily the nuclear programs of their adversaries. See Matthew Fuhrmann and Sarah E. Kreps, "Targeting Nuclear Programs in War and Peace: A Quantitative Empirical Analysis, 1941–2000," *Journal of Conflict Resolution* 54, no. 6 (2010): 831–859.

50. Gene Gerzhoy, "Alliance Coercion and Nuclear Restraint: How the United States Thwarted West Germany's Nuclear Ambitions," *International Security* 39, no. 4 (2015): 91–129.

51. Stephen Van Evera, "Offense, Defense, and the Causes of War," *International Security* 22, no. 4 (1998): 9–10. This window of opportunity might become all the more tempting to exploit if the adversary believes that the ally would try to acquire nuclear weapons. See Alexandre Debs and Nuno Monteiro, "Known Unknowns: Power Shifts, Uncertainty, and War," *International Organization* 68, no. 1 (2014): 1–31.

52. Jonathan Kirshner, "The Microfoundations of Economic Sanctions," *Security Studies* 6, no. 3 (1997): 36–37.

53. See Jean-Marc F. Blanchard and Norrin M. Ripsman, "Asking the Right Question: When Do Economic Sanctions Work Best?," *Security Studies* 9, no. 1 (1999): 226.

54. Albert O. Hirschman, *National Power and the Structure of Foreign Trade* (Berkeley: University of California Press, 1945).

55. Robert Pape, "Why Economic Sanctions Do Not Work," *International Security* 22, no. 2 (1997): 93.

56. Daniel Drezner, *The Sanctions Paradox: Economic Statecraft and International Relations* (Cambridge: Cambridge University Press, 1999), 20–21.

57. Drezner, *Sanctions Paradox*, 54.

58. Eugene B. Kogan, "Coercing Allies: Why Friends Abandon Nuclear Plans" (PhD diss., Brandeis University, 2013). Nuclear denial of the sort described here may have become harder to achieve since the end of the Cold War. Writing in 2017, former deputy secretary of energy Daniel B. Poneman argues that "lopsided demands for [nonproliferation] concessions by [nuclear] suppliers only work in a sellers' market and the global nuclear market is anything but that." See Daniel B. Poneman, "The Case for American Nuclear Leadership," *Bulletin of the Atomic Scientists* 73, no. 1 (2017): 45. On the circumstances under which states provide others with nuclear technologies, see Matthew Fuhrmann, "Spreading Temptation: Proliferation and Peaceful Nuclear Cooperation Agreements," *International Security* 34, no. 1 (2009): 7–41; and Kroenig, *Exporting the Bomb*. On the use of positive incentives as opposed to denial, see Tristan A. Volpe, "Atomic Inducements: The Case for 'Buying Out' Nuclear Latency," *Nonproliferation Review* 23, no. 3–4 (2016): 481–483.

59. Francis J. Gavin, "Strategies of Inhibition: US Grand Strategy, the Nuclear Revolution, and Nonproliferation," *International Security* 40, no. 1 (2015): 9–46.

60. On how these dynamics affect commitment choices, see Keren Yarhi-Milo, Alexander Lanoszka, and Zack Cooper, "To Arm or to Ally? The Patron's Dilemma and the Strategic Logic of Arms Transfers and Alliances," *International Security* 41, no. 2 (2016): 90–139.

61. Stephen M. Walt, *The Origin of Alliances* (Ithaca, NY: Cornell University Press, 1997). See also Sagan, "Why Do States Build," 60.

62. Jeffrey W. Legro and Andrew Moravcsik, "Is Anybody Still a Realist?," *International Security* 24, no. 2 (1999): 12–13.

63. Etel Solingen, *Nuclear Logics: Contrasting Paths in East Asia and the Middle East* (Princeton, NJ: Princeton University Press, 2007), 17. For another theory of nuclear proliferation that emphasizes regime characteristics, see Christopher Way and Jessica L. P. Weeks, "Making It Personal: Regime Type and Nuclear Proliferation," *American Journal of Political Science* 58, no. 3 (2014): 705–719.

64. Sagan, "Why Do States Build," 73–77.

65. Jacques E. C. Hymans, *The Psychology of Nuclear Proliferation: Identity, Emotions, and Foreign Policy* (New York: Cambridge University Press, 2006), 13.

66. See Peter J. Katzenstein, *Cultural Norms and National Security: Police and Military in Postwar Japan* (Ithaca, NY: Cornell University Press, 1996); and Thomas U. Berger, *Cultures of Antimilitarism: National Security in Germany and Japan* (Baltimore, MD: Johns Hopkins University Press, 1998). For another norm-centric argument, see Maria Rost Rublee, *Nonproliferation Norms: Why States Choose Nuclear Restraint* (Athens: University of Georgia Press, 2009).

67. See, e.g., Helen V. Milner and Keiko Kubota, "Why the Move to Free Trade? Democracy and Trade Policy in the Developing World," *International Organization* 59, no. 1 (2005): 107–143.

68. On complex causality, see Alexander L. George and Andrew Bennett, *Case Studies and Theory Development in the Social Sciences* (Cambridge, MA: MIT Press, 2004), 157.

69. Sagan, "Why Do States Build," 85.

70. John J. Mearsheimer, *The Tragedy of Great Power Politics* (New York: W. W. Norton, 2001), 382.

2. American Security Guarantees during the Cold War, 1949–1980

1. Numerous explanations for the origins of the Cold War are available in the historical and political science literatures. See, inter alia, Deborah Welch Larson, *Origins of Containment: A Psychological Explanation* (Princeton, NJ: Princeton University Press, 1989); Daniel Yergin, *Shattered Peace: The Origins of the Cold War* (New York: Penguin Books, 1990); Melvyn Leffler, *A Preponderance of Power: National Security, the Truman Administration, and the Cold War* (Stanford, CA: Stanford University Press, 1993); John Lewis Gaddis, *Strategies of Containment: A Critical Appraisal of American National Security Policy* (New York: Oxford University Press, 1982); Marc Trachtenberg, *A Constructed Peace: The Making of the European Settlement, 1945–1963* (Princeton, NJ: Princeton University Press, 1999); and Andrew H. Kydd, *Trust and Mistrust in International Politics* (Princeton, NJ: Princeton University Press, 2005).

2. See Michael Goodman, "British Intelligence and the Soviet Atomic Bomb, 1945–1950," *Journal of Strategic Studies* 26, no. 2 (2003): 120–151.

3. David Alan Rosenberg, "American Strategy and the Hydrogen Bomb Decision," *Journal of American History* 66, no. 1 (1979): 71.

4. Rosenberg, "American Strategy," 72–73. On Soviet conventional military power in the immediate postwar period, see Philip A. Karber and Jerald A. Combs, "The United States, NATO, and the Soviet Threat to Europe," *Diplomatic History* 22, no. 3 (1998): 403–417.

5. On how American decision makers confronted this danger, see Marc Trachtenberg, "A 'Wasting Asset': American Strategy and the Shifting Nuclear Balance, 1949–1954," *International Security* 13, no. 3 (1988–1989): 5–49.

6. Aaron L. Friedberg, *In the Shadow of the Garrison State: America's Anti-Statism and Its Cold War Strategy* (Princeton, NJ: Princeton University Press, 2000), 98–107.

7. Friedberg, *In the Shadow*, 158–178.

8. See Phil Williams, *The Senate and US Troops in Europe* (New York: Macmillan, 1985); Ted Galen Carpenter, "United States' NATO Policy at the Crossroads: The 'Great Debate' of 1950–1951," *International History Review* 8, no. 3 (1986): 389–415; and Benjamin O. Fordham, *Building the Cold War Consensus: The Political Economy of U.S. National Security Policy, 1949–51* (Ann Arbor: University of Michigan Press, 1998). In a January 1950 address delivered to the National Press Club, Secretary of State Dean Acheson failed to include South Korea in the East Asian "defense perimeter" of the United States. See Russell D. Buhite, "'Major Interests': American Policy toward China, Taiwan, and Korea, 1945–1950," *Pacific Historical Review* 47, no. 3 (1978): 440–451.

9. Hal Brands, *What Good Is Grand Strategy?: Power and Purpose in American Statecraft from Harry S. Truman to George W. Bush* (Ithaca, NY: Cornell University Press, 2014), 22.

10. Historians disagree over whether NSC-68 represented a major change in American Cold War strategy. See Gaddis, *Strategies of Containment*, 87–124 and Leffler, *Preponderance*, 355–360.

11. Secretary of State Dean Acheson noted that "Korea came along and saved us." Acheson quoted in Walter LaFeber, *America, Russia, and the Cold War*, 3rd ed. (New York: John Wiley and Sons, 1976), 100. See Robert Jervis, "The Impact of the Korean War on the Cold War," *Journal of Conflict Resolution* 24, no. 4 (1980): 579–581.

12. On early NATO as a weak security institution, see Robert O. Keohane and Celeste A. Wallander, "Risk, Threat, and Security Institutions," in *Imperfect Unions: Security Institutions across Time and Space*, ed. Helga Haftendorn, Robert O. Keohane, and Celeste A. Wallander (Oxford: Oxford University Press, 1999), 41.

13. See Final Act of the London Conference, October 3, 1954, accessed October 16, 2017, http://www.nato.int/archives/1st5years/appendices/1b.htm.

14. Trachtenberg, *Constructed Peace*, 128.

15. Timothy D. Temerson, "Double Containment and the Origins of the U.S.-Japan Security Alliance" (working paper 91-14, MIT-Japan Program, Cambridge, MA, 1991), 3.

16. Bilateral Security Treaty between the United States of America and Japan, September 8, 1951.

17. Figures reported in Friedberg, *In the Shadow*, 125.

18. Data on American military personnel deployed overseas collected by the Heritage Foundation, accessed October 16, 2017, http://www.heritage.org/defense/report/global-us-troop -deployment-1950-2003.

19. David Alan Rosenberg, "The Origins of Overkill: Nuclear Weapons and American Strategy, 1945–1960," *International Security* 7, no. 4 (1983): 22–24.

20. Rosenberg, "Origins of Overkill," 22–23. US Air Force Chief of Staff Hoyt Vandenburg quoted ibid., 22.

21. Friedberg, *In the Shadow*, 125.

22. Friedberg, *In the Shadow*, 94–95.

23. Raymond J. Saulnier, *Constructive Years: The US Economy under Eisenhower* (Lanham, MD: University Press of America, 1991), 2.

24. Quotations pulled from Basic National Security Policy, October 30, 1953, Foreign Relations of the United States (FRUS) 1952–1954 2: 578–598. The phrase "massive retaliation" was first used by Secretary of State John Foster Dulles in a foreign policy address to the Council of Foreign Relations. See idem, "The Evolution of Foreign Policy," Before the Council of Foreign Relations, New York, Department of State, Press Release No. 81 (January 12, 1954). See also Glenn H. Snyder, "The 'New Look' of 1953," in *Strategy, Politics, and Defense Budgets*, eds. Warner R. Schilling, Paul Y. Hammond, and Glenn H. Snyder (New York: Columbia University Press, 1962); Gaddis, *Strategies of Containment*, 127–163; and Saki Dockrill, *Eisenhower's New-Look National Security Policy, 1953–61* (New York: St. Martin's, 1996). On nuclear war planning in the early Cold War, see Rosenberg, "Origins of Overkill."

25. Susanna Schrafstetter and Stephen Twigge, *Avoiding Armageddon: Europe, the United States, and the Struggle for Nuclear Proliferation, 1945–1970* (Westport, CT: Praeger, 2004), 206.

26. A later policy document reiterated this view. See Report to the NSC by the NSC Planning Board, February 11, 1954, FRUS 1952–1954 2: 611.

27. Report to the National Security Council by the Executive Secretary (Lay), October 30, 1953, FRUS 1952–1954 2: 578, 590.

28. This figure appears in an NSC document presumably drafted in 1953. See Draft Memorandum Prepared for the National Security Council, undated 1953, FRUS 1952–1954 2: 284.

29. Robert J. Watson, *The Joint Chiefs of Staff and National Policy, 1953–54*, Vol. 5 of *History of the Joint Chiefs of Staff* (Washington, DC: US Government Printing Office, 1986), 61. Unsurprisingly, the US Army hated the New Look. See Andrew J. Bacevich, "The Paradox of Professionalism: Eisenhower, Ridgway, and the Challenge to Civilian Control, 1953–1955," *Journal of Military History* 61, no. 2 (1997): 314–316.

30. Scott D. Sagan, *Moving Targets: Nuclear Strategy and National Security* (Princeton, NJ: Princeton University Press, 1989), 19–27.

31. Pavel Podvig, ed., *Russian Strategic Nuclear Forces* (Cambridge, MA: MIT Press, 2001), 4–5.

32. Karber and Combs, "United States," 423.

33. Karber and Combs, "United States," 424.

34. The United States did not believe that China would launch an assault over the Taiwan Straits. See, e.g., Special National Intelligence Estimate, April 9, 1957, FRUS 1955–1957 3: 515–518.

35. Gordon H. Chang, "To the Nuclear Brink: Eisenhower, Dulles, and the Quemoy-Matsu Crisis," *International Security* 12, no. 4 (1988): 96–123.

36. Nancy Bernkopf Tucker, *The China Threat: Memories, Myths, and Realities in the 1950s* (New York: Columbia University Press, 2012), 141. On the American military commitment to Taiwan, see Keren Yarhi-Milo, Alexander Lanoszka, and Zack Cooper, "To Arm or to Ally? The Patron's Dilemma and the Strategic Logic of Arms Transfers and Alliances," *International Security* 41, no. 2 (2016): 103–119.

37. Peter Hayes, *Pacific Powderkeg: American Nuclear Dilemmas in Korea* (Lexington, KY: Lexington Books, 1991), 35.

38. For this discussion, I rely on Francis J. Gavin, *Gold, Dollars, and Power: Money, Security, and the Politics of the U.S. Balance of Payments, 1958–1971* (Durham: University of North Carolina Press, 2004), 17–32.

39. On this paradox regarding the balance-of-payments problem that the United States confronted in the early 1960s, see Robert Triffin, *Gold and the Dollar Crisis: The Future of Convertibility* (New Haven, CT: Yale University Press, 1960).

40. Another problem facing American decision makers in the immediate postwar era was the "dollar gap" facing potential allies. See Leffler, *Preponderance*, 17. On helping allies "get back on their feet," see Letter from the Representative at the United Nations (Lodge) to the Secretary of State, October 29, 1957, FRUS 1955–1957, 9: 328. On the increasing awareness of the problems posed by the balance-of-payments deficit, see Memorandum from the Deputy Under Secretary of State for Economic Affairs (Prochnow) to the Secretary of State, October 29, 1956, FRUS 1955–1957 9: 308–310; and Letter from the Special Assistant in the Office of the Secretary of State (Greene) to the Representative at the United Nations (Lodge), October 24, 1957, FRUS 1955–1957 9: 326–328.

41. Gavin, *Gold*, 24.

42. See Christopher A. Preble, ""Who Ever Believed in the 'Missile Gap'?": John F. Kennedy and the Politics of National Security," *Presidential Studies Quarterly* 33, no. 4 (2003): 801–826.

43. "Special Message to the Congress on the Defense Budget," March 28, 1961, *Public Papers of the Presidents of the United States: John F. Kennedy (1961)* (Washington, DC: US Government Printing Office, 1962), 230–231.

44. Karber and Combs, "United States," 427.

45. Karber and Combs, "United States," 424.

46. Friedberg, *In the Shadow*, 143–148.

47. Numbers drawn from "Outlays by Superfunction and Function: 1940–2018," *Office of Management and Budget*, Historical Tables, accessed October 16, 2017, https://www.whitehouse.gov/omb/budget/Historicals.

48. Fred Kaplan, *The Wizards of Armageddon* (New York: Simon and Schuster, 1983), 307–314.

49. Francis J. Gavin, "The Myth of Flexible Response: United States Strategy in Europe during the 1960s," *International History Review* 23, no. 4 (2001): 847–865. See also Marc Trachtenberg, *The Cold War and After: History, Theory, and the Logic of International Politics* (Princeton, NJ: Princeton University Press, 2012), 164–166.

50. Sagan, *Moving Targets*, 34.

51. Gavin, "Myth of Flexible Response," 862–863.

52. Gavin, *Gold*, 63. The United States and its allies eventually negotiated significant tariff reductions in Geneva between 1960 and 1962 during the Dillon Round, a series of talks on tariff levels named after the U.S. Treasury Secretary Douglas Dillon.

53. Gavin, *Gold*, 68.

54. Memorandum from Secretary of the Treasury Dillon to President Kennedy, October 9, 1962, FRUS 1961–1963 9: 35–42; Memorandum for the Record, February 27, 1963, FRUS 1961–1963 9: 45–47; and Memorandum from Secretary of Defense McNamara to President Kennedy, June 4, 1963, FRUS 1961–1963 9: 64–66.

55. For an exemplary primary source, see Memorandum of Conversation, June 24, 1963, FRUS 1961–63, 9: 170–174. Gavin makes this point in "Myth of Flexible Response," 859–860. See

also Arthur M. Schlesinger, *A Thousand Days: John F. Kennedy in the White House* (Boston: Houghton Mifflin, 1965), 654–655; Walt W. Rostow, *The Diffusion of Power: An Essay in Recent History* (New York: Macmillan, 1972): 136; and Frank Costigliola, "The Failed Design: Kennedy, de Gaulle, and the Struggle for Europe," *Diplomatic History* 8, no. 3 (1984): 227–252.

56. Gavin, "Myth of Flexible Response." For an argument about how the United States decided on a permanent troop presence in Western Europe during the Kennedy years, see Brendan Rittenhouse Green, "Two Concepts of Liberty: US Cold War Grand Strategies and the Liberal Tradition," *International Security* 37, no. 2 (2012): 9–43.

57. Matthew Jones, *After Hiroshima: The United States, Race and Nuclear Weapons in Asia, 1945–1965* (Cambridge: Cambridge University Press, 2010), 412–413.

58. Jones, *After Hiroshima*, 420.

59. Gavin argues that by showing some willingness to support existing nuclear weapons programs through the provision of such missile systems as Polaris to Great Britain and France, the United States inconsistently sought to centralize authority so as to manage nuclear escalation. Yet such offers of support were more exceptional than normal. Many contemporary allied decision makers interpreted American diplomacy as serving to monopolize tactical nuclear weapons within the Western alliance. Gavin, "Myth of Flexible Response," 856.

60. University of Michigan Commencement Address by Secretary of Defense Robert McNamara, Ann Arbor, Michigan, July 9, 1962.

61. James B. Solomon, "The Multilateral Force: America's Nuclear Solution for NATO, 1960–1965," *USNA Trident Scholar Project Report no. 269* (Annapolis, MD: United States Naval Academy, 1999), 6–9.

62. Keith W. Baum, "Treating the Allies Properly: The Eisenhower Administration, NATO, and the Multilateral Force," *Presidential Studies Quarterly* 13, no. 1 (1983): 86–88.

63. For a text of this speech, see *Public Papers of the Presidents of the United States: John F. Kennedy, 1961*, 382–387.

64. The agreement in question is the Nassau Agreement. See the discussion on Great Britain in chapter 6.

65. These views are captured in Steering Group on Implementing the Nassau Decisions: Post-Nassau Strategy, January 2, 1963, folder: "NATO, Weapons, Nassau Sub-Group IV, Multilateral Force Planning," National Security Files, Regional Security, box 230, John F. Kennedy Presidential Library and Museum, Boston, MA (hereafter abbreviated as JFKL).

66. Quote from Telegram from Kennedy to Macmillan, May 29, 1963, folder: "Multilateral Force Subjects, Macmillan Correspondence," National Security Files, Regional Security, box 219, JFKL. See also MLF Congressional Presentation Book (pp. 6–9), June 1, 1964, folder: "Multilateral Force, General, vol. I [1 of 3]," National Security Files, Regional Security, box 22a, LBJ Presidential Library, Austin, TX (hereafter abbreviated as LBJL).

67. Brief Talking Points on Offset Agreements, December 26, 1963, folder: "Germany: 12/28–29/63," National Security File, Country File, box 190, LBJL.

68. Memorandum for the President, December 13, 1963, folder: "Germany 12/63 [1 of 3]," National Security File, Country File, box 190, LBJL.

69. The expanding Soviet submarine fleet was partly how the Soviet Union reached nuclear parity with the United States. More plentiful survivable ICBM launchers were another reason. See Daryl G. Press, *Calculating Credibility: How Leaders Assess Military Threats* (Ithaca, NY: Cornell University Press, 2005), 89. Another reason was the increase in fixed ICBM launchers. See Austin Long and Brendan Rittenhouse Green, "Stalking the Second Strike: Intelligence, Counterforce, and Nuclear Strategy," *Journal of Strategic Studies* 38, no. 1–2 (2015): 42.

70. Victor Gobarev, "Soviet Policy toward China: Developing Nuclear Weapons, 1949–1969," *Journal of Slavic Military History* 12, no. 4 (1999): 17–31.

71. William Burr and Jeffrey T. Richelson, "Whether to 'Strangle the Baby in the Cradle': The United States and the Chinese Nuclear Program, 1960–64," *International Security* 25, no. 3 (2000–2001): 54–99. See also Rachel Elizabeth Whitlark, "Nuclear Beliefs: A Leader-Focused Theory of Counter-Proliferation," *Security Studies* 26, no. 4 (2017): 545–574.

72. Fredrik Logevall, *Choosing War: The Lost Chance for Peace and the Escalation of the War in Vietnam* (Berkeley: University of California Press, 1999), 368–369.

73. Bruce W. Jentleson, "American Commitments in the Third World: Theory vs. Practice," *International Organization* 41, no. 4 (1987): 667–668. Consider the domino theory, according to which the fall of one country to communism would make the fall of another country to communism more likely.

74. Numbers drawn from "Outlays by Superfunction and Function: 1940–2018," *Office of Management and Budget*, Historical Tables, accessed October 16, 2017, https://www.whitehouse.gov/omb/budget/Historicals.

75. Memorandum of Conversation, January 19, 1969, FRUS 1969–1976, 6: 2–3; and Memorandum from the President's Assistant for National Security Affairs (Kissinger) to President Nixon, March 10, 1969, FRUS 1969–1976, 6: 100.

76. National Security Study Memorandum 36, April 10, 1969, FRUS 1969–1976, 6: 195–196; and *Public Papers of the Presidents of the United States, Richard Nixon: 1969* (Washington, DC: Government Printing Office, 1971), 901–909. Nixon also escalated hostilities by approving a secret bombing campaign against Khmer Rouge targets in Cambodia shortly after becoming president. Critics subsequently alleged that his Vietnam policy suffered from a "credibility gap."

77. *Public Papers, Richard Nixon: 1969*, 549.

78. *Public Papers, Richard Nixon: 1969*, 905.

79. On the Nixon Shock, see Joanne S. Gowa, *Closing the Golden Window: Domestic Politics and the End of Bretton Woods* (Ithaca, NY: Cornell University Press, 1983); and Gavin, *Gold*, 195–196. On how the Nixon Shock demonstrated American power, see Susan Strange, "The Persistent Myth of Lost Hegemony," *International Organization* 41, no. 4 (1987): 569.

80. Some argue that Congress was not serious in legislating the War Powers Act, preferring instead to evade responsibility on foreign policy matters. See John Hart Ely, "Suppose Congress Wanted a War Powers Act That Worked," *Columbia Law Review* 88, no. 7 (1988): 1385.

81. Phil Williams, "Whatever Happened to the Mansfield Amendment?," *Survival* 18, no. 4 (1976): 146–153.

82. Quotations and argument drawn from Francis J. Gavin, *Nuclear Statecraft: History and Strategy in America's Atomic Age* (Ithaca, NY: Cornell University Press, 2012), 104–119.

83. Joshua Rovner, *Fixing the Facts: National Security and the Politics of Intelligence* (Ithaca, NY: Cornell University Press, 2011), 92–96.

84. Quotations drawn from Gavin, *Nuclear Statecraft*, 112.

85. In Nixon's time, however, the missiles still did not carry MIRVs with high yields.

86. William Burr, "The Nixon Administration, the 'Horror Strategy,' and the Search for Limited Nuclear Options, 1969–1972," *Journal of Cold War Studies* 7, no. 3 (2005): 34–78.

87. Earl C. Ravenal, "Counterforce and Alliance: The Ultimate Connection," *International Security* 6, no. 4 (1982): 26–43.

88. See Kristina Spohr Readman, "Conflict and Cooperation in Intra-Alliance Nuclear Politics: Western Europe, the United States, and the Genesis of NATO's Dual-Track Decision, 1977–1979," *Journal of Cold War Studies* 13, no. 2 (2011): 39–89.

89. Richard K. Betts, *Nuclear Blackmail and Nuclear Balance* (Washington, DC: Brookings Institution Press, 1987).

3. West Germany, 1954–1970

1. John J. Mearsheimer, *The Tragedy of Great Power Politics* (New York: W. W. Norton, 2001), 382.

2. I thank Andreas Lutsch for clarifying this issue for me.

3. Thomas U. Berger, *Cultures of Antimilitarism: National Security in Germany and Japan* (Baltimore, MD: Johns Hopkins University Press, 1998), 58–59, 61–62, and 64.

4. On West German party differences in the early Cold War, see Andrew Moravcsik, *The Choice for Europe: Social Purpose and State Power from Messina to Maastricht* (Ithaca, NY: Cornell University Press, 1998), 90–103.

5. Berger, *Cultures of Antimilitarism*, 58.

6. Berger, *Cultures of Antimilitarism*, 43–44; and Peter J. Katzenstein, *Cultural Norms and National Security: Police and Military in Postwar Japan* (Ithaca, NY: Cornell University Press, 1996), 178–179.

7. My translation. Adenauer quoted in Colette Barbier, "Les négociations franco-germano-italiennes en vue de l'établissement d'une cooperation militaire nucléaire au cours des années 1956–1958," *Revue d'histoire diplomatique* 104, no. 3 (1990): 93.

8. Barbier, "Les négociations franco-germano-italiennes," 112–113. See also Eckart Conze, "La coopération franco-germano-italienne dans le domaine nucléaire dans les années 1957–1958," *Revue d'histoire diplomatique* 104, no. 3 (1990): 115–132; and Beatrice Heuser, *NATO, Britain, France, and the FRG: Nuclear Strategies and Forces for Europe, 1949–2000* (New York: St. Martin's, 1997).

9. The secrecy was perhaps due to the premature state of the initiative rather than a deliberate effort to evade American detection. See Leopoldo Nuti, "The F-I-G Story Revisited," *Storia delle Relazioni Internazionali* 13, no. 1 (1998): 77–84.

10. Quoted in Aleksandr Fursenko and Timothy Naftali, *Khrushchev's Cold War: The Inside Story of an American Adversary* (New York: W. W. Norton, 2006), 186–187. Statesmen back then used imprecise terminology to refer to nuclear weapons. The Colomb-Béchar Protocol, signed by West Germany and France in 1957, referred to "armes nouvelles," sparking historiographical controversy over how to interpret this secret mutual rearmament agreement. See Barbier, "Les négociations franco-germano-italiennes," 91; and Conze, "La coopération franco-germano-italienne," 115–132.

11. Conze, "La coopération franco-germano-italienne," 127–128. See also Hans-Peter Schwarz, *Adenauer: The Statesman: 1952–1967* (Oxford: Berghahn Books, 1997), vol. 2, 311–324.

12. Andreas Lutsch, "In Favor of 'Effective' and 'Non-Discriminatory' Non-Dissemination Policy: The FRG and the NPT Negotiation Process (1962–1966)," in *Negotiating the Nuclear Non-Proliferation Treaty: Origins of the Nuclear Order*, ed. Roland Popp, Liviu Horovitz, and Andreas Wenger (Oxon, UK: Routledge, 2017), 38–39.

13. For a contemporary account of West German posturing, see Catherine McArdle Kelleher, *Germany and the Politics of Nuclear Weapons* (New York: Columbia University Press, 1975).

14. George H. Quester, "The Nuclear Nonproliferation Treaty and the International Atomic Energy Agency," *International Organization* 24, no. 2 (1970): 164.

15. Letter from President Kennedy to Prime Minister Macmillan, November 22, 1961, FRUS 1961–1962 14: 633. According to a later conversation recorded by British defence minister Peter Thorneycroft in September 1962, Kennedy remarked that "if the Germans embarked on work in the nuclear sphere which constituted a breach of the 1954 Agreement the United States would have to consider her own guarantees to station forces in Europe." This reconsideration could involve "haul[ing]out." See Ministry of Defence, "Notes on Talks During the Minister of Defence's Visit to the United States, September 1962, Nuclear Problems in Europe," September 19, 1962, DEFE [Defence] 13/323, British National Archives.

16. Memorandum of Conversation, November 21, 1961, FRUS 1961–1962 14: 616.

17. Charles E. Bohlen, recorded interview by Arthur M. Schlesinger, May 21, 1964, p. 36, John F. Kennedy Presidential Library and Museum, Boston, MA (hereafter abbreviated as JFKL), Oral History Program.

18. German Nuclear Developments and rebus sic stantibus, July 6, 1962, folder: "NATO, Weapons, Cables, Germany, 3/61–9/63," National Security Files, Regional Security, box 226A, JFKL.

19. Telegram 3161 from Paris to the Secretary of State, December 20, 1961, folder: "NATO, Weapons, Cables, Germany, FRG-French Nuclear Cooperation," National Security Files, Regional Security, box 226A, JFKL.

20. Telegram 3165 from Paris to the Secretary of State, June 25, 1962, same box and folder as footnote 19.

21. Telegram 1538 from Bonn to the Secretary of State, December 10, 1962, same box and folder as footnote 19.

22. Telegram 243 from Bonn to the Secretary of State, July 25, 1962, same box and folder as footnote 19.

23. Memorandum for the President (p. 2), February 26, 1963, same box and folder as above.

24. Quoted in Frank Costigliola, "The Failed Design: Kennedy, de Gaulle, and the Struggle for Europe," *Diplomatic History* 8, no. 3 (1984): 236.

25. Post-Nassau Strategy (pp. 4, 20), January 2, 1963, folder: "NATO, Weapons, Sub-Group V, Post-Nassau Strategy," National Security Files, Regional Security, box 230, JFKL.

26. Quoted in Susanna Schrafstetter and Stephen Twigge, *Avoiding Armageddon: Europe, the United States, and the Struggle for Nuclear Proliferation, 1945–1970* (Westport, CT: Praeger, 2004), 155–156.

27. "National Intelligence Estimate, NIE 4-66, 'The Likelihood of Further Nuclear Proliferation,'" January 20, 1966, History and Public Policy Program Digital Archive, obtained and contributed by William Burr and included in Nuclear Proliferation International History Project (NPIHP) Research Update no. 11, http://digitalarchive.wilsoncenter.org/document/116887.

28. Address by the Polish Foreign Minister (Rapacki) to the UN General Assembly in *Documents on Disarmament, 1945–1959 [Volume II, 1957–1959]* (Washington, DC: Department of State), 889–892. See also Jeremi Suri, "America's Search for a Technological Solution to the Arms Race: The Surprise Attack Conference of 1958 and a Challenge for 'Eisenhower Revisionists,'" *Diplomatic History* 21, no. 3 (1997): 440–442.

29. Laurien Crump, *The Warsaw Pact Reconsidered: International Relations in Eastern Europe, 1955–69* (New York: Routledge, 2015), 98–129.

30. These issues touched on the diplomatic status of East Germany as well. See Telegram from the Department of State to the Embassy in France, October 2, 1961, FRUS 1961–1962 14: 459.

31. Carl Walske, "Nuclear Electric Power and the Proliferation of Nuclear Weapon States," *International Security* 1, no. 3 (1977): 97.

32. William W. Lowrance, "Nuclear Futures for Sale: To Brazil from West Germany, 1975," *International Security* 1, no. 2 (1976): 147.

33. See William W. Kaufmann, *The Requirements of Deterrence, Memorandum #7* (Princeton, NJ: Center for International Studies, 1954).

34. Memorandum of Discussion at the 285th Meeting of the National Security Council, May 17, 1956, FRUS 1955–1957 19: 307.

35. My translation. Conze, "La coopération franco-germano-italienne," 119.

36. Kelleher, *Germany*, 36.

37. Hubert Zimmermann, "The Sour Fruits of Victory: Sterling and Security in Anglo-German Relations during the 1950s and 1960s," *Contemporary European History* 9, no. 2 (2000): 231.

38. Heuser, *NATO*, 28–34.

39. Memorandum of Discussion at the 166th Meeting of the NSC, October 13, 1953, FRUS 1952–1954 2: 548.

40. Memorandum by the President to the Secretary of State, September 8, 1953, FRUS 1952–1954 2: 461.

41. Memorandum by the Secretary of State to the President, October 21, 1953, FRUS 1952–1954 2: 550.

42. Memorandum for the Record by the President, November 11, 1953, FRUS 1952–1954 2: 597.

43. Hubert Zimmermann, *Money and Security: Troops, Monetary Policy, and West Germany's Relations with the United States and Britain, 1950–1971* (Cambridge: Cambridge University Press, 2002), 90. Several months later, the secretary of the Air Force explained the basis for the *New York Times* report. He told Adenauer that it was "a staff proposal which was prepared for discussion by the Joint Chiefs of Staff. This plan had neither the approval of the Chairman of the Joint Chiefs of Staff, Admiral Arthur W. Radford, nor had it been officially presented to the Government. In working out the draft paper, the question under study was an examination of how the strength of the forces could be adjusted to the constantly increasing costs which arise from equipping the individual soldier with the newest weapons. In view of the increased costs and the accompanying increase in striking power, one could not maintain the same number of soldiers under arms. It was therefore a question of establishing a balance between these two factors." Memorandum of a Conversation, September 10, 1956, FRUS 1955–1957 26: 159–160.

44. Memorandum of a Conversation, July 17, 1956, FRUS 1955–1957 26: 131–135.

45. Letter from Adenauer to Dulles (p. 3), July 22, 1956, folder: "(5)," box 23, Files Relating to John Foster Dulles, White House Memoranda Series, Seeley Mudd Library, Princeton, NJ.

46. Zimmermann, *Money and Security*, 90.

47. Memorandum of Conference with the President, Washington, October 2, 1956, FRUS 1955–1957 4: 99. The United States issued assurances regarding American conventional military commitments to Adenauer. Memorandum from the Secretary of State to the President, October 1, 1956, FRUS 1955–1957 4: 96–99.

48. Telegram from the United States Delegation at the North Atlantic Ministerial Meeting to the Department of State, December 11, 1957, FRUS 1955–1957 4: 106–110.

49. See Vladislav Martinovich Zubok and Konstantin Pleshakov, *Inside the Kremlin's Cold War: From Stalin to Khrushchev* (Cambridge, MA: Harvard University Press, 1996); and Fursenko and Naftali, *Khrushchev's Cold War*.

50. These quotes are pulled from a larger discourse on the problems with troop withdrawals. Memorandum of Discussion at the 424th Meeting of the NSC, November 12, 1959, FRUS 1955–1957 7: 508–509.

51. Promoting Strauss also helped Adenauer deflect potential criticisms regarding his country's nuclear intentions away from himself. Nuti, "F-I-G Story," 83.

52. Schwarz writes that in early 1956 Adenauer informed the French ambassador Maurice Couve de Murville that he lost "confidence" in Eisenhower's approach toward the Soviet Union. Yet the primary source Schwarz uses is dated October 3, 1956, thereby fitting the timeline advanced here. See Schwarz, *Adenauer*, 236.

53. Christoph Bluth, *Britain, Germany and Western Nuclear Strategy* (Oxford: Clarendon Press, 1995), 110.

54. John S. Duffield, *Power Rules: The Evolution of NATO's Conventional Force Posture* (Stanford, CA: Stanford University Press, 1995), 156–157.

55. Bluth, *Britain*, 111–113.

56. Memorandum quoted in Bluth, *Britain*, 124.

57. Quoted in Werner D. Lippert, "Richard Nixon's Détente and Willy Brandt's Ostpolitik: The Politics and Economic Policy of Engaging the Past" (PhD diss., Vanderbilt University, 2005): 25–26.

58. Quoted in Marc Trachtenberg, *The Cold War and After: History, Theory, and the Logic of International Politics* (Princeton, NJ: Princeton University Press, 2012), 166.

59. Duffield, *Power Rules*, 168.

60. Duffield, *Power Rules*, 170.

61. "German Nuclear Developments and rebus sic stantibus," July 6, 1962, folder: "NATO, Weapons, Cables, Germany, 3/61–9/63," National Security Files, Regional Security, box 226A, JFKL.

62. William Glenn Gray, *Germany's Cold War: The Global Campaign to Isolate East Germany, 1949–1969* (Durham: University of North Carolina Press, 2003), 39.

63. Matthew Evangelista, "'Why Keep Such an Army?' Khrushchev's Troop Reductions," *Cold War International History Project*, Working Paper No. 19 (Washington, DC: Woodrow Wilson Center, 1997).

64. Marc Trachtenberg, *A Constructed Peace: The Making of the European Settlement, 1945–1963* (Princeton, NJ: Princeton University Press, 1999).

65. Quoted in Schwarz, *Adenauer*, 35.

66. Schwarz, *Adenauer*, 36.

67. Schwarz, *Adenauer*, 175.

68. Georges-Henri Soutou, "Les accords de 1957 et 1958: Vers une communauté stratégique nucléaire entra la France, l'Allemagne et l'Italie," *Matériaux pour l'histoire de notre temps* 31: 2.

69. Schwarz, *Adenauer*, 192–193.

70. Schwarz, *Adenauer*, 256.

71. German Nuclear Developments and rebus sic stantibus (p. 2), July 6, 1962, folder: "NATO, Weapons, Cables, Germany, 3/61–9/63," National Security Files, Regional Security, box 226A, JFKL.

72. Gene Gerzhoy, "Alliance Coercion and Nuclear Restraint: How the United States Thwarted West Germany's Nuclear Ambitions," *International Security* 39, no. 4 (2015): 91–129; Trachtenberg, *Constructed Peace*; and Francis J. Gavin, "Strategies of Inhibition: US Grand Strategy, the Nuclear Revolution, and Nonproliferation," *International Security* 40, no. 1 (2015): 43–44.

73. G. John Ikenberry, "Power and Liberal Order: America's Postwar World Order in Transition," *International Relations of the Asia-Pacific* 5, no. 2 (2005): 146.

74. Michael Middeke, "Anglo-American Nuclear Weapons Cooperation after the Nassau Conference: The British Policy of Independence," *Journal of Cold War Studies* 2, no. 2 (2000): 77.

75. Telegram from the Department of State to the Embassy in Italy, January 30, 1963, FRUS 1961–1963 13: 155.

76. Memorandum from Gerald C. Smith to Dean Rusk (p. 4), May 5, 1964, folder: "Multilateral Force, General, vol. 1 [1 of 3]," National Security Files, Regional Security, box 22a, LBJ Presidential Library, Austin, TX (hereafter abbreviated as LBJL).

77. Telegram from Athens to Rusk, March 12, 1963, folder: "Multilateral Force, Cables: 3/11/63–3/15/63," National Security Files, Regional Security, box 219, JFKL.

78. Memorandum of Conversation, February 18, 1963, FRUS 1961–1963 13: 502 and 504. During this meeting, American decision makers affirmed their interest to preserve American veto power over nuclear decision-making in the alliance.

79. Middeke, "Anglo-American Nuclear Weapons Cooperation," 77–78.

80. For an American description of de Gaulle's views on the MLF, see "De Gaulle and Atlantic Nuclear Matters," November 2, 1964, folder: "Multilateral Force, Vol. 2 [3 of 3]," National Security File, Subject File, box 23, LBJL. See also Memorandum of Conversation, May 28, 1963, FRUS 1961–1963 13: 583.

81. Memorandum of Conversation, May 28, 1963, FRUS 1961–1963 13: 585. See Middeke, "Anglo-American Nuclear Weapons Cooperation."

82. Memorandum by Ambassador Aristov, April 1, 1963, translation, KC PZPR (Komitet Centralny Polskiej Zjednoczonej Partii Robotniczej [Central Committee of the Polish United Workers' Party]), syn. 2639, 335–337, http://digitalarchive.wilsoncenter.org/document/111581.

83. Letter from Gomułka to Khrushchev, Marked "Final Version," translation, Archiwum Act Nowych [New Files Archive] (AAN), KC PZPR, sign. 2637, 267–282, http://digitalarchive.wilsoncenter.org/document/111619.

84. Memorandum for the President, December 4, 1964, folder: "Multilateral Force, General Vol. 3 [3 of 3]," National Security File, Subject File, box 23, LBJL.

85. Research Memorandum for the Acting Secretary of State, December 16, 1964, folder: "Multilateral Force, General Vol. 3 [2 of 3]," National Security File, Subject File, box 23, LBJL; and Telegram from Embassy in Bonn to Dean Rusk, October 26, 1963, folder: "Germany, Erhard Visit 12/63 [2 of 3]," National Security File, Country File, box 190, LBJL.

86. Telegram from Hyannis Port to the Department of State, May 11, 1963, FRUS 1961–1963 13: 1204.

87. Telegram from Embassy in Bonn to Dean Rusk, July 23, 1964, folder: "Multilateral Force—Cables, Vol. 2 [1 of 3]," National Security File, Subject File, box 24, LBJL.

88. Research Memorandum to Dean Rusk (p. iii), October 28, 1964, folder: "Multilateral Force, General Vol. 2 [3 of 3]," National Security File, Subject File, box 23, LBJL.

89. Memorandum from David Klein to McGeorge Bundy (p. 2), December 5, 1963, folder: "Germany, Erhard Visit 12/63 [1 of 3]," National Security File, Country File, box 190, LBJL. See also Airgram from Embassy in Bonn to Department of State, July 2, 1964, folder: "Multilateral Force—Cables, Vol. 2 [1 of 3]," National Security File, Subject File, box 24, LBJL.

90. On Erhard's confidence in American security guarantees, see Garret Joseph Martin, *General de Gaulle's Cold War: Challenging American Hegemony, 1963–1968* (New York: Berghahn Books, 2013), 34.

91. MLF Congressional Presentation Book (p. 9), June 1, 1964, folder: "Multilateral Force, General Vol. 1 [1 of 3]," National Security File, Subject File, box 22a, LBJL. Erhard made public statements disavowing nuclear weapons, but he would also press for a "hardware" solution. John W. Young, "Killing the MLF?: The Wilson Government and Nuclear Sharing in Western Europe, 1964–1966," *Diplomacy and Statecraft* 14, no. 2 (2003): 311, 315.

92. Despite earlier reservations, Erhard indicated an interest in "go[ing] alone with the US." Intelligence Note to the Secretary of State (p. 2), October 7, 1964, folder: "Multilateral Force, General, Vol. 2 [3 of 3]," National Security File, Subject File, box 23, LBJL. For a summer 1964 statement by Erhard that a bilateral arrangement was infeasible, see Telegram from the Embassy in Bonn to Dean Rusk, June 25, 1964, folder: "Multilateral Force—Cables, Vol. 2 [1 of 3]," National Security File, Subject File, box 24, LBJL. For an intelligence note that summarizes Western European and Soviet views on such a bilateral arrangement, see Intelligence Note to Dean Rusk, October 7, 1964, folder: "Multilateral Force, Vol. 2 [3 of 3]," National Security File, Subject File, box 23, LBJL.

93. See, e.g., National Security Action Memorandum no. 322, December 17, 1964, FRUS 1964–1968 13: 165–167.

94. To clarify, NATO considered various nuclear sharing arrangements in the mid-1960s. Great Britain advanced the idea of the Atlantic Nuclear Force in 1964. Thereafter in 1965 West Germany proposed a mixed force that had elements of the Atlantic Nuclear Force (a British counter-proposal to the MLF that would involve the use of V bombers and nuclear-armed Polaris submarines) and the MLF, with land-based MRBMs. Such hardware solutions were eventually abandoned by 1966. See Susanna Schraftstetter and Stephen Twigge, "Trick or Truth? The British ANF Proposal, West Germany and US Nonproliferation Policy, 1964–1968," *Diplomacy and Statecraft* 11, no. 2 (2000): 161–184.

95. US/FRG Offset Arrangements (p. 1), December 26, 1963, folder: "Germany, Visit of Chancellor Erhard, 12/28–29/63," National Security Files, Country File, box 190, LBJL.

96. Statistics drawn from Zimmermann, *Money and Security*, 246–249.

97. Joint Chiefs of Staff Telegram 5152, June 27, 1962, folder: "NSAM [National Security Action Memorandum] 171, Department of Defense Actions to Reduce Its Overseas Expenditures," National Security Files, Meetings and Memoranda, box 337, JFKL; and Department of State Telegram, July 19, 1962, folder: "NSAM 171, Department of Defense Actions to Reduce its Overseas Expenditures," National Security Files, Meetings and Memoranda, box 337, JFKL.

98. Duffield, *Power Rules*, 158–162.

99. Zimmermann, "Sour Fruits," 224.

100. Francis J. Gavin, *Gold, Dollars, and Power: Money, Security, and the Politics of the U.S. Balance of Payments, 1958–1971* (Durham: University of North Carolina Press, 2004), 64.

101. Zimmermann, *Money and Security*, 133.

102. Zimmermann, *Money and Security*, 134, 136–137.

103. Report to the President by the Cabinet Committee on Balance of Payments (p. 1), July 27, 1962, folder: "Balance of Payments, 1963," Papers of Francis M. Bator, Subject Files, box 14, LBJL.

104. Michael D. Bordo, Owen F. Humpage, and Anna J. Schwartz, *Bretton Woods and the US Decision to Intervene in the Foreign-Exchange Market, 1957–1962* (Cleveland, OH: Federal Reserve Bank of Cleveland, 2006), 7.

105. Quoted in Zimmermann, *Money and Security*, 147.

106. Zimmermann, *Money and Security*, 147–152.

107. Trachtenberg, *Constructed Peace*, 283–297.

108. Summary Record NSC Executive Committee Meeting No. 38 (Part 2), January 25, 1963, FRUS 1961–1963 13: 488–489.

109. Rusk quoted in Hubert Zimmermann, "The Improbable Permanence of a Commitment: American Presence in Europe during the Cold War," *Journal of Cold War Studies* 11, no. 1 (2009): 15.

110. Zimmermann, "The Improbable Permanence of a Commitment."

111. Trachtenberg, *Constructed Peace*, 383–387.

112. Gray, *Germany's Cold War*, 143–144.

113. In fact, a background paper prepared for Johnson suggested that Erhard was so pro-American that the chancellor might be liable to domestic and international criticism. Background Paper: Atlantic Partnership and European Integration (p. 1), December 20, 1963, folder: "Germany Briefing Book—Erhard Visit, 12/28–29/63 [2 of 2]," National Security File, Country File, box 190, LBJL.

114. Memorandum for the President, June 10, 1964, folder: "Germany—Erhard Visit [6/64], 6/12–6/13 [1 of 3]," National Security File, Country File, box 191, LBJL.

115. Quoted in Zimmermann, *Money and Security*, 165.

116. Zimmermann, *Money and Security*, 168.

117. Defense Minister Kai-Uwe von Hassel "said that prices are going up, and that the capital market has 'broken down.' He said that, if this goes on, the stability of the DM [Deutschmark] will be endangered, and 'all Germans remember 1923 and 1948.'" Memorandum of Conversation (p. 3), July 26, 1966, folder: "Offset (US/UK/FRG) [1 of 3]," Papers of Francis M. Bator, Subject Files, box 20, LBJL.

118. Memorandum for the President, September 13, 1966, same folder and box as footnote 117.

119. United States Information Agency—Office of Policy and Research, "German Malaise over Growing Differences with the U.S. on Offset and NATO Issues," August 1966, same folder and box as footnote 117.

120. Briefing Memorandum for the President, undated, and Memorandum for McNamara, July 18, 1966, folder: "Offset (US/UK/FRG) [2 of 3]," Papers of Francis M. Bator, Subject File, box 20, LBJL.

121. Telegram from Bonn to Rusk, September 8, 1966, folder: "Offset (US/UK/FRG) [3 of 3]," Papers of Francis M. Bator, Subject File, box 20, LBJL.

122. Zimmermann, "Sour Fruits," 235.

123. Gavin, *Gold*, 165.

124. Gavin, *Gold*, 190.

125. Jonathan Kirshner, *Currency and Coercion: The Political Economy of International Monetary Power* (Princeton, NJ: Princeton University Press, 1995), 194. Of course, the United States ultimately succeeded in forcing its allies to bear adjustment costs disproportionately when the system collapsed in 1971. See Michael Mastanduno, "System Maker and Privilege Taker: U.S. Power and the International Political Economy," *World Politics* 61, no. 1 (2009): 121–154.

126. Trachtenberg, *Constructed Peace*, 377.

127. Ronald F. Bunn, "The Spiegel Affair and the West German Press: The Initial Phase," *Public Opinion Quarterly* 30, no. 1 (1966): 55–57.

128. Bunn, "Spiegel Affair."

129. I thank Jonas Schneider for this point.

130. Memorandum of Conversation, February 23, 1968, FRUS 1964–1968 15: 637.

131. Gerzhoy, "Alliance Coercion," 123.

132. Jonas Schneider and Gene Gerzhoy, "Correspondence: The United States and West Germany's Quest for Nuclear Weapons," *International Security* 41, no. 1 (2016): 183; and Letter from Rusk to Director of the U.S. Arms Control and Disarmament Agency quoted in Makreeta Lahti, "Security Cooperation as a Way to Stop the Spread of Nuclear Weapons? Nuclear Nonproliferation Policies of the United States toward the Federal Republic of Germany and Israel, 1945–1968" (PhD diss., University of Potsdam, 2008), 334.

133. Schneider and Gerzhoy, "Correspondence," 183–184.

134. Even so, Strauss opposed the NPT much more so than Kiesinger.

135. Schneider and Gerzhoy, "Correspondence," 184.

136. On the Gilpatric Committee, see Francis J. Gavin, "Blasts from the Pasts: Proliferation Lessons from the 1960s," *International Security* 29, no. 3 (2004–2005): 100–135; and Hal Brands, "Non-Proliferation and the Dynamics of the Middle Cold War: The Superpowers, the MLF, and the NPT," *Cold War History* 7, no. 3 (2007): 389–423.

137. Report by the Committee on Nuclear Proliferation, January 21, 1965, FRUS 1964–1968 11: 175.

138. Brands, "Non-Proliferation," 394.

139. Brands, "Non-Proliferation," 406–408.

140. Andrew Priest, "From Hardware to Software: The End of the MLF and the Rise of the Nuclear Planning Group," in *Transforming NATO in the Cold War: Challenges Beyond Deterrence in the 1960s* (London: Routledge, 2006), 148–161.

141. On the emergence of the NPG, see Bluth, *Britain*, 179–194; and Priest, "From Hardware."

142. David James Gill, *Britain and the Bomb: Nuclear Diplomacy, 1964–1970* (Stanford, CA: Stanford University Press, 2014), 165–166.

143. The United States negotiated the language of articles 1 and 2 of the treaty so as to protect alliance consultations. Letter from Katzenbach to Clifford, April 10, 1968, National Security Archive: Nuclear Vault, George Washington University, http://www.gwu.edu/~nsarchiv/nukevault/ebb253/index.htm (hereafter, Nuclear Vault).

144. Telegram 7557 from the Embassy in Bonn to Dean Rusk, January 23, 1968, Nuclear Vault.

145. Department of State Cable 113607 to Rusk, February 10, 1968, Nuclear Vault.

146. Telegram 7557 from the Embassy in Bonn to Dean Rusk, January 23, 1968, Nuclear Vault.

147. Schrafstetter and Twigge, *Avoiding Armageddon*, 170–171. Nuclear safeguards are measures intended to ensure that nuclear materials would not be used for military purpose. International organizations can have their own standards with respect to nuclear safeguards.

148. Telegram 7557 from the Embassy in Bonn to Dean Rusk, January 23, 1968, Nuclear Vault.

149. Schrafstetter and Twigge, *Avoiding Armageddon*, 185.

150. Statements recorded in Schrafstetter and Twigge, *Avoiding Armageddon*, 182–183.

151. Schrafstetter and Twigge, *Avoiding Armageddon*, 189.

152. U.S. Embassy Bonn Cable 10869 to State Department, April 10, 1968, Nuclear Vault; and State Department Memorandum of Conversation, July 23, 1968, Nuclear Vault.

153. On *Ostpolitik*, see Mary Elise Sarotte, *Dealing with the Devil: East Germany, Détente, and Ostpolitik, 1969–1973* (Durham: University of North Carolina Press, 2001).

154. Brandt quoted in Lippert, "Richard Nixon's Détente," 45.

155. Gray, *Germany's Cold War*, 203.

156. An artifact of the immediate postwar period, these articles gave the right of victor states to intervene in the domestic affairs of their defeated adversaries. Gray, *Germany's Cold War*, 206.

157. Gray, *Germany's Cold War*, 207–208.

158. The Nixon administration generally stood aloof as this process unfolded. Indeed, one document argues that progress was finally achieved because an "absence of pressure . . . has substantially decreased emotional resistance in Germany." Memorandum from Eliot to Kissinger, October 29, 1969, FRUS 1969–1976 E-2: 2.

159. Sarotte, *Dealing with the Devil*, 27. Ostpolitik did not mean that West Germany recognized East Germany in international law, however. Bluth, *Britain*, 169.

160. Memorandum from Kissinger to Nixon, February 11, 1969, FRUS 1969–1976 40: 14–19. For a summary of Kiesinger's position on the NPT in February 1969, see Memorandum of Conversation, February 3, 1969, FRUS 1969–1976 E-2: 1–3.

161. Emphasis mine. Draft Memorandum of Conversation, February 26, 1969, FRUS 1969–1976 40: 37.

162. Sarotte, *Dealing with the Devil*, 30–31.

163. Ostpolitik arguably built on the NATO-approved Harmel Report that emphasized strong defense and positive diplomatic relations with the Warsaw Pact in the spirit of détente. Bluth, *Britain*, 174.

164. Henry A. Kissinger, *White House Years* (New York: Simon and Schuster, 1979), 409–411.

165. Georges-Henri Soutou, *L'Alliance incertaine: Les rapports politico-stratégiques franco-allemands, 1954–1996* (Paris: Fayard, 1996), 319.

166. See Trachtenberg, *Cold War and After*, 167; and Sarotte, *Dealing with the Devil*, 35–36.

167. Jonas Schneider, "Nuclear Nonproliferation within the Context of US Alliances: Protection, Status, and the Psychology of West Germany's Nuclear Reversal" (paper presented at the convention of the International Studies Association, Toronto, March 26–29, 2014). See also Jonas Schnieder, *Amerikanische Allianzen und nukleare Nichtverbreitung: Die Beendigung von Kernwaffenktivitäten bei Allianzpartnern der USA* [US alliances and nuclear proliferation: Why US allies give up their nuclear weapons activities] (Baden-Baden, Germany: Nomos Publishers, 2016).

168. Indeed, Brandt and his adviser Egon Bahr saw NPT accession as the first step toward denuclearizing Germany so as to dissolve the Cold War blocs and to allow for the emergence of a new European security system. I thank Andreas Lutsch for this observation.

169. Brandt, Bahr, and Kiesinger quoted in Jonas Schneider, "Beyond Assurance and Coercion: U.S. Alliances and the Psychology of Nuclear Reversal," (working paper, Center for Security Studies, ETH Zurich, January 2016), 30–31.

170. Gray, *Germany's Cold War*, 229.

171. Trachtenberg, *Cold War and After*, 167.

172. Etel Solingen, *Nuclear Logics: Contrasting Paths in East Asia and the Middle East* (Princeton, NJ: Princeton University Press, 2007), 8.

173. Schrafstetter and Twigge, *Avoiding Armageddon*, 182.

174. Berger, *Cultures of Antimilitarism*, 49.

4. Japan, 1952–1980

1. Ariel E. Levite, "Never Say Never: Nuclear Reversal Revisited," *International Security* 27, no. 3 (2003): 59–88.

2. John Wilson Lewis and Hua Di, "China's Ballistic Missile Programs: Technologies, Strategies, Goals," *International Security* 17, no. 2 (1992): 14–18.

3. On Japan's political factions, see Thomas U. Berger, *Cultures of Antimilitarism: National Security in Germany and Japan* (Baltimore, MD: Johns Hopkins University Press, 1998), 56–64; and Nathaniel Bowman Thayer, *How the Conservatives Rule Japan* (Princeton, NJ: Princeton University Press, 1969).

4. Etel Solingen, *Nuclear Logics: Contrasting Paths in East Asia and the Middle East* (Princeton, NJ: Princeton University Press, 2007), 70.

5. Solingen, *Nuclear Logics*, 80.

6. Solingen, *Nuclear Logics*, 67.

7. Kurt M. Campbell and Tsuyoshi Sunohara, "Japan: Thinking the Unthinkable," in *Nuclear Tipping Point: Why States Reconsider Their Nuclear Choices*, ed. Kurt M. Campbell, Robert J. Einhorn, and Mitchell B. Reiss (Washington, DC: Brookings Institution Press, 2004), 129.

8. Quoted in Telegram from the Embassy in Japan to the Department of State, May 8, 1957, FRUS 1955–1957 23: 285.

9. Telegram from the Embassy in Japan to the Department of State, May 8, 1957, FRUS 1955–1957 23: 285. For a summary of Japanese leaders' views on nuclear weapons, see Ayako Kusunoki, "The Sato Cabinet and the Making of Japan's Non-Nuclear Policy," *Journal of American-East Asian Relations* 15 (2008): 28–29.

10. Quotes from Background Paper Prepared by Sidney Weintraub of the Office of Northeast Asian Affairs, June 17, 1957, FRUS 1955–1957 23: 354–355.

11. In fact, the Japanese government commissioned seventeen studies on nuclear policy when Sato was prime minister. See Toshimitsu Kishi, "Deliberations on Japanese Nuclear Policy During the SATO Administration: Studies by the Cabinet Research Office," *National Graduate Institute for Policy Studies (GRIPS) Discussion Paper 17–15*, February 2018.

12. Toshimitsu Kishi, "Sato Administration's Reaction to the Chinese Nuclear Test: Examination of Nuclear Scenarios by the Cabinet Research Office in the 1960s," *Journal of the Graduate School of Asia-Pacific Studies* 30 (2015): 21.

13. Kusunoki, "Sato Cabinet," 44.

14. Yuri Kase, "The Costs and Benefits of Japan's Nuclearization: An Insight into the 1968/70 Internal Report," *Nonproliferation Review* 8, no. 2 (2001): 59.

15. Matthew Fuhrmann and Benjamin Tkach, "Almost Nuclear: Introducing the Nuclear Latency Dataset," *Conflict Management and Peace Science* 32, no. 4 (2015): 451.

16. On Japan's incipient centrifuge program and enrichment technology, see Ronald Scott Kemp, "Nonproliferation in the Centrifuge Age" (PhD diss., Princeton University, 2010), 64–65; and John E. Endicott, *Japan's Nuclear Option: Political, Technical, and Strategic Factors* (New York: Praeger, 1975), 118–125. To be sure, throughout the 1960s, Japan experienced difficulty in

developing domestic fuel reprocessing and plutonium procurement. Interestingly, President Johnson did not oppose Japan's efforts to develop reprocessing capabilities. See Akira Kurosaki, "Nuclear Energy and Nuclear-Weapon Potential: A Historical Analysis of Japan in the 1960s," *Nonproliferation Review* 24, No. 1–2 (2017): 60–63.

17. R. Scott Kemp, "Centrifuges: A New Era for Nuclear Proliferation," in *Nuclear Proliferation: Moving beyond Pretense; Preliminary Findings of NPEC's Project on Nonproliferation Policy*, ed. Henry Sokolski (Arlington, VA: Nonproliferation Policy Education Center), 62, 64.

18. Some argue that Japan's nuclear energy program is "not designed to hedge against abandonment by the United States, but rather is embedded in a far broader portfolio of policies designed to decrease perceived risks associated with on external energy supplies." Neither motive is mutually exclusive, however. That Japan would try to obtain certain nuclear technologies strictly without having any geopolitical uses in mind is hard to believe. See Llewelyn Hughes, "Why Japan Will Not Go Nuclear (Yet): International and Domestic Constraints on the Nuclearization of Japan," *International Security* 31, no. 4 (2007): 81.

19. Quoted in Kemp, "Nonproliferation," 64.

20. Kase, "Costs and Benefits." One study argues that the study group "acted on its own initiative and not under instructions from Prime Minister Sato." The report did see limited circulation among Japanese officials. See Kurosaki, "Nuclear Energy," 52, 56–57.

21. Memorandum of Conversation (p. 2), October 3, 1967, folder: "DEF-18-4 Non-Proliferation Treaty (NPT). Press Comments, 1967," Records Relating to Japanese Political Affairs 1960–1975, box 3, RG 59, National Archives and Records Administration (hereafter abbreviated as NARA).

22. Memorandum of Conversation (p. 2), October 3, 1967, folder: "DEF-18-4 Non-Proliferation Treaty (NPT). Press Comments, 1967," Records Relating to Japanese Political Affairs 1960–1975, box 3, RG 59, NARA.

23. Hughes, "Why Japan Will Not Go Nuclear (Yet)," 86.

24. Quoted in Yukinori Komine, "Okinawa Confidential, 1969: Exploring the Linkage between the Nuclear Issue and the Base Issue," *Diplomatic History* 37, no. 4 (2013): 826.

25. Japan had already secretly permitted the United States to introduce nuclear weapons into its territory under certain conditions during the treaty negotiations in 1960. See Description of Consultation Arrangements under the Treaty of Mutual Cooperation and Security with Japan, June 1960, National Security Archive: Nuclear Vault, George Washington University, Washington, DC (hereafter Nuclear Vault); Summary of Unpublished Agreements, June 1960, Nuclear Vault, document available at http://nsarchive2.gwu.edu//nukevault/ebb291/index.htm; and Telegram 2335 from Tokyo to the Department of State, April 4, 1963, Nuclear Vault.

26. Endicott, *Japan's Nuclear Option*, 42–43.

27. Memorandum of Conversation, Washington, July 31, 1973, 11 a.m., FRUS 1969–1976 E-12: 6.

28. Memorandum of Conversation, May 21, 1974, folder: "May 21, 1974—Nixon, Japanese Foreign Minister Masayoshi Ohira," National Security Adviser, Memoranda of Conversation, box 4, Gerald R. Ford Library (hereafter abbreviated as GRFL).

29. National Security Decision Memorandum 13, May 28, 1969, Nuclear Vault.

30. Memorandum of Conversation, September 21, 1974, FRUS 1969–1976 E-14: 283. Raising the specter of Japanese nuclear proliferation was a ploy that the Nixon administration used to justify a military presence in East Asia. Yukinori Komine, "The 'Japan Card' in the United States Rapprochement, 1969–1972," *Diplomacy and Statecraft* 20, no. 3 (2009): 494–514.

31. Zhou quoted in William R. Kintner, "Arms Control for a Five-Power World," in *SALT: Implications for Arms Control in the 1970s*, ed. William R. Kintner and Robert L. Pfaltzgraff Jr. (Pittsburgh, PA: University of Pittsburgh Press, 1973), 173.

32. Kissinger to Nixon, "My October China Visit: Discussion of the Issues," November 11, 1971, Negotiating US-Chinese Rapprochement, National Security Archive Electronic Briefing Book No. 70, http://www.gwu.edu/~nsarchiv/NSAEBB/NSAEBB70/.

33. Memorandum of Conversation, April 7, 1974, FRUS 1973–1976 E-12: 2.

34. See Kemp, "Nonproliferation," 64–65.

35. Matake Kamiya, "Nuclear Japan: Oxymoron or coming soon?," *Washington Quarterly* 26, no. 1 (2010): 69–71.

36. The United States had no issue with undertaking partial military withdrawals from Japan. See Memorandum from the Joint Chiefs of Staff to the Secretary of Defense, April 1, 1955, FRUS 1955–1957 23: 33–34; National Security Council Report, April 9, 1955, FRUS 1955–1957 23: 60; Memorandum of a Conversation, August 30, 1955, FRUS 1955–1957 23: 97–104; and Memorandum of Discussion at the 266th Meeting of the NSC, November 15, 1955, FRUS 1955–1957 23: 137–39.

37. Memorandum from the Assistant Secretary of State for Far Eastern Affairs to the Secretary of State, July 28, 1955, FRUS 1955–1957 23: 79–80.

38. On Japanese postwar attitudes toward the United States, see John W. Dower, *Embracing Defeat: Japan in the Wake of the World War II* (New York: W. W. Norton, 1999).

39. Memorandum of Conversation, August 31, 1955, 10 a.m., FRUS 1955–1957 23: 107.

40. Memorandum from the Assistant Secretary of State for Far Eastern Affairs to the Secretary of State, July 28, 1955, FRUS 1955–1957 23: 80. Whatever the substance of Japanese elite opinion, surveys of the Japanese public revealed an aversion toward the use of nuclear weapons in East Asia, especially because of Hiroshima and Nagasaki. See Matthew Jones, *After Hiroshima: The United States, Race and Nuclear Weapons in Asia, 1945–1965* (Cambridge: Cambridge University Press, 2010), 322–323. That said, polls indicate that the level of support for Japan to acquire nuclear weapons fell by half between 1955 and 1981. See Akitoshi Miyashita, "Where Do Norms Come From? Foundations of Japan's Postwar Pacifism," *International Relations of the Asia-Pacific* 7, no. 1 (2006): 109.

41. Thomas J. Christensen, *Worse than a Monolith: Alliance Politics and Problems of Coercive Diplomacy in Asia* (Princeton, NJ: Princeton University Press, 2011).

42. See Gordon H. Chang, "To the Nuclear Brink: Eisenhower, Dulles, and the Quemoy-Matsu Crisis," *International Security* 12, no. 4 (1988): 96–123.

43. Letter from the Ambassador in Japan (MacArthur) to the Secretary of State, May 25, 1957, FRUS 1955–1957 23: 326–327.

44. Report to the National Security Council by the Executive Secretary, October 30, 1953, FRUS 1952–1954 2: 592.

45. Memorandum of Discussion at the 244th Meeting of the NSC, April 7, 1955, FRUS 1955–1957 23: 44.

46. I thank Kazuto Suzuki for this point.

47. National Intelligence Estimate, March 16, 1955, FRUS 1955–1957 2: 377.

48. Memorandum of a Conference with the President, May 14, 1956, FRUS 1955–1957 19: 302.

49. Memorandum of Discussion at the 285th Meeting of the NSC, May 17, 1956, FRUS 1955–1957 19: 307. See also Jones, *After Hiroshima*, 304–305. On implementing New Look in East Asia, see Jones, *After Hiroshima*, 308–309.

50. Memorandum from the Assistant Secretary of State for Far Eastern Affairs (Robertson) to the Secretary of State, July 28, 1955, FRUS 1955–1957 23: 80; and Telegram from the Consulate General at Naha to the Department of State, December 15, 1957, FRUS 1955–1957 23: 548.

51. Memorandum of a Conversation between Foreign Secretary Macmillan and Secretary of State Dulles, June 21, 1955, FRUS 1955–1957 23: 73.

52. Memorandum from the Acting Assistant of State for Far Eastern Affairs (Sebald) to the Secretary of State, August 26, 1955, FRUS 1955–1957 23: 89.

53. Memorandum from the Assistant Secretary of State for Far Eastern Affairs (Robertson) to the Secretary of State, January 7, 1957, FRUS 1955–1957 23: 241. On the domestic debates regarding rearmament in early 1950s Japan, see Jennifer M. Miller, "The Struggle to Rearm Japan: Negotiating the Cold War State in US-Japanese Relations," *Journal of Contemporary History* 46, no. 1 (2011): 82–108.

54. Memorandum of a Conversation between Dulles and Kishi, June 20, 1957, 4 p.m., FRUS 1955–1957 23: 401. Japanese policy toward China involved separating political issues from economic ones. This theme continued at least through the 1960s. Memorandum from Norred to Green, August 19, 1964, folder: "POL. Japan, Communist China (CHICOM), 1965," RG 59, Records Relating to Japanese Political Affairs, box 1, NARA.

55. Memorandum of a Conversation, August 31, 1955, FRUS 1955–1957 23: 105.

56. Memorandum for the Record of a Meeting between the Secretary of State and the President's Special Consultant (Nash), June 5, 1957, FRUS 1955–1957 23: 340.

57. John Swenson-Wright, *Unequal Allies?: United States Security and Alliance Policy toward Japan* (Stanford, CA: Stanford University Press, 2005).

58. On American base politics on Okinawa, see Nicholas Evan Sarantakes, *Keystone: The American Occupation of Okinawa and U.S.-Japanese Relations* (College Station: Texas A&M University Press, 2000).

59. National Intelligence Estimate, February 7, 1961, FRUS 1961–1963 22: 674–675.

60. Michael Schaller, *Altered States: The United States and Japan since the Occupation* (New York: Oxford University Press, 1997), 163.

61. Roger Buckley, *US-Japan Alliance Diplomacy, 1945–1990* (Cambridge: Cambridge University Press, 1992), 100.

62. Buckley, *US-Japan Alliance Diplomacy*, 99.

63. Kase, "Costs and Benefits," 63.

64. Kishi, "Sato Administration's Reaction," 21.

65. Quotes drawn from Memorandum of Conversation, January 12, 1965, FRUS 1964–1968 29: 76–77.

66. Sato quoted in Francis J. Gavin, "Blasts from the Pasts: Proliferation Lessons from the 1960s," *International Security* 29, no. 3 (2004–2005): 117.

67. Lyndon B. Johnson: "Joint Statement Following Meetings With the Prime Minister of Japan," January 13, 1965. Online by Gerhard Peters and John T. Woolley, *The American Presidency Project*, http://www.presidency.ucsb.edu/ws/?pid=26852.

68. Quoted in Kusunoki, "Sato Cabinet," 31.

69. Sato also supported the United States on Vietnam in order to manage trade links and to revert Okinawa back to Japan. See Thomas R. H. Havens, *Fire across the Sea: The Vietnam War and Japan, 1965–1975* (Princeton, NJ: Princeton University Press, 1987), 25–26.

70. Lyndon B. Johnson, *Public Papers of the Presidents of the United States: Lyndon B. Johnson, 1968–1969 [Book 1]* (Washington, DC: Government Printing Office, 1970), 469–476.

71. Johnson statements recorded in Editorial Note, FRUS 1964–1968 29: 270.

72. Editorial Note, FRUS 1964–1968 29: 270.

73. Memorandum from Straus to Sneider, April 25, 1968, folder: "DEF-1 Japan. Defense Policy, 1967," Records Relating to Japanese Political Affairs 1960–1975, box 3, RG 59, NARA.

74. Telegram from the Embassy in Japan to the Department of State, June 5, 1968, FRUS 1965–1968 29: 277–278.

75. Memorandum from the President's Special Assistant (Rostow) to President Johnson, March 1, 1967, FRUS 1964–1968 29: 168.

76. Memorandum from the President's Special Assistant (Rostow) to President Johnson, March 1, 1967, FRUS 1964–1968 29: 166.

77. Victor D. Cha, *Alignment despite Antagonism: The United States-Korea-Japan Security Triangle* (Stanford, CA: Stanford University Press, 1999), 68–69.

78. Aichi quoted in Cha, *Alignment despite Antagonism*, 70.

79. I privilege conservative views because of the influence conservatives had on Japanese policy-making during this period.

80. Endicott, *Japan's Nuclear Option*, 6.

81. Economic relations also shaped Japanese perceptions of the United States. See Japanese Public Opinion Relevant to U.S.-Japan Relations, July 26, 1973, folder: "POL 2-6 Public Opinion Polls, 1973," Records Relating to Japanese Political Affairs 1960–1975, box 9, RG 59, NARA.

82. Japanese Public Opinion Relevant to US-Japan Relations after Vietnam, July 28, 1975, folder: "POL 2, Public Opinion Polls, 1975," Records Relating to Japanese Political Affairs 1960–1975, box 12, RG 59, NARA.

83. Kemp, "Nonproliferation," 64–65.

84. Nakasone quoted in Cha, *Alignment despite Antagonism*, 71.

85. Komine, "Okinawa Confidential"; and Kusunoki, "Sato Cabinet," 48.

86. Kusunoki, "Sato Cabinet," 45.

87. Cha, *Alignment despite Antagonism*, 72.

88. See, e.g., Lawrence S. Wittner, *The Struggle against the Bomb, Volume 2* (Stanford, CA: Stanford University Press, 1993), 39–55.

89. Kusunoki, "Sato Cabinet," 35–36.

90. "Albin Krebs, Eisaku Sato Ex-Premier of Japan, Dies at 75," *New York Times*, June 3, 1975.

91. Memorandum of Conversation, November 23, 1964, FRUS 1964–1968 11: 123.

92. Memorandum from the Joint Chiefs of Staff to Secretary of Defense McNamara, January 16, 1965, FRUS 1964–1968 30: 145.

93. Christopher Hemmer and Peter J. Katzenstein, "Why Is There No NATO in Asia? Collective Identity, Regionalism, and the Origins of Multilateralism," *International Organization* 56, no. 3 (2002): 591–598.

94. Memorandum from Secretary of State Rusk to President Johnson, September 4, 1967, FRUS 1964–1968 29: 207.

95. Key Judgments from Research Study OPR-4 Prepared in the Central Intelligence Agency, May 1974, FRUS 1969–1974 E-12: 1–3.

96. Endicott, *Japan's Nuclear Option*, 8–9.

97. Memorandum of Bureau of International Scientific and Technology Affairs, October 31, 1972, folder: "AE-13. Safeguards (NPT), 1972," Records Relating to Japanese Political Affairs 1960–1975, box 9, RG 59, NARA.

98. Memorandum of Conversation, May 21, 1974, folder: "May 21, 1974—Nixon, Japanese Foreign Minister Masayoshi Ohira," National Security Adviser, Memoranda of Conversation, box 4, GRFL.

99. Memorandum for Major General Brent Scowcroft, August 26, 1974, folder: "Japan (1)," National Security Adviser, Presidential Country Files for East Asia and the Pacific, box 6, GRFL.

100. Memorandum for the President from Henry A. Kissinger, folder: "Japan (7)," National Security Adviser, Presidential Country Files for East Asia and the Pacific, box 7, GRFL.

101. Talking Points for Meeting with Japanese Prime Minister Takeo Miki, August 4, 1976, same folder and box as footnote 99.

102. Memorandum of Conversation, July 7, 1966, FRUS 1964–1968 19: 152.

103. Schaller, *Altered States*, 177–181.

104. Schaller, *Altered States*, 181.

105. Schaller, *Altered States*, 198–199.

106. Schaller, *Altered States*, 201.

107. Memorandum from Robert Hormats of the NSC Staff to the President's Assistant for National Security Affairs (Kissinger), April 12, 1973, FRUS 1969–1976 E-12: 1.

108. All quotes found in Memorandum from the Deputy Secretary of Defense to President Kennedy, February 8, 1963, FRUS 1961–1963 22: 767.

109. Memorandum from the Deputy Secretary of Defense to President Kennedy, February 8, 1963, FRUS 1961–1963 22: 768. See also Telegram from the Embassy in Japan to the Department of State, November 1, 1963, FRUS 1961–1963 22: 797; and Letter from Secretary of Defense McNamara to Secretary of State Rusk, November 16, 1963, FRUS 1961–1963 22: 801–803.

110. See, e.g., Memorandum of Conversation, December 8, 1962 and Position Paper: Military Offset Negotiations with Japan, December 3–5, 1962 in folder: "FN-12 Military Offsets (Buildup of Gilpatric Visit), 10/15/62–2/4/63," Records Relating to Japanese Political Affairs 1960–1975, box 1, RG 59, NARA. The United States eventually did obtain Japanese offsets in negotiations that began in the late 1970s. See Tatsuro Yoda, "Japan's Host Nation Support Program for the U.S.-Japan Security Alliance: Past and Prospects," *Asian Survey* 46, no. 6 (2006): 939–942.

111. Schaller, *Altered States*, 212.

112. "Secret Pact with US on Textile Curbs Revealed," *Japan Times*, November 27, 2010, https://www.japantimes.co.jp/news/2010/11/27/national/secret-pact-with-u-s-on-textile-curbs-revealed/.

113. Mike M. Mochizuki, "Japan and the Strategic Quadrangle," in *The Strategic Quadrangle: Russia, China, Japan, and the United States in East Asia*, ed. Michael Mandelbaum (Washington, DC: Council of Foreign Relations Press, 1995), 107–153.

114. Editorial Note, FRUS 1973–1976 E-12: 1. Original citation as National Archives, Nixon Presidential Materials, White House Tapes, Oval Office, Conversation No. 114-1.

115. Conversation between President Nixon and John B. Connally, January 31, 1973, FRUS 1969–1976: 1. Connally was secretary of the Treasury in 1971 and 1972.

116. Memorandum of Conversation, January 4, 1973, FRUS 1969–1876 E-12: 3.

117. See Japan-U.S. Energy Relations Talking Points, undated, folder: "POL 2: 16th US-Japan Planning Talks, 1972," Records Relating to Japanese Political Affairs 1960–1975, box 9, RG 59, NARA.

118. Motoya Kitamura, "Japan's Plutonium Program: A Proliferation Threat?," *Nonproliferation Review* 3, no. 2 (1996): 4.

119. Kitamura, "Japan's Plutonium Program."

120. See Eugene Skolnikoff, Tatsujiro Suzuki, and Kenneth Oye, "International Responses to Japanese Plutonium Programs" (Cambridge, MA: Center for International Studies, 1995), 6.

121. Endicott, *Japan's Nuclear Option*, 30. See also Kurosaki, "Nuclear Energy," 61–64.

122. Kitamura, "Japan's Plutonium Program," 7.

123. Jayita Sarkar, "India's Nuclear Limbo and the Fatalism of the Nuclear Non-Proliferation Regime, 1974–1983," *Strategic Analysis* 37, no. 3 (2013): 322–337.

124. Skolnikoff, Suzuki, and Oye, "International Responses," 21.

125. Memorandum Prepared by Counselor and Chairman of the Policy Planning Council (Owen), July 12, 1966, FRUS 1964–1968 29: 153–154.

126. Telegram from the Embassy in Japan to the Department of State, March 1, 1967, FRUS 1964–1968 29: 168.

127. George H. Quester, "Japan and the Nuclear Non-Proliferation Treaty," *Asian Survey* 10, no. 9 (1970): 765.

128. Komine, "'Japan Card.'"

129. Interview with former ambassador Yoichi Funabashi, Tokyo, March 2013. On Nakasone's efforts to reorient Japan's defense policy between 1969 and 1971, see Fintan Hoey, "The Nixon Doctrine and Nakasone Yasuhiro's Unsuccessful Challenge to Japan's Defense Policy, 1969–1971," *Journal of American-East Asian Relations* 19, no. 1 (2012): 52–74.

130. Komine, "'Japan Card,'" 496.

131. Francis J. Gavin, *Nuclear Statecraft: History and Strategy in America's Atomic Age* (Ithaca, NY: Cornell University Press, 2012), 118.

132. Paper Prepared by the NSC Under Secretaries Committee, June 21, 1976, 1969–76 E-14: 132–133.

133. Paper Prepared by the NSC Under Secretaries Committee, June 21, 1976, 1969–76 E-14: 137.

134. Special National Intelligence Estimate 4-1-74, August 23, 1974, FRUS 1969–1976 E-14: 221.

135. Key Judgments from Research Study OPR-4 Prepared in the Central Intelligence Agency, May 1974, FRUS 1969–1974 E-12: 1–3.

136. Talking Points for Meeting with Japanese Prime Minister Takeo Miki, August 4, 1976, folder: "Japan (7)," National Security Adviser, Presidential Country Files for East Asia and the Pacific, box 7, GRFL.

137. See Chalmers Johnson, "Tanaka Kakuei, Structural Corruption, and the Advent of Machine Politics in Japan," *Journal of Japanese Studies* 12, no. 1 (1986): 1–28.

138. Memorandum for Secretary Kissinger from Rodman, June 25, 1975, folder: "Japan (7)," National Security Adviser, Presidential Country Files for East Asia and the Pacific, box 6, GRFL.

139. K. V. Kesavan, "Japan and the Nuclear Non-Proliferation Treaty," *India Quarterly* 32, no. 1 (1976): 13; and Maria Rost Rublee, *Nonproliferation Norms: Why States Choose Nuclear Restraint* (Athens: University of Georgia Press, 2009), 68.

140. John E. Endicott, "The 1975–76 Debate over Ratification of the NPT in Japan," *Asian Survey* 17, no. 3 (1977): 275–292.

141. Endicott, "1975–76 Debate," 278.

142. Kesavan, "Japan," 14.

143. Kissinger understood Miyazawa's objectives when he alerted Ford that the meeting was "to demonstrate the high importance we attach to our alliance with Japan" and "to reaffirm US determination to continue our vital role as regards the future peace and stability of Asia, particularly in light of the current Indochina crisis." Kissinger acknowledged that "we have had reports that our inability to react to recent events in Indochina has caused some second thoughts in Japan about ratifying the Non-Proliferation Treaty." Note for Meeting with the Japanese Foreign Minister Kiichi Miyazawa, April 12, 1975, folder: "Japan (7)," National Security Adviser, Presidential Country Files for East Asia and the Pacific, box 7, GRFL.

144. Endicott, "1975–76 Debate," 282.

145. Kesavan, "Japan,"14.

146. See Memorandum for Major General Brent Scowcroft, August 26, 1974, folder: "Japan (1)," National Security Adviser, Presidential Country Files for East Asia and the Pacific, box 6, GRFL; and Memorandum for the President from Henry A. Kissinger, folder: "Japan (7)," National Security Adviser, Presidential Country Files for East Asia and the Pacific, box 7, GRFL. Some American government officials—like Secretary of Defense James Schlesinger—advocated for the United States to adopt "somewhat more forceful means of persuasion" to obtain Japanese NPT ratification. See also Memorandum from Secretary of Defense Schlesinger to Secretary of State Kissinger, March 24, 1975, FRUS 1969–1976 E-14: 426. See also Memorandum from the Director of the Arms Control and Disarmament Agency (Iklé) to President Ford, February 18, 1975, FRUS 1969–1976 E-14: 403–405.

147. Memorandum of Conversation, November 19, 1974, FRUS 1969–1976 E-12: 11.

148. Memorandum of Conversation, November 19, 1974, FRUS 1969–1976 E-12: 12.

149. Memorandum for Zbigniew Brzezinski, March 23, 1977, Jimmy Carter, Remote Archives Capture (RAC) Project Number NLC-10-1-7-11-0.

150. Memorandum for the President from Warren Christopher, April 2, 1977, JCL, RAC Project Number NLC-132-4-3-10-6.

151. Kitamura, "Japan's Plutonium Program," 7.

152. "Japan on Short End of A-Plant Compromise," EIR 4, no. 37 (September 12, 1977): 1.

153. Emphasis in original. Memorandum for the President from Zbigniew Brzezinski, February 26, 1977, JCL, RAC Project Number NLC-SAFE 39 D-41-128-2-0.

154. Charles S. Costello III, "Nuclear Nonproliferation: A Hidden but Contentious Issue in US-Japan Relations during the Carter Administration (1977–1981)," Asia Pacific Perspectives 3, no. 1 (2003): 1.

155. Memorandum for the President from Cyrus Vance, undated, JCL, RAC Project Number NLC-15-24-1-21-5.

156. Memorandum for the President from Warren Christopher, April 2, 1977, JCL, RAC Project Number NLC-132-4-3-10-6.

157. "The Japanese Reprocessing Plant at Tokai," JCL, RAC Project Number NLC-132-4-3-9-8; and Embassy Telegram (4460) from Tokyo to the Secretary of State, September 9, 1977, JCL, RAC Project Number NLC-16-11-1-16-4.

158. Memorandum for Zbigniew Brzezinski, March 23, 1977, JCL, RAC Project Number NLC-10-1-7-11-0.

159. Memorandum for the President from Cyrus Vance, undated, JCL, RAC Project Number NLC-15-24-1-21-5.

160. "The Nuclear Non-Proliferation Treaty: Looking toward the 1980 Review Conference," CIA Research Paper, Jimmy Carter Library, RAC Project Number NLC-17-144-8-1-5.

161. Memorandum on Non-Proliferation Country Problems, undated, JCL, RAC Project Number NLC-31-14-5-2-5.

162. Memorandum for Zbigniew Brzezinski, May 3, 1977, JCL, RAC Project Number NLC-10-2-4-10-3.

163. For more on this episode, see Costello III, "Nuclear Nonproliferation."

164. Sung Chull Kim, "Endangering Alliance or Risking Proliferation: US-Japan and US-Korea Nuclear Energy Cooperation Agreements," Pacific Review 30, no. 5 (2017): 698–699. In the late 1980s, the United States gave Japan programmatic consent, allowing Japan to reprocess spent nuclear fuel from American-supplied uranium.

165. Masafumi Takubo and Frank von Hippel, "Forty Years of Impasse: The United States, Japan, and the Plutonium Problem," *Bulletin of the Atomic Scientists* 73, no. 5 (2017): 337–343.

166. Solingen, *Nuclear Logics*, 80.

167. Michael J. Green and Benjamin L. Self, "Japan's Changing China Policy: From Commercial Liberalism to Reluctant Realism," *Survival* 38, no. 2 (2008): 38.

168. Joseph M. Ha and John Guinasso, "Japan's Rearmament Dilemma: The Paradox of Recovery," *Pacific Affairs* 53, no. 2 (1980): 250.

169. Ha and Guinasso, "Japan's Rearmament Dilemma," 260.

170. Jennifer M. Lind, "Pacifism or Passing the Buck?: Testing Theories of Japanese Security Policy," *International Security* 29, no. 1 (2004): 92–121. On how Japan indigenized its defense industry during the Cold War, see Michael J. Green, *Arming Japan: Defense Production, Alliance Politics, and the Postwar Search for Autonomy* (New York: Columbia University Press, 1995); and Richard J. Samuels, *"Rich Nation, Strong Army": National Security and the Technological Transformation of Japan* (Ithaca, NY: Cornell University Press, 1994).

171. Kitamura, "Japan's Plutonium Program," 13.

172. Kusunoki, "Sato Cabinet"; Komine, "Okinawa Confidential"; Yukinori Komine, "Whither a 'Resurgent Japan': The Nixon Doctrine and Japan's Defense Buildup, 1969–1976," *Journal of Cold War Studies* 16, no. 3 (2014): 88–128; Hoey, "Nixon Doctrine"; and Fintan Hoey, "Japan and Extended Nuclear Deterrence: Security and Non-proliferation," *Journal of Strategic Studies* 39, no. 4 (2016): 484–501. Kurosaki provides one crucial exception but argues "Japan . . . developed and maintained its latent capability to produce plutonium bombs, despite the absence of any common purpose to do so within the Japanese government." See Kurosaki, "Nuclear Energy," 64. I resist the view that Japan's latent nuclear capability is like what was said of the British Empire: that it was acquired in an absence of mind. Still, Kurosaki's scholarship is the best on the subject.

173. Rublee, *Nonproliferation Norms*, 68.

174. Lind, "Pacifism or Passing the Buck?," 93.

5. South Korea, 1968–1980

1. The Department of the Army to the Commander in Chief, United Nations Command (Hull), September 15, 1954, FRUS 1952–1954, 9: 1877–1878.

2. Alice Amsden, *Asia's Next Giant: South Korea and Late Industrialization* (New York: Oxford University Press, 1989).

3. Memorandum from Director of Central Intelligence Helms to Secretary of Defense McNamara, January 23, 1968, FRUS 1964–1968 29: 464–465; and Summary Minutes of Meeting, January 24, 1968, FRUS 1964–1968 29: 469–474.

4. Memorandum from the President's Military Adviser (Haig) to the President's Assistant for National Security Affairs (Kissinger), April 16, 1969, FRUS 1969–1972 19: 26–27.

5. Minutes of a National Security Council Meeting, April 16, 1969, FRUS 1969–1972 19: 31.

6. Sung Gul Hong, "The Search for Deterrence: Park's Nuclear Option," in *The Park Chung Hee Era: The Transformation of South Korea*, ed. Byung-Kook Kim (Cambridge, MA: Harvard University Press, 2011), 484.

7. Se Jin Kim, "South Korea's Involvement in Vietnam and Its Economic and Political Impact," *Asian Survey* 10, no. 6 (1970): 519.

8. See, e.g., Memorandum of Conversation, May 18, 1965, 10 a.m., FRUS 1964–1968 29: 102.

9. Chalmers Johnson, *MITI and the Japanese Miracle: The Growth of Industrial Policy, 1925–1975* (Stanford, CA: Stanford University Press, 1982); and Peter B. Evans, *Embedded Autonomy: States and Industrial Transformation* (Princeton, NJ: Princeton University Press, 1995).

10. Ezra F. Vogel, *The Four Little Dragons: The Spread of Industrialization in East Asia* (Cambridge, MA: Harvard University Press, 1991).

11. Seung-Young Kim, "Security, Nationalism, and the Pursuit of Nuclear Weapons and Missiles: The South Korean Case, 1970–82," *Diplomacy and Statecraft* 12, no. 4 (2001): 58. A Central Intelligence Agency (CIA) report claims that Park authorized the program in August

1974. See National Foreign Assessment Center, "South Korea: Nuclear Development and Strategic Decisionmaking," CIA, June 1978. I thank Robert Reardon for providing me this document.

12. Sheila Jasanoff and Sang-Hyung Kim, "Containing the Atom: Sociotechnical Imaginaries and Nuclear Power in the United States and South Korea," *Minerva* 47, no. 2 (2009): 132.

13. Jungmin Kang and Harold A. Feiveson, "South Korea's Shifting and Controversial Interest in Spent Fuel Reprocessing," *Nonproliferation Review* 8, no. 1 (2001): 74.

14. Hong, "Search," 486–489.

15. Kim, "Security," 58.

16. Hong, "Search," 490.

17. Hong, "Search," 59.

18. To be sure, I have come across in my research a large range of estimates on the size of South Korean nuclear facilities, from there being a minimal industrial footprint to there being a significant one, by the time the United States began its efforts to suppress the program actively.

19. Memorandum of Conversation, January 19, 1969, FRUS 1969–1976 6: 2–3; and Memorandum from the President's Assistant for National Security Affairs (Kissinger) to President Nixon, March 10, 1969 FRUS 1969–1976 6: 100.

20. National Security Study Memorandum 36, April 10, 1969, FRUS 1969–1976 6: 195–196; and Address to the Nation on the War in Vietnam, November 3, 1969.

21. See Paper Prepared by the Policy Planning Council of the Department of State, June 15, 1968, FRUS 1964–1968 29: 435. A 1965 NIE observed that "[the ROK Government] will also, like all its predecessors, oppose any withdrawals of US forces from the ROK, both because of the impact on South Korean morale, and because in recent years the ROK has earned some $50 million annually from expenditures by US forces." NIE 42/14.2-65, "The Korean Problem" (p. 8), January 22, 1965, folder: "South Korea (42)," box 6, National Intelligence Estimates, National Security File, LBJ Presidential Library, Austin, TX (hereafter abbreviated as LBJL).

22. On the impact of the Nixon Doctrine on South Korea, see Joo-Hong Nam, *America's Commitment to South Korea: The First Decade of the Nixon Doctrine* (Cambridge: Cambridge University Press, 1986).

23. Memorandum of Conversation, August 21, 1969, FRUS 1969–1972 19: 96–100. In a private conversation with Kissinger, South Korean prime minister Kim Jong Pil later referred to this exchange to reproach the Nixon administration for having provided misleading assurances. Kissinger did not dispute the substance of Park and Nixon's conversation but added that no decision was made at the time regarding American deployments. Memorandum of Conversation, December 2, 1970, FRUS 1969–1972 19: 213–216.

24. Memorandum from President Nixon to the President's Assistant for National Security Affairs (Kissinger), November 24, 1969, FRUS 1969–1972 19: 117.

25. National Security Decision Memorandum 48, "U.S. Programs in Korea," March 20, 1970, box H-208, National Security Council Institutional Files, Richard M. Nixon Library (hereafter abbreviated as RMNL).

26. For other evidence that Seoul feared American abandonment, see Victor D. Cha, *Alignment despite Antagonism: The United States-Korea-Japan Security Triangle* (Stanford, CA: Stanford University Press, 1999), 64–67.

27. Memorandum from the President's Assistant for National Security Affairs (Kissinger) to President Nixon, November 25, 1969, FRUS 1969–1972 19: 117–118.

28. Chae-jin Lee, *A Troubled Peace: U.S. Policy and the Two Koreas* (Baltimore, MD: Johns Hopkins University Press, 2006), 68.

29. See Telegram from the Department of State to the Embassy in Korea, January 29, 1970, FRUS 1969–1972 19: 121–122.

30. Oh Won-Chul, *Pakjonghi-wa Kimilsung-ui Ogissaum* [The contest of guts between Park Chung-hee and Kim Il-sung], *ShinDongA* (June 1996): 482.

31. See Jung-ryum Kim, *Hangukgyongjegonsol 30 nyonsa: Kim Jongryom Hoegorok* [History of Korean economic construction for thirty years: Memoir] (Seoul, South Korea: Joongang Ilbosa, 1995), 316.

32. Kim, *Hangukgyongjegonsol 30 nyonsa.*

33. Secretary of State William Rogers stated that he, Laird, and other American officials made hints regarding troop withdrawals that Park chose to ignore. Telegram from the Department of State, April 23, 1970, FRUS 1969–1972 19: 150–151.

34. Telegram from the Embassy in Korea to the Department of State, May 29, 1970, FRUS 1969–1972 19: 155. In a June 1970 letter intended for Nixon, Park reiterated the domestic difficulties of accepting the troop reductions: "On my part, it would be impossible to persuade the Korean people to accept the partial withdrawal by the end of June 1971, as mentioned in your letter, because of the unexpected shock it would give to them and the shortness of time involved." Telegram from the Embassy in Korea to the Department of State, June 15, 1970, FRUS 1969–1972, 19: 161.

35. Telegram from the Embassy in Korea to the Department of State, June 1, 1970, FRUS 1969–1972 19: 158.

36. Telegram from the Embassy in Korea to the Department of State, August 4, 1970, FRUS 1969–1972 19: 174–179.

37. Kim, "Security," 55.

38. Memorandum of Conversation, December 2, 1970, FRUS 1969–1972 19: 216. This unease reflected Park's views on why the Korean War began. In his 1963 memoirs, he wrote, "Our relationship with the US can be traced back since the dawn of our independence. . . . We are also bonded by a common fate, that is the Korean War, and needless to say, how the victors of the WWII are responsible for it." Park Chung-hee, *Kukga-wa Hyokmyung-gwa Na* [State, revolution and me] (Seoul, South Korea: Chiguchon, 1997 [originally published by Hyangmunsa, 1963]), 227–231.

39. Richard M. Nixon, "Asia after Viet Nam," *Foreign Affairs* 46, no. 1 (1967): 113–125.

40. Memorandum from President Nixon to His Assistant for National Security Affairs (Kissinger), February 1, 1969, FRUS 1969–1972 17: 7.

41. Park used the occasion to consolidate his political rule further. See Lyong Choi, "The Foreign Policy of Park Chunghee, 1968–1978" (PhD diss., London School of Economics, 2012), 92–97.

42. Kim, "Security," 55. The South Korean Foreign Ministry did make official statements regarding how the rapprochement might encourage the Chinese to restrain North Korea. See Lee, *Troubled Peace*, 71. Privately, Seoul was apprehensive. Telegram from the Embassy in Korea to the Department of State, December 13, 1971, FRUS 1969–1972 19: 302–305; and Memorandum from John H. Holdridge of the National Security Staff to the President's Assistant for National Security Affairs (Kissinger), February 12, 1972, FRUS 1969–1972 19: 316–317.

43. A former diplomat recounts how "on the surface, the South Korean government reacted positively towards the rapprochement negotiation between the United States and China and expressed its hope for easing of tension in the Korean peninsula, but internally, many were concerned that the Taiwan issue, China's request for the withdrawal of the US forces in Korea, and negotiation regarding the Vietnam war would be brought up during the discussion. This concern was exemplified when the US did not inform the schedule of the meeting with the Chinese to the South Korean government." Kim Yong-Shik, *Huimang-gwa Tojon-Kim Yongsik Oegyohoegorok* [Hope and challenge: Memoir of Kim Yong-shik's diplomacy] (Seoul, South Korea: Dong-A Ilbo sa, 1987), 246.

44. Telegram from the Embassy in Korea to the Department of State, June 15, 1970. FRUS 1969–1972, 19: 159–161. See also Telegram from the Commander in Chief, Pacific (McCain) to the Department of State, July 23, 1970, FRUS 1969–1972 19: 170–173.

45. Letter from President Nixon to Korean President Park, May 26, 1970, FRUS 1969–1972 19: 152–154.

46. Telegram from the Embassy in Korea to the Department of State, May 29, 1970, FRUS 1969–1972 19: 154–155.

47. Park told Ambassador Porter, "If United States [*sic*] proceeds to reduce he will not object but he will not cooperate. . . . Perhaps it would be said that [the South Korean government] is uncooperative and intransigent but same holds true for United States because [the South Korean government] was not consulted in advance of this decision and must have assurances." Telegram from the Embassy in Korea to the Department of State, August 4, 1970, FRUS 1969–1972 19: 174–179.

48. At a minimum, documents show a change in the tenor of South Korea's démarche. See, e.g., Telegram from the Department of State to the Embassy in Korea, October 26, 1970, FRUS 1969–1972 19: 185–189.

49. Porter hypothesized that domestic opposition and congressional pressure might have prompted this behavioral change. Telegram from the Embassy in Korea to the Department of State, November 7, 1970, FRUS 1969–1972 19: 193–194.

50. Memorandum from Secretary of State Rogers to President Nixon, November 10, 1970, FRUS 1969–1972 19: 197–198.

51. Telegram from the Embassy in Korea to the Department of State, February 2, 1971, FRUS 1969–1972 19: 224.

52. Telegram from the Embassy in Korea to the Department of State, November 3, 1971, FRUS 1969–1972 19: 290–293. Seoul eventually agreed to postpone its withdrawals. Memorandum from John H. Holdridge of the NSC Staff to the President's Deputy Assistant for National Security Affairs (Haig), February 5, 1972, FRUS 1969–1972 19: 315–316.

53. Memorandum of Conversation, September 28, 1971, FRUS 1969–1972 19: 282–285; Telegram from the Embassy in Korea to the Department of State, December 22, 1971, FRUS 1969–1972 19: 307–311; and Letter from President Nixon to Korean President Park, May 19, 1972, FRUS 1969–1972 19: 351–353.

54. North Korea also moderated its diplomacy toward South Korea between 1970 and 1972. Nevertheless, the problem of troop withdrawals is that they might offer a "window of opportunity" for an adversary to exploit. To be sure, some domestic opponents of Park argued that he deliberately inflated threats to improve his political stature. Memorandum of Conversation, February 1, 1972, FRUS 1969–1972 19: 313–315.

55. Despite articulating these criticisms, Vance and Park reiterated their countries' Vietnam War and alliance commitments, respectively. Memorandum from Cyrus R. Vance to President Johnson, February 20, 1968, FRUS 1964–1968 29: 384–391.

56. Vipin Narang, *Nuclear Strategy in the Modern Era: Regional Powers and Regional Conflict* (Princeton, NJ: Princeton University Press, 2014), 15–17.

57. Byung-Kook Kim, "Introduction: The Case for Political History," in *The Park Chung Hee Era: The Transformation of South Korea*, ed. Byung-Kook Kim and Ezra F. Vogel (Cambridge, MA: Harvard University Press, 2011), 26–27.

58. The same memorandum highlighted a loophole in American civilian nuclear agreements with South Korea. The recentness of the Indian "peaceful nuclear explosion" (PNE) raised concerns that South Korea would divert plutonium "specifically for PNE use." NSC Memorandum for General Scowcroft, "Sale of Canadian Nuclear Reactor to South Korea," November 18, 1974, folder: "Korea (?)," box 9, National Security Adviser, Presidential Country Files for East Asia and the Pacific, GRFL.

59. Memorandum for Lieutenant General Brent Scowcroft, October 19, 1974, folder: "Korea (4)," box 9, National Security Adviser, Presidential Country Files for East Asia and the Pacific, GRFL.

60. Department of State Telegram, "ROK Plans to Develop Nuclear Weapons and Missiles," December 1974, folder: "Korea—State Department Telegrams from SECSTATE—NODIS (2)," box 11, National Security Adviser, Presidential Country Files for East Asia and the Pacific, GRFL.

61. Memorandum from Smyser and Elliott for Secretary Kissinger, February 28, 1975, folder: "Korea (4)," box 9, National Security Adviser, Presidential Country Files for East Asia and the Pacific, GRFL.

62. See also Telegram 2685 from the Embassy in the Republic of Korea to the Department of State, April 18, 1975, FRUS 1973–1976 E-12.

63. George Perkovich, *India's Nuclear Bomb: The Impact on Global Proliferation* (Berkeley: University of California Press, 2001), 186–187.

64. Quoted in Don Orberdorfer, *The Two Koreas: A Contemporary History*, 2nd ed. (New York: Basic Books, 2001), 72.

65. Kim, "Security," 66.

66. President Gerald R. Ford, "Statement on Nuclear Policy," October 28, 1976, http://www.presidency.ucsb.edu/ws/?pid=6561.

67. Draft Department of State Cable (p. 5), "ROK Plans to Develop Nuclear Weapons and Missiles," February 24, 1975, folder: "Korea (4)," box 9, National Security Adviser, Presidential Country Files for East Asia and the Pacific, GRFL.

68. Study Prepared by the Office of International Security Affairs in the Department of Defense, undated, FRUS 1973–1976 E-12.

69. Department of State Telegram, "Vice President's Meeting with ROK Prime Minister Kim Chong-Pil," April 1975, folder: "Korea—State Department Telegrams: From SECSTATE to NODIS (3)," box 11, National Security Adviser, Presidential Country Files for East Asia and the Pacific, GRFL.

70. Memorandum from Smyser for Secretary Kissinger, March 5, 1975, folder: "Korea (5)," box 9, National Security Adviser, Presidential Country Files for East Asia and the Pacific, GRFL.

71. Memorandum from Kissinger for President Ford, April, 1975?, folder: "Korea (6)," same box as footnote 70.

72. Memorandum from Kissinger for the Secretary of Defense, undated, same folder and box as footnote 70. That American decision makers themselves saw the linkage between troop redeployments and South Korea's nuclear program also builds confidence for my theory. They may be relying on private insights drawn from information that remains classified.

73. Gerald R. Ford, *A Time to Heal: The Autobiography of Gerald R. Ford* (New York: Harper and Row, 1979), 212–213. Kissinger says nothing about the South Korean nuclear weapons program in Henry Kissinger, *White House Years* (New York: Simon and Schuster, 1979), *Years of Upheaval* (New York: Simon and Schuster, 1982), or *Years of Renewal* (New York: Simon and Schuster, 1999).

74. CIA, "South Korea Nuclear Development and Strategic Decisionmaking," June 1978: 6.

75. Etel Solingen, *Nuclear Logics: Contrasting Paths in East Asia and the Middle East* (Princeton, NJ: Princeton University Press, 2007), 90–91.

76. Young-sun Ha, *Nuclear Proliferation, World Order, and Korea* (Seoul, South Korea: Seoul National University Press, 1983), 234.

77. Daniel Drezner, *The Sanctions Paradox: Economic Statecraft and International Relations* (Cambridge: Cambridge University Press, 1999), 260–261.

78. By 1978, Kori 1 was still undergoing tests, while construction had just begun on another light water reactor and the Canada Deuterium Uranium (CANDU) heavy water reactor. Seoul planned for six plants to be operational with a total capacity of almost five thousand megawatts by the mid-1980s. See CIA, "South Korea Nuclear Development and Strategic Decisionmaking," June 1978.

79. Memorandum of Conversation, August 26, 1975, folder: "Korea (12)," box 9, National Security Adviser, Presidential Country Files for East Asia and the Pacific, GRFL; and Exchange of Remarks, Office of the White House Press Secretary, June 25, 1975, folder: "Korea (10)," box 9, National Security Adviser, Presidential Country Files for East Asia and the Pacific, GRFL.

80. Don Oberdorfer, *The Two Koreas: A Contemporary History*, 3rd ed. (New York: Basic Books, 2011), 59–66.

81. Cécile Menétrey-Moncau, "The *Mayaguez* Incident as an Epilogue to the Vietnam War and Its Reflection of the Post-Vietnam Political Equilibrium in Southeast Asia," *Cold War History* 5, no. 3 (2005): 337–357.

82. Quoted in Oberdorfer, *Two Koreas*, 58.

83. Oberdorfer, *Two Koreas*, 479.

84. Kim, "Security," 66.

85. Oberdorfer, *Two Koreas*, 58.

86. Kim, "Security," 66.

87. Note of a Conversation with the American Ambassador, undated, Foreign and Commonwealth Office (FCO) 96/583, British National Archives.

88. One hundred congressmen signed a petition renouncing human rights violations in South Korea during the Ford presidency. This congressional effort further strained the relationship between the two countries. See Han Sungjoo, "South Korea and the United States: The Alliance Survives," *Asian Survey* 20, no. 11 (1980): 1075–1086.

89. Larry A. Niksch, "U.S. Troop Withdrawal from South Korea: Past Shortcomings and Future Prospects," *Asian Survey* 21, no. 3 (1981): 325–327.

90. William H. Gleysteen, *Massive Entanglement, Marginal Influence: Carter and Korea in Crisis* (Washington, DC: Brookings Institution Press, 1999), 17.

91. Presidential Review Memorandum/NSC-13, January 26, 1977, folder: "Presidential Review Memorandum (11-35)," box 105, Vertical File, Jimmy Carter Presidential Library, Atlanta, GA (hereafter abbreviated as JCL).

92. On the discord within the Carter administration, see Gleysteen, *Massive Entanglement*, 24.

93. Memorandum, July 20, 1977, JCL, RAC Project Number NLC-1-3-2-42-9.

94. At least, such was the assessment of American intelligence officials. See Intelligence Memorandum: The Value of the United States to China's National Security, March 1977, Jimmy Carter, RAC Project Number NLC-26-54-3-1-0.

95. Memorandum from Brzezinski to Carter (p. 3), June 10, 1977, Jimmy Carter, RAC Project Number NLC-15-125-8-1-8.

96. Kim, "Security," 67.

97. Kim, "Security."

98. Jonathan D. Pollack and Mitchell B. Reiss, "South Korea: The Tyranny of Geography and the Vexations of History," in *The Nuclear Tipping Point: Why States Reconsider Their Nuclear Choices*, ed. Kurt M. Campbell, Robert J. Einhorn, and Mitchell B. Reiss (Washington, DC: Brookings Institution Press, 2004), 263.

99. The oil crisis provided additional impetus for the Minister of Science and Technology's announcement. See Solingen, *Nuclear Logics*, 93.

100. Young-sun Ha, "Nuclearization of Small States and World War: The Case of South Korea," *Asian Survey* 18, no. 11 (1978): 1142. That said, when these statements were made, neither the United States nor the IAEA detected any major effort to develop nuclear weapons. See Drezner, *Sanctions Paradox*, 265.

101. Mitchell B. Reiss, *Without the Bomb: The Politics of Nuclear Nonproliferation* (New York: Columbia University Press, 1988), 85–86, 93–94.

102. For additional evidence of South Korean apprehensions with Carter, see Cha, *Alignment Despite Antagonism*, 149–152.

103. Telegram 1062 from Embassy in Seoul to the Department of State, February 7, 1977, Jimmy Carter, RAC Project Number NLC-26-39-6-3-2.

104. Telegram 2723 from Embassy in Seoul to the Department of State, April 5, 1977, Jimmy Carter, RAC Project Number NLC-16-11-1-18-2.

105. Telegram from Embassy in Seoul to the Department of State, April 19, 1977, Jimmy Carter, RAC Project Number NLC-10-2-2-23-1.

106. Memorandum of Conversation (p. 3), May 21, 1977, folder: "5/16–23/77," National Security Affairs, Staff Material: Far East, JCL.

107. Telegram from Embassy in Seoul to the Department of State, June 13, 1977, Jimmy Carter, RAC Project Number NLC-16-11-2-17-2.

108. Telegraph 8951 from Embassy in Seoul to the Department of State, October 21, 1977, NLC-17-144-9-1-4.

109. Central Intelligence Agency, "South Korea Nuclear Development and Strategic Decisionmaking," June 1978.

110. South Korea also sought to develop surface-to-surface missile technology in the 1970s. See Kim, "Security."

111. Paul Kerr, "IAEA: Seoul's Nuclear Sins in Past," *Arms Control Today*, December 1, 2004, accessed October 30, 2017, http://www.armscontrol.org/print/1714.

112. On post-Park changes in South Korean defense policy, see Kim, "Security," 69. Still, Kim argues that the desire to maintain positive relations with the United States drove South Korea to abandon nuclear weapons development. Kim, "Security," 70–71.

113. Memorandum from Brzezinski to Carter, July 19, 1978, Jimmy Carter, RAC Project Number NLC-126-13-25-1-9; and Memorandum of Conversation, January 23, 1979, Jimmy Carter, RAC Project Number NLC-7-37-2-3-9.

114. Memorandum from Mike Armacost to Zbigniew Brzezinski, June 29, 1977, folder: "6/28–30/77," box 2, National Security Affairs, Staff Material: Far East, JCL.

115. Memorandum from Nick Platt for Brzezinski (p. 2), May 7, 1979, folder: "5/16–31/79," box 67, National Security Affairs, Staff Material, Far East, JCL.

116. Memorandum for Brzezinski, October 9, 1979, Jimmy Carter, RAC Project Number NLC-10-24-3-7-4.

117. Kim, "Security," 64.

118. Oberdorfer, *Two Koreas*, 52–54.

119. Solingen, *Nuclear Logics*, 90.

120. Park quoted in Solingen, *Nuclear Logics*, 93.

121. This passage, drawn from Solingen, *Nuclear Logics*, includes a quote by Park, 93.

122. Orberdorfer, *Two Koreas*, 44–45.

123. Accordingly, Park declared: "The first step in accomplishing nationalistic democracy is to stand on our own feet. Self-reliance is the foundation of every democracy, and through self-reliance, we can retain our national identity. Without self-reliance, democracy and national identity mean nothing." On nationalism, he wrote: "What came from the outside—knowledge, ideology, political system—we must mend them to fit our unique environment and characteristics. This is what I call 'nationalism.'" Put differently, nationalism required the adaptation of externally generated ideas, institutions, and goods to serve the purposes of state and society. It did not entail closure to the outside world. Translated quote from Shim Yoong-Taek, *Jarip-e-ui uiji: Pak jonghi Daetongryong orok* [The will for self-reliance: The words of President Park Chung-hee] (Seoul, South Korea: Hanlim Ch'ulpansa, 1972), 228–234. Translation thanks to research assistance.

124. Jasanoff and Kim, "Containing the Atom," 133.

125. Kim, "Security," 57.

126. Airgram from the Embassy in Korea to the Department of State, December 10, 1972, FRUS 1969–1972 19: 436–445. This view appears to have support. In an exchange with Habbib's predecessor in August 1970, Park "went on rapidly, saying that time has come for Korea to develop her economy and her defense self-reliance, and he fully intended that his country would stand on her own feet but the only thing required is our understanding that this could not be done in day or two." Telegram from the Embassy in Korea to the Department of State, August 4, 1970, FRUS 1969–1972 19: 174–179.

127. Memorandum of Conversation, November 22, 1974, box 7, National Security Adviser, Memoranda of Conversation, GRFL.

128. See Peter Hayes and Chung-in Moon, "Park Chung Hee, the CIA, and the Bomb," *NAPSNET Special Reports*, September 23, 2011, accessed November 10, 2017, https://nautilus .org/napsnet/napsnet-special-reports/park-chung-hee-the-cia-and-the-bomb/.

6. Nuclear Proliferation and Other American Alliances

1. On how the Battle of Britain influenced later British strategic thinking, see Matthew Grant, *After the Bomb: Civil Defence and Nuclear War in Britain, 1945–68* (Basingstoke, UK: Palgrave Macmillan, 2010).

2. Simon J. Ball, "Military Nuclear Relations between the United States and Great Britain under the Terms of the McMahon Act, 1946–1958," *Historical Journal* 38, no. 2 (1995): 439–454.

3. Lorna Arnold and Mark J. Smith, *Britain, Australia and the Bomb: The Nuclear Tests and Their Aftermath* (Basingstoke, UK: Palgrave Macmillan, 2006), 3.

4. Quoted in John Baylis and Kristan Stoddart, "The British Nuclear Experience: The Role of Ideas and Beliefs (Part One)," *Diplomacy and Statecraft* 23, no. 2 (1995): 335.

5. Margaret Gowing, *Independence and Deterrence: Britain and Atomic Energy 1945–1952*, vol. 1: *Policy Making* (Basingstoke, UK: Macmillan, 1974), 74.

6. David James Gill, *Britain and the Bomb: Nuclear Diplomacy, 1964–1970* (Stanford, CA: Stanford University Press, 2014), 19.

7. Justin Bronk, "Britain's 'Independent' V-Bomber Force and US Nuclear Weapons, 1957–1962," *Journal of Strategic Studies* 37, no. 6–7 (2014): 974–997.

8. Beatrice Heuser, *NATO, Britain, France, and the FRG: Nuclear Strategies and Forces for Europe, 1949–2000* (New York: St. Martin's, 1997), 34.

9. John Baylis, "The 1958 Anglo-American Mutual Defence Agreement: The Search for Nuclear Interdependence," *Journal of Strategic Studies* 31, no. 3 (2008): 457–458.

10. Diana B. Kunz, *Economic Diplomacy of the Suez Crisis* (Chapel Hill: University of North Carolina Press, 1991).

11. Jan Melissen, "The Thor Saga: Anglo-American Nuclear Relations, US IRBM Development and Deployment in Britain, 1955–1959," *Journal of Strategic Studies* 15, no. 2 (1992): 178–180.

12. Ian Clark and David Angell, "Britain, the United States, and the Control of Nuclear Weapons: The Diplomacy of the Thor Deployment 1956–1958," *Diplomacy and Statecraft* 2, no. 3 (1991): 153.

13. Baylis, "1958 Anglo-American Mutual Defence Agreement," 443–444.

14. Jan Melissen, "The Restoration of the Nuclear Alliance: Great Britain and Atomic Negotiations with the United States, 1957–1958," *Contemporary Record* 6, no. 1 (1992): 87.

15. For more on Blue Steel, see John Baylis, *Ambiguity and Deterrence: British Nuclear Strategy, 1945–1964* (Oxford: Clarendon Press, 1995), 349–351. On Blue Streak, see Baylis, *Ambiguity and Deterrence*, 279–288.

16. Baylis, *Ambiguity and Deterrence*, 290–291.

17. Permanent Secretary of the Ministry of Defense and Chairman of the British Nuclear Deterrent Study Group, Sir Robert Scott, quoted Baylis, *Ambiguity and Deterrence*, 278.

18. Richard E. Neustadt, *Alliance Politics* (New York: Columbia University Press, 1970).

19. Dean Acheson, "Our Atlantic Alliance: The Political and Economic Strands," speech delivered at US Military Academy, West Point, New York, December 5, 1962. Reprinted in *Vital Speeches of the Day* 24, no. 6 (1963): 162–166.

20. "Skybolt Missile (Talks)," House of Commons Debate, 17 December 1962, vol. 669, cc893–900.

21. On these debates, see Michael Middeke, "Anglo-American Nuclear Weapons Cooperation after the Nassau Conference: The British Policy of Independence," *Journal of Cold War Studies* 2, no. 2 (2000): 69–96. See also Andrew Priest, "In American Hands: Britain, the United States and the Polaris Nuclear Project 1962–1968," *Contemporary British History* 19, no. 3 (2005): 355–357.

22. Stephen Blank, "Britain: The Politics of Foreign Economic Policy, the Domestic Economy, and the Problem of Pluralistic Stagnation," *International Organization* 31, no. 4 (1977): 674.

23. On British immediate postwar recovery, see Blank, "Britain," 678–679.

24. Kunz, *Economic Diplomacy*.

25. Ball quoted in Gill, *Britain and the Bomb*, 157.

26. Andrew J. Pierre, "Nuclear Diplomacy: Britain, France, and America," *Foreign Affairs* 49, no. 2 (1971): 288.

27. Thomas Robb, "Antelope, Poseidon or a Hybrid: The Upgrading of the British Strategic Nuclear Deterrent, 1970–1974," *Journal of Strategic Studies* 33, no. 6 (2010): 811–812.

28. See John Baylis, "British Nuclear Doctrine: The 'Moscow Criterion' and the Polaris Improvement Programme," *Contemporary British History* 19, no. 1 (2005): 53–65.

29. Judith Reppy and Harry Dean, "Britain Buys the Trident," *Bulletin of the Atomic Scientists* 36, no. 9 (1980): 26–31.

30. Gill, *Britain and the Bomb*, 158.

31. Jacques Bounolleau and Jean-Claude Levain, "Les brevets nucléaires de l'équipe Joliot en Grande-Bretagne et aux États-Unis (1939–1968)," in *La France et l'atome: Études d'histoire nucléaire*, ed. Maurice Vaïsse (Brussels, Belgium: Bruylant, 1994).

32. Maurice Vaïsse, "Le choix atomique de la France (1945–1958)," *Vingtième Siècle: Revue d'histoire* 36 (1992): 22.

33. Gabrielle Hecht, "Political Designs: Nuclear Reactors and National Policy in Postwar France," *Technology and Culture* 35, no. 4 (1994): 675.

34. On French nuclear experiments, see Yves Le Baut, "Les essais nucléaires français," in *La France et l'atome: Études d'histoire nucléaire*, ed. Maurice Vaïsse (Brussels, Belgium: Bruylant, 1994).

35. Leopoldo Nuti, "The F-I-G Story Revisited," *Storia delle Relazioni Internazionali* 13, no. 1 (1998): 80, 90.

36. Quoted in Marc Trachtenberg, *The Cold War and After: History, Theory, and the Logic of International Politics* (Princeton, NJ: Princeton University Press, 2012), 147.

37. My translation of the French quote in Dominique Mongin, "Genèse de l'armement nucléaire français," *Revue Historique des Armées*, no. 262 (2011): 9–19, accessed February 11, 2016, http://rha.revues.org/7187.

38. My translation of the French quoted in Vaïsse, "Le choix atomique," 27. Vaïsse contends that the Suez crisis catalyzed the French nuclear program, but many preparations for the nuclear program were already in place by 1956.

39. This debate had a precedent. The French National Assembly deliberated in the early 1950s over France's nuclear program. The Communist Party advanced one motion to forbid nuclear weapons production that was roundly rejected. See Mongin, "Genèse de l'armement nucléaire français."

40. Avery Goldstein, *Deterrence and Security in the 21st Century: China, Britain, France, and the Enduring Legacy of the Nuclear Proliferation* (Stanford, CA: Stanford University Press), 185–191.

41. David S. Yost, "France's Deterrent Posture and Security in Europe, Part I: Capabilities and Doctrine," Adelphi Paper No. 194 (London: International Institute for Strategic Studies, 1984–1985), 4.

42. Quoted in Bradley A. Thayer, "The Causes of Nuclear Proliferation and the Utility of the Nuclear Non-Proliferation Regime," *Security Studies* 4, no. 3 (1995): 489.

43. Maurice Vaïsse, *La grander: Politique étrangère du général de Gaulle, 1958–1969* (Paris: Athème Fayard, 1998).

44. Andrew Moravcsik, "Charles de Gaulle and Europe: The New Revisionism," *Journal of Cold War Studies* 14, no. 1 (2012): 53–77.

45. Philip Nord, *France's New Deal: From the Thirties to the Postwar Era* (Princeton, NJ: Princeton University Press, 2010), 7.

46. William I. Hitchcock, *France Restored: Cold War Diplomacy and the Quest for Leadership in Europe, 1944–1954* (Durham: University of North Carolina Press, 1998).

47. Barry Eichengreen, "Institutions and Economic Growth: Europe after World War II," in *Economic Growth in Europe since 1945*, ed. Nicholas Crafts and Gianni Toniolo (Cambridge: Cambridge University Press, 1996), 39.

48. Fred L. Block, *The Origins of International Economic Disorder: A Study of United States International Monetary Policy from World War II to the Present* (Berkeley: University of California Press, 1977), 133.

49. Éric Monnet, "Une coopération à la française: La France, le dollar et le système de Bretton Woods, 1960–1965," *Histoire@Politique. Politique, culture, société*, no. 19 (January–April 2013).

50. To be sure, these efforts did not succeed partly because de Gaulle had no concrete objectives aside from frustrating the United States. See Jonathan Kirshner, *Currency and Coercion: The Political Economy of International Monetary Power* (Princeton, NJ: Princeton University Press, 1995), 192–203.

51. Frank Costigliola, "The Failed Design: Kennedy, de Gaulle, and the Struggle for Europe," *Diplomatic History* 8, no. 3 (1984): 227–252.

52. Maurice Vaïsse, "La réconciliation franco-allemande: Le dialogue de Gaulle-Adenauer," *Politique Étrangère* 58, no. (1993): 963–972; and Garret Joseph Martin, *General de Gaulle's Cold War: Challenging American Hegemony, 1963–1968* (New York: Berghahn Books, 2013), 34.

53. See Andrew Moravcsik, "De Gaulle between Grain and Grandeur: The Political Economy of EC Policy, 1958–1970 (Part 1)," *Journal of Cold War Studies* 2, no. 2 (2000): 3–43; and Andrew Moravcsik, "De Gaulle between Grain and Grandeur: The Political Economy of EC Policy, 1958–1970 (Part 2)," *Journal of Cold War Studies* 2, no. 3 (2000): 4–66.

54. Marc Trachtenberg, "The French Factor in US Foreign Policy during the Nixon-Pompidou Period, 1969–1974," *Journal of Cold War Studies* 13, no. 1 (2011): 4–59.

55. Matthew Fuhrmann and Benjamin Tkach, "Almost Nuclear: Introducing the Nuclear Latency Dataset," *Conflict Management and Peace Science* 32, no. 4 (2015): 443–461.

56. Astrid Forland, "Norway's Nuclear Odyssey: From Optimistic Proponent to Nonprolif-erator," *Nonproliferation Review* 4, no. 2 (1997): 14.

57. Forland, "Norway's Nuclear Odyssey," 1.

58. To be sure, the Soviet Union did occupy parts of northern Norway at the end of World War II. I thank Henriik Hiim for this point.

59. Forrestal quoted in Matts R. Berdal, *The United States, Norway and the Cold War, 1954–60* (London: Springer, 1997), 17.

60. Berdal, *United States*, 16.

61. United States General Accounting Office, "Status of the Marine Corps Prepositioning Pro-gram in Norway," GAO/NSIAD-89-110 (Washington, DC: General Accounting Office, 1989).

62. Forland, "Norway's Nuclear Odyssey," 13.

63. Berdal, *United States*, 8.

64. Ole Waever, "Nordic Nostalgia: Northern Europe after the Cold War," *International Af-fairs* 68, no. 1 (1992): 78–79.

65. Gary Milhollin, "Heavy Water Cheaters," *Foreign Policy*, no. 69 (1987–1988): 100.

66. Jim Walsh, "Surprise Down Under: The Secret History of Australia's Nuclear Ambitions," *Nonproliferation Review* 5, no. 1 (1997): 10.

67. Quoted in Walsh, "Surprise Down Under," 12.

68. Walsh, "Surprise Down Under."

69. Christine M. Leah, *Australia and the Bomb* (New York: Palgrave Macmillan, 2014), 27.

70. The remaining residual British forces in Southeast Asia were part of the Five Power De-fense Arrangements (with Australia, New Zealand, Malaysia, and Singapore). This agreement did not include security guarantees or promises to mount an intervention.

71. Walsh, "Surprise Down Under," 9.

72. Leah, *Australia and the Bomb*, 62–63; and Walsh, "Surprise Down Under," 12.

73. Leah, *Australia and the Bomb*, 59 and 75.

74. Walsh, "Surprise Down Under," 12.

75. Leah, *Australia and the Bomb*, 59–79

76. Jacques E. C. Hymans, *The Psychology of Nuclear Proliferation: Identity, Emotions, and For-eign Policy* (New York: Cambridge University Press, 2006), 136.

77. This case study draws on work I did for Henry Sokolsky and the Nonproliferation Pol-icy Education Center's project on intelligence and nuclear proliferation.

78. David Albright and Corey Gay, "Taiwan: Nuclear Nightmare Averted," *Bulletin of the Atomic Scientists* 54, no. 1 (1998): 54–60.

79. See Gordon H. Chang, "To the Nuclear Brink: Eisenhower, Dulles, and the Quemoy-Matsu Crisis," *International Security* 12, no. 4 (1988): 96–123.

80. Telegram from the Embassy in the Republic of China to the Department of State, Au-gust 3, 1968, FRUS 1961–1963 30: 697–698.

81. Jay Taylor, *The Generalissimo: Chiang Kai-shek and the Struggle for Mainland China* (Cam-bridge, MA: Harvard University Press, 2009), 529.

82. Taylor, *Generalissimo*, 527–529.

83. Keren Yarhi-Milo, Alexander Lanoszka, and Zack Cooper, "To Arm or to Ally? The Pa-tron's Dilemma and the Strategic Logic of Arms Transfers and Alliances," *International Security* 41, no. 2 (2016): 103–119.

84. US Embassy Tel Aviv, Airgram 793, March 19, 1966, National Archives, RG 59, Depart-ment of State Records, Subject-Numeric Files, 1964–1966, AE 7 Chinat, pulled from William Burr, ed., "New Archival Evidence on Taiwanese 'Nuclear Intentions,' 1966–1976," National Security Archive Electronic Briefing Book No. 20, http://nsarchive2.gwu.edu/NSAEBB/NSAEBB20/ (hereafter abbreviated as NSA); and US Mission to the European Communities, April 7, 1966, cable ECBUS 898, Subject-Numeric 1964–66, FSE 13 Chinat, NSA.

85. US Embassy Taipei, Airgram 1037, June 20, 1966, Subject-Numeric 1964–66, DEF 12-1 Chi-nat, NSA. This issue transpired at the same time as negotiations for the NPT. See US Mission to the European Communities, April 7, 1966, cable ECBUS 898, Subject-Numeric 1964–66, FSE 13 Chinat, NSA.

86. State Department to Embassies Taipei and Bonn, Cable 16187, March 20, 1967, Subject-Numeric 1967–69, FSE 13 Chinat, NSA.

87. State Department Memorandum of Conversation, November 22, 1972, RG 59, Department of State Records, Subject-Numeric Files, 1970–1973, AE 11-2 Chinat, NSA.

88. Memorandum from Office of Republic China Affairs to Assistant Secretary for East Asian and Pacific Affairs, December 14, 1972, Subject-Numeric 1970–73, FSE 13 Chinat, NSA.

89. Embassy Taipei to State Department, Cable 0338, January 17, 1973, Subject-Numeric 1970–73, FSE 13 Chinat, NSA.

90. State Department to Embassies in Bonn, Brussels, and Taipei, Cable 12137, January 20, 1973, Subject-Numeric 1970–73, FSE 13 Chinat, NSA; and Embassy Taipei to State Department, Cable 685, January 31, 1973, Subject-Numeric 1970–73, FSE 13 Chinat, NSA.

91. Jeffrey Richelson, *Spying on the Bomb: American Nuclear Intelligence from Nazi Germany to Iran and North Korea* (New York: W. W. Norton, 2006), 267.

92. Embassy Taipei to State Department, Cable 1197, February 24, 1973, Subject-Numeric 1970–73, FSE 13 Chinat, NSA.

93. State Department Memorandum of Conversation (p. 3), April 5, 1973, Subject-Numeric 1970–73, AE 1 Chinat, NSA.

94. State Department Memorandum of Conversation (p. 4), August 29, 1973, Subject-Numeric 1970–73, AE 1 Chinat, NSA.

95. Quoted in Richelson, *Spying on the Bomb*, 270.

96. Albright and Gay, "Taiwan," 57.

97. Memorandum from Burton Levin, Office of Republic of China Affairs, to Oscar Armstrong, Deputy Assistant Secretary for East Asian Affairs, October 12, 1976, RG 59, Policy Planning Staff (Director's Files), 1969-7, box 377, WL China Sensitive Chron 10/1–12/31/76, NSA. In September 1976, a State Department telegram sent to the embassy in Taipei noted vaguely that "should the ROC [Taiwan] or any other government seek national reprocessing capabilities, this would risk jeopardizing additional highly important relations with the US." State Department cable 91733 to Embassy Taiwan, "ROC's Nuclear Intentions," September 4, 1976, National Security Archive: Nuclear Vault, George Washington University, http://www.gwu.edu/~nsarchiv/nukevault/ebb221/ (hereafter, Nuclear Vault). In December 1978, the United States informed Taiwan that it and China "have agreed to establish diplomatic relations" and that "the United States will recognize the People's Republic of China as the government of China." Yet this diplomatic move had more to do with exploiting the Sino-Soviet split than fulfilling a threat made with regard to Taiwan's nuclear proliferation-related behavior. See Backchannel Message from Secretary of State Vance and the President's Assistant for National Security Affairs (Brzezinski) to the Ambassador to the Republic of China (Unger), December 15, 1978, FRUS 1977–1980 13: 650.

98. State Department Memorandum of Conversation, November 18, 1976, RG 84, Records of Foreign Service Posts, Top Secret Foreign Service Post Files, Embassy Taipei, 1959–1977, box 1, DEF 12 NWT-1977, box 1, DEF 12 NWT-1976 ROC [Republic of China], NSA.

99. State Department cable 67316 to Embassy Taiwan, March 26, 1977, Nuclear Vault.

100. Zbigniew Brzezinski to President Carter, "Weekly National Security Report #11," April 29, 1977, Nuclear Vault.

101. William Burr, "The Taiwanese Nuclear Case: Lesson for Today," *Carnegie Endowment of Peace*, August 9, 2007, http://carnegieendowment.org/2007/08/09/taiwanese-nuclear-case-lessons-for-today/6cq.

102. "IAEA Investigating Egypt and Taiwan," *Arms Control Association*, January 1, 2005, https://www.armscontrol.org/act/2005_01-02/Egypt_Taiwan.

103. Albright and Gay, "Taiwan," 59–60.

104. Albright and Gay, "Taiwan," 43.

105. Nicholas L. Miller, "The Secret Success of Nonproliferation Sanctions," *International Organization* 68, no. 4 (2014): 932.

106. Burr, "Taiwanese Nuclear Case."

Conclusion

1. Jonathan Mercer, *Reputation and International Politics* (Ithaca, NY: Cornell University Press, 1996); and Daryl G. Press, *Calculating Credibility: How Leaders Assess Military Threats* (Ithaca, NY: Cornell University Press, 2005), 21.

2. Alex Weisiger and Keren Yarhi-Milo, "Revisiting Reputation: How Past Actions Matter in International Politics," *International Organization* 69, no. 2 (2015): 473–495.

3. John Mitton, "Selling Schelling Short: Reputations and American Coercive Diplomacy in Syria," *Contemporary Security Policy* 36, no. 3 (2015): 408–431.

4. Rex W. Douglass and Alexander Lanoszka, "Two Warheads Passing in the Night: On Modeling Nuclear Proliferation," paper presented at the annual meeting of the American Political Science Association, September 3–6, 2015.

5. John J. Mearsheimer, *Conventional Deterrence* (Ithaca, NY: Cornell University Press, 1983); and Stephen Biddle, *Military Power: Explaining Victory and Defeat in Modern Battle* (Princeton, NJ: Princeton University Press, 2004). Some recent exceptions exist. See Caitlin Talmadge, "Would China Go Nuclear? Assessing the Risk of Chinese Nuclear Escalation in a Conventional War with the United States," *International Security* 41, no. 4 (2017): 50–92; and Walter C. Ladwig III, "Indian Military Modernization and Conventional Deterrence in South Asia," *Journal of Strategic Studies* 38, no. 5 (2015): 729–772.

6. See Vipin Narang, "What Does It Take to Deter? Regional Power Nuclear Postures and International Conflict," *Journal of Conflict Resolution* 57, no. 3 (2013): 478–508.

7. Francis J. Gavin, "What We Talk about When We Talk about Nuclear Weapons: A Review Essay," *H-Diplo/International Security Studies Forum* (2): 11–36.

8. Todd S. Sechser, "Goliath's Curse: Coercive Threats and Asymmetric Power," *International Organization* 64, no. 4 (2010): 627–660.

9. Todd S. Sechser and Matthew Fuhrmann, "Crisis Bargaining and Nuclear Blackmail," *International Organization* 67, no. 1 (2013): 173–195.

10. Dianne Pfundstein Chamberlain, *Cheap Threats: Why the United States Struggles to Coerce Weak States* (Washington, DC: Georgetown University Press, 2016).

11. Dan W. Altman, "By Fait Accompli, Not Coercion: How States Wrest Territory from Their Adversaries," *International Studies Quarterly* 61, no. 3 (2017): 881–891.

12. Kyle Beardsley and Victor Asal, "Winning with the Bomb," *Journal of Conflict Resolution* 53, no. 2 (2009): 296; and Matthew Kroenig "Nuclear Superiority and the Balance of Resolve: Explaining Nuclear Crisis Outcomes," *International Organization* 67, no. 1 (2013): 141–171.

13. Etel Solingen, ed., *Sanctions, Statecraft, and Nuclear Proliferation* (New York: Cambridge University Press, 2012).

14. Stéfanie Von Hlatky, *American Allies in Times of War: The Great Asymmetry* (Oxford: Oxford University Press, 2013); and Marina E. Henke, "The International Security Cooperation Market: Coalition Building in Pursuit of Peace" (PhD diss., Princeton University, 2013).

15. David A. Lake, *Hierarchy in International Relations* (Ithaca, NY: Cornell University Press, 2009); and G. John Ikenberry, *Liberal Leviathan: The Origins, Crisis, and Transformation of the American World Order* (Princeton, NJ: Princeton University Press, 2011).

16. Daniel Deudney, "Unipolarity and Nuclear Weapons," in *International Relations Theory and the Consequences of Unipolarity*, ed. G. John Ikenberry, Michael Mastanduno, and William C. Wohlforth (Cambridge: Cambridge University Press, 2011), 315.

17. Francis J. Gavin, "Strategies of Inhibition: US Grand Strategy, the Nuclear Revolution, and Nonproliferation," *International Security* 40, no. 1 (2015): 43–44.

18. John J. Mearsheimer, *The Tragedy of Great Power Politics* (New York: W. W. Norton, 2001), 32.

19. See Matthew Kroenig, "Force or Friendship? Explaining Great Power Nonproliferation Policy," *Security Studies* 23, no. 1 (2014): 1–32.

20. For some defensive realists, nuclear proliferation is desirable because of its allegedly pacifying effect on interstate relations. See Kenneth N. Waltz, "Nuclear Myths and Political Realities," *American Political Science Review* 84, no. 3 (1990): 731–745.

21. This discussion draws from Alexander Lanoszka, "Nuclear Proliferation and Nonproliferation among Soviet Allies," forthcoming in *Journal of Global Security Studies* 3, no. 2 (2018): 217–233.

22. On northern-southern dynamics within the Warsaw Pact, see Eliza Gheorghe, "Nuclear Alliances: Strategies of Extended Nuclear Deterrence and the Pursuit of Hegemony," paper presented at the convention of the International Studies Association, San Francisco, April 4–7, 2018.

23. Eliza Gheorghe, "Atomic Maverick: Romania's Negotiations for Nuclear Technology, 1964–1970," *Cold War History* 13, no. 3 (2013): 373–392.

24. Chen Jian, *Mao's China and the Cold War* (Chapel Hill, NC: University of North Carolina Press, 2001), 60–64; and Charles K. Armstrong, *Tyranny of the Weak: North Korea and the World, 1950–1992* (Ithaca, NY: Cornell University Press, 2013), 44.

25. Lanoszka, "Nuclear Proliferation and Nonproliferation."

26. Armstrong, *Tyranny of the Weak*, 108; and "Journal of Soviet Ambassador in the DPRK A. M. Puzanov for 20 May 1958," May 1958, Wilson Center Digital Archive, accessed September 17, 2017, http://digitalarchive.wilsoncenter.org/document/116269.

27. Jonathan D. Pollack, *No Exit: North Korea, Nuclear Weapons and International Security* (London: International Institute for Strategic Studies, 2011), 47.

28. Eleanor Albert, "The China–North Korea Relationship," *Council of Foreign Relations*, July 5, 2017, accessed September 20, 2017, https://www.cfr.org/backgrounder/china-north-korea-relationship.

29. Jeremy Page and Alastair Gale, "Behind North Korea's Nuclear Advance: Scientists Who Bring Technology Home," *Wall Street Journal*, September 9, 2017, accessed October 28, 2017, https://www.wsj.com/articles/behind-north-koreas-nuclear-advance-scientists-who-bring-technology-home-1504711605?.

30. On the symbolic politics of nuclear weapons within alliances, see Barry O'Neill, *Honor, Symbols, and War* (Ann Arbor: University of Michigan Press, 2001): 215–239.

31. Michael A. Hunzeker and Alexander Lanoszka, "Landpower and American Credibility," *Parameters* 45, no. 4 (2015–2016): 17–26.

32. For a similar but outdated view, see Christopher W. Hughes, "North Korea's Nuclear Weapons: Implications for the Nuclear Ambitions of Japan, South Korea, and Taiwan," *Asia Policy* 3, no. 1 (2007): 75–104. That said, South Korea has expressed an interest in reprocessing and can do limited experimentation on a type of reprocessing called pyroprocessing according to a 2015 nuclear cooperation agreement signed with the United States. See Jungmin Kang and Frank von Hippel, "Reprocessing Policy and South Korea's New Government," *Bulletin of the Atomic Scientists* (May 15, 2017), accessed November 15, 2017, https://thebulletin.org/reprocessing-policy-and-south-korea%E2%80%99s-new-government10768.

33. Jeffrey Michaels and Heather Williams, "The Nuclear Education of Donald J. Trump," *Contemporary Security Policy* 38, no. 1 (2017): 65–68.

34. See Paul J. Bracken, *The Second Nuclear Age: Strategy, Danger, and the New Power Politics* (New York: Times Books, 2012), 2.

35. Stephen G. Brooks and William C. Wohlforth, *America Abroad: The United States' Global Role in the 21st Century* (New York: Oxford University Press, 2016); and Andrea Gilli and Mauro Gilli, "Military-Technological Superiority: Systems Integration and the Challenges of Imitation, Reverse Engineering, and Cyber-Espionage" forthcoming in *International Security*.

Index